THE BATTLE OF AN LOC

Twentieth-Century Battles

Spencer C. Tucker, editor

THE
BATTLE
OF
AN LOC

JAMES H. WILLBANKS

INDIANA UNIVERSITY PRESS

BLOOMINGTON AND INDIANAPOLIS

This book is a publication of

Indiana University Press
601 North Morton Street
Bloomington, IN 47404-3797 USA

Manufactured in the United States of America

ISBN 0-253-34481-6

This book is dedicated to all the American men and women who answered their nation's call and served in the Republic of Vietnam, but especially to those who made the supreme sacrifice with their lives, including Brigadier General Richard J. Tallman, Lieutenant Colonel Stanley J. Kuick, Major Peter M. Bentson, First Lieutenant John A. Todd Jr., all killed by incoming artillery in An Loc on 9 July 1972, and Lieutenant Colonel William B. Nolde, the last American who died in Vietnam before the negotiated cease-fire went into effect. Colonel Nolde was killed by an incoming artillery shell in An Loc on 27 January 1973, just 11 hours before the guns stopped firing. This book is also dedicated to the brave South Vietnamese officers and soldiers who stood their ground against overwhelming odds during the desperate battle for An Loc in 1972.

An Loc held—and held. Where Dien Bien Phu lasted 56 days before collapse, An Loc held on for 70 days before driving the Communists out leaving the town strewn with the wreckage of field guns and derelict Soviet T-54s. . . . [The] An Loc victory was not only that of the RVN Armed Forces over three enemy divisions, but also a victory of the free world's democracy over Communist totalitarianism.

—PRESIDENT NGUYEN VAN THIEU

CONTENTS

FIGURES

MAPS

PHOTOS

PREFACE

THE GENESIS OF this book goes back to 1972 in the surgical ward at 3rd Field Hospital in Saigon, Republic of Vietnam. Having just been evacuated from the besieged city of An Loc, I thought that someday I would attempt to write of the desperate battle that was fought there during the massive North Vietnamese Easter Offensive.

Twenty years after the fact, as part of a master's degree program at the University of Kansas, I made a first effort to draw together the many aspects of this key battle that blocked the North Vietnamese attack on Saigon. The resulting manuscript was published as a short monograph by the Combat Studies Institute Press of Fort Leavenworth, Kansas, in 1993.

Several years ago I decided to expand on my original effort. The body of literature on the war in Vietnam grows daily, but the emphasis of most of these works falls within two categories: historical overviews and first-person accounts. These books usually focus on the period of the war representing the height of American involvement, when large numbers of U.S. troops and units were actively conducting combat operations. However, in recent years, more and more has been written about the American commitment in the latter part of the war, when U.S. participation was embodied mostly in a few advisers who remained with the South Vietnamese units as they assumed more responsibility for the war.

The battle of An Loc, although one of the key battles in the entire Vietnam War, has been discussed only briefly in the literature about the conflict. With the exception of Dale Andradé's excellent *America's Last Vietnam Battle: Halting Hanoi's 1972 Easter Offensive* (University Press of Kansas, 2001), very little has been written about the South Vietnamese victory in blunting the massive North Vietnamese invasion.

Whereas Andradé gave a comprehensive and impeccably documented account of the entire Easter Offensive, including the major battles at Quang Tri and Kontum as well as those in Military Region III, this book will focus solely on An Loc. As an adviser with the ARVN (Army of the Republic of Vietnam) defenders at An Loc, I have relied on my own personal experiences for context, but since memories are somewhat perishable and no one participant can see the whole battle, I have attempted to document the story of the battle from multiple sources. My research drew heavily on primary sources, such as unit histories, official communiqués, operational summaries, intelligence reports, and a limited number of first-person accounts and interviews. The research also considered the South Vietnamese point of view by examining the U.S. Army Center of Military History Indochina Monograph Series, in which former senior South Vietnamese military leaders discuss a variety of issues germane to the Vietnam War, including ARVN performance during the 1972 North Vietnamese invasion.

One of the reasons for taking on this topic again is the increasing availability of North Vietnamese sources, which were decidedly limited when I first wrote about the battle of An Loc. While these works are official accounts and very political in nature, they provide a glimpse of the Communist perspective, the strategy that led to the North Vietnamese decision to launch a large-scale offensive in 1972, and the tactics they used in trying to take the city.

Thus, the objective of this book is not to provide merely a personal account of the battle from one participant's limited perspective, but rather to tell the whole complex story from the perspectives of many of the participants, including other U.S. advisers, our South Vietnamese counterparts, army helicopter pilots, and the pilots and air crews from the air force, navy, and Marine Corps who provided critical air support, while at the same time considering the actions and perspectives of our opponents during the fierce fighting. It is my hope that this approach will provide a more comprehensive story of this pivotal battle.

ACKNOWLEDGMENTS

THERE ARE A number of groups and persons whom I would like to thank for their contribution to this book. First, I would like to thank Colonel William Miller, senior adviser to the 5th ARVN Division in An Loc during April–May 1972, for his stalwart leadership during the battle and for his friendship in the years after; he has always epitomized the best of the warrior spirit. His papers, which he was kind enough to loan to me, were invaluable in the preparation of this book. Colonel Miller passed away in 2003; may he rest in peace.

I am in debt to the staffs of the Center of Military History, Washington, D.C.; the National Archives, College Park, Maryland; the Texas Tech University Center for the Study of the Vietnam Conflict, Lubbock, Texas; the Military History Institute, Carlisle Barracks, Pennsylvania; and the Combined Arms Research Library, Fort Leavenworth, Kansas. Without their superb and timely assistance during my research, this project would never have been completed.

I would also like to thank Dr. Ted Wilson of the University of Kansas and Mr. Dale Andradé of the U.S. Army Center of Military History for their friendship and encouragement in what has become a reconstruction of one of the most significant emotional events in my life. I greatly appreciate their patience, indulgence, and wise counsel.

Special recognition is due Mr. Merle L. Pribbenow, not only for his seminal translation of *Victory in Vietnam: The Official History of the People's Army of Vietnam, 1954–1975* (2002), but also for his many kindnesses and generous efforts in translating a number of Vietnamese documents, both North Vietnamese and South Vietnamese. Without his assistance, the story that follows would have been quite one-sided.

I would also like to thank Ms. Robin Kern of Leavenworth, Kansas, for her superb work on the maps and charts in this book; her professionalism and skill added much to the finished product.

I could not have told the whole story of the desperate battle at An Loc without the assistance and encouragement of my good friend Bill Carruthers, who flew over the city as a forward air controller during the height of the fighting in 1972. In addition to providing photographs, he has been tireless in helping me find many of the air force pilots and crewmen who made such a difference during the battle. In the same vein, Mike Sloniker, formerly of the 229th Aviation Battalion, was instrumental in providing information on his unit's operations and putting me in touch with his fellow helicopter pilots who provided such courageous support during the battle for Binh Long Province.

I would also like to thank Neal Ulevich, who reported on the offensive in 1972 as correspondent and photographer for Associated Press, and Chad Richmond, who flew helicopters for the 229th Aviation Battalion during the battle, for the photographs they kindly provided.

A special heartfelt thanks goes to my wife, Diana, who served on the home front and supported me through the difficult times addressed in this book. I would also like to thank our son Russell, our daughter Jennifer, and her husband, Captain Bob Beuerlein, U.S. Army, for their support and encouragement during the preparation of this book.

Lastly, I am grateful to my parents, Sergeant First Class (U.S. Army, Ret.) and Mrs. James E. Willbanks, for their unfailing love and support over the years. They have always been there for me, and no one could ask for better parents. My father passed away during the production of this book, but his memory will always be with me.

INTRODUCTION

ON THE AFTERNOON of 12 April 1972, Major Raymond M. Haney and I flew from Lai Khe into An Loc, the capital city of Binh Long Province. Artillery rounds and rockets had been falling steadily on the city since earlier that day; the helicopter hovered only long enough for us to jump off the aircraft into a freshly dug hole in the city soccer field. As the aircraft departed, artillery rounds began to impact near the landing zone. This was our introduction to An Loc.

Major Haney and I were both from Advisory Team 87, the division combat assistance team with the 18th ARVN (Army of the Republic of Vietnam) Division. We were normally based at Xuan Loc in Long Khanh Province, to the east of Saigon. A two-battalion task force from the 18th, called TF 52, had been placed under the operational control of the 5th ARVN Division in March 1972 and had been operating in Binh Long Province in the area between Loc Ninh near the Cambodian border and An Loc to the south. When the 1972 North Vietnamese offensive began, the NVA (North Vietnamese Army) attacked Loc Ninh on 5 April. Within 48 hours, the North Vietnamese overran the South Vietnamese defenders there and turned south. They then pushed TF 52 from its positions. The ARVN attempted to withdraw to An Loc under heavy enemy pressure, but in the process of that withdrawal, the three American advisers from the task force were encircled, wounded, and eventually evacuated by helicopter in the midst of heavy contact. Major Haney and I had flown into An Loc to replace these advisers and join the survivors of TF 52 in An Loc. Haney was the cavalry squadron adviser, and I was an adviser with one of the other infantry regiments of the 18th Division. When the advisers with TF 52 were extracted, Colonel Frank S. Plummer, senior adviser to the 18th, asked for volunteers to join the task force in An Loc. Haney and I raised our hands and headed for Lai Khe to catch a helicopter into the city.

After arriving, we joined the unit in the northern part of the city. During the night, the situation was relatively quiet with regard to enemy probes and ground attacks, but there was a dramatic increase in the number of incoming rockets and artillery rounds later in the evening and into the early morning hours as the South Vietnamese soldiers prepared for the inevitable North Vietnamese attack.

Early the next morning, I went onto the roof of the building that the task force was using for a headquarters to put up a radio antenna. As I finished installing the radio antenna, I heard a tremendous explosion and ran down the stairs to the front of the building. Panic-stricken South Vietnamese soldiers ran by shouting, *"Thiet Giap!!"* Although I had been to a short Vietnamese-language course before arriving in country, I had never heard this phrase before. However, as I ran around the corner of the building, it became all too apparent that the ARVN were yelling "Tanks!" Rumbling down the street toward us from the north was a column of North Vietnamese T-54s. So began the Battle of An Loc, described by Douglas Pike as "the single most important battle in the war."[1]

For the better part of the next three months, a desperate struggle raged between three North Vietnamese divisions (estimated at over 36,000 troops) and the greatly outnumbered South Vietnamese defenders and their U.S. Army advisers. What would prove to be the longest siege of the entire war resulted in horrendous losses on both sides and culminated with the South Vietnamese forces blocking the North Vietnamese thrust toward the South Vietnamese capital in Saigon.

Although this battle occurred after the high point of American commitment in Vietnam, American forces were active and key participants in the action. The American advisory effort had become increasingly more important as American combat troops were withdrawn. During the battle of An Loc, American advisers and U.S. airpower would play major roles in the South Vietnamese victory. The story that follows tells how a very small band of South Vietnamese defenders and their American advisers held out against almost overwhelming odds in what journalist Philip Clarke called "the battle that saved Saigon."[2]

ABBREVIATIONS

AAR	after-action report
AB	air base
AID	Agency for International Development
AO	area of operation
APC	armored personnel carrier
ARVN	Army of the Republic of Vietnam
ARC LIGHT	B-52 bombing strike
bde	brigade
CARP	Computerized Aerial Drop System
cav	cavalry
CBU	cluster bomb unit
CCK	Ching Chuan Kang
CDR	commander
CG	commanding general
CIA	Central Intelligence Agency
CIDG	Civilian Irregular Defense Group
CJCS	Chairman, Joint Chiefs of Staff
COMUSMACV	Commander, U.S. Military Assistance Command, Vietnam
CORDS	Civil Operations and Revolutionary Development Support
COSVN	Central Office for South Vietnam
CP	command post
CPT	captain
CTZ	corps tactical zone

CWO	chief warrant officer
DCAT	division combat assistance team
DCG	deputy commanding general
DepCORDS	Deputy to COMUSMACV for Civil Operations and Revolutionary Development Support
DIA	Defense Intelligence Agency
DMZ	Demilitarized Zone
DOD	Department of Defense
DRAC	Delta Regional Assistance Command
DRV	Democratic Republic of Vietnam (North Vietnam)
DSA	district senior adviser
DZ	drop zone
FAC	forward air controller
FRAC	First Regional Assistance Command
FSB	fire support base
GVN	Government of [South] Vietnam
GRADS	Ground Radar Directed Air Delivery System
HALO	high-altitude, low-opening
HEDP	high-explosive, dual purpose
Huey	UH-1 utility helicopter (also known as a "slick")
JCS	Joint Chiefs of Staff
JGS	Joint General Staff (RVNAF)
KIA	killed in action
LAW	light antitank weapon
LOC	line(s) of communication
LZ	landing zone
MACV	Military Assistance Command, Vietnam
MATT	mobile advisory training team
medevac	medical evacuation (helicopter)
MIA	missing in action
MR	military region
MTT	mobile training team
NCO	noncommissioned officer
NLF	National Liberation Front
NVA	North Vietnamese Army
NVN	North Vietnam
OPLAN	operations plan
PAVN	People's Army of [North] Vietnam
PF	Popular Forces

POL	petroleum, oil, and lubricants
POW	prisoner of war
PRG	Provisional Revolutionary Government
PSA	province senior adviser
PSDF	People's Self-Defense Force
PZ	pickup zone
RDF	radio direction finding
RF	Regional Forces
RPG	rocket-propelled grenade
RVN	Republic of (South) Vietnam
RVNAF	Republic of Vietnam Armed Forces
SAC	Strategic Air Command
SAM	surface-to-air missile
SRAC	Second Regional Assistance Command
SVN	South Vietnam
tac air	tactical air support
TASS	Tactical Air Support Squadron
TOC	tactical operations center
TRAC	Third Regional Assistance Command
VC	Viet Cong
VCI	Viet Cong infrastructure
VNAF	(South) Vietnamese Air Force
VNMC	(South) Vietnamese Marine Corps
VNN	(South) Vietnamese Navy
TRAC	Third Regional Assistance Command
WIA	wounded in action
WO	warrant officer

THE BATTLE OF AN LOC

CHAPTER ONE

PRELUDE TO BATTLE

Nixon's Vietnamization Program

DURING THE 1968 election campaign, Republican candidate Richard Nixon had pledged to bring American troops home and secure an honorable peace in Vietnam. After taking office, he and his advisers devised a plan that called for a "highly forceful approach" to be taken to cause President Nguyen Van Thieu and the South Vietnamese government to assume greater responsibility for the war.[1] This program, first called "Vietnamization" by Secretary of Defense Melvin Laird and announced by Nixon and Thieu at Midway in June 1969, sought to gradually turn over the conduct of the war to the South Vietnamese forces. This was to be accomplished by a steady buildup and improvement of South Vietnamese forces and institutions, accompanied by increased military pressure on the enemy, while steadily withdrawing American troops. The ultimate objective was to strengthen ARVN capabilities and bolster the Thieu government such that the South Vietnamese could stand on their own against the Communists from North Vietnam after U.S. forces had departed.

In order to accomplish program objectives, Nixon directed General Creighton W. Abrams, commander of Military Assistance Command, Vietnam (MACV), senior U.S. military headquarters in Vietnam, to provide maximum assistance to the South Vietnamese to build up their forces, support the pacification program, and to reduce the flow of supplies and matériel to Communist forces in the south. Between 1969 and 1972, the Thieu government, with American aid, increased the size of its military forces from 825,000 to over a million. The South Vietnamese combat strength included about 120 infantry battalions in 11 divisions supported by 58 artillery battalions, 19 battalion-size armored units, and many engineer and signal formations.

By 1972, the regular ARVN divisions were robust organizations with modern equipment and weapons. They included three infantry regiments of three battalions each, one artillery regiment of three battalions, a cavalry squadron, an engineer battalion, and various logistics units. Figure 1 shows the organization of the ARVN division in 1972.

In addition to the ARVN divisions, there were 37 border ranger battalions, 21 ranger battalions, and the airborne and marine divisions. Complementing the regular forces were the Territorial Forces that included 300,000 Regional Forces and 250,000 Popular Forces (RF/PF) soldiers, and more than 500,000 People's Self-Defense Forces (PSDF).[2]

Along with the increase in size, there was also an effort to modernize the South Vietnamese forces in terms of weapons and equipment. American military aid provided the ARVN and Regional and Popular Forces over one million M16 rifles, 12,000 M60 machine guns, 40,000 M79 grenade

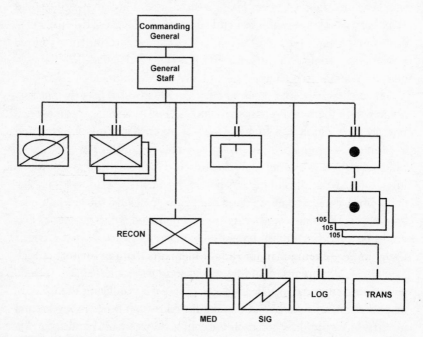

Figure 1. ARVN Division, 1972

launchers, and 2,000 heavy mortars.[3] The U.S. also provided them with 40,000 radios, 20,000 quarter-ton trucks, and 56 M-48 tanks. The objective was to equip the South Vietnamese forces with modern weapons that were on a par with the weapons and equipment being provided North Vietnam by the Soviet Union and China.

Although South Vietnamese ground forces were the primary focus of this modernization effort, the other services were also expanded and modernized during this period. By 1972, the Vietnamese Navy (VNN) had 43,000 men and operated 1,680 ships and boats. The Vietnamese Air Force (VNAF) more than doubled in size by this time, increasing to nine tactical wings, 40,000 personnel, and nearly 1,000 aircraft, including new A-1E, A-37, and F-5 fighters. The Vietnamese Marine Corps (VNMC) was also expanded to twice its original strength. By 1972, the Republic of Vietnam Armed Forces (RVNAF) was one of the largest and best equipped militaries in the world.

Equipment and numbers were not the only answers to the problem of the South Vietnamese becoming self-sufficient on the battlefield. In order to improve the quality of the ARVN force, MACV put new emphasis on improving the training of the South Vietnamese armed forces. The South Vietnamese military schools and training centers were improved and expanded to handle over 100,000 students a year. Similarly, the Pentagon brought more than 12,000 ARVN officers to the United States for advanced training at a number of military schools, including the U.S. Army Command and General Staff College at Fort Leavenworth, Kansas.

Concurrent with the renewed emphasis on training, MACV also took measures to improve the advisory effort. The U.S. advisory program was not new; Americans had been serving with Vietnamese units since 1955.[4] However, the emphasis on the advisory program had been lessened with the arrival of U.S. ground combat units in 1965. With the institution of Nixon's Vietnamization program in 1969 and the subsequent U.S. troop withdrawals, the advisory effort was returned to the front burner. The size and quality of the advisory corps increased as the number of American combat units dwindled; by the end of 1970, there was "an infusion of top-flight military professionals into South Vietnam's training advisory effort."[5] Part of the effort included putting more advisers in the field; this included a new program that dispatched more than 350 five-man teams of American advisers to train Regional and Popular Forces, which were having to carry more and more of the burden of fighting the Communists as the number of U.S. troops decreased.

The American military advisory structure very closely paralleled that of the Vietnamese military command and control organization. Headquarters, MACV, provided the advisory function to the Joint General Staff (JGS), the senior headquarters of the RVNAF.

Just below the JGS level were four South Vietnamese corps commanders who were responsible for the four military regions (MRs) that made up South Vietnam.[6] The corps commanders controlled from two to three ARVN divisions. The South Vietnamese corps commanders' U.S. counterparts were the commanders of the four regional assistance commands, whose responsibilities included providing assistance, advice, and support to the South Vietnamese corps commander and his staff in planning and executing operations, training, and logistical efforts. As the corps senior adviser, the regional assistance commander, usually an army major general, exercised operational control over the subordinate U.S. Army advisory groups in the military region. Map 1 depicts the military regions, associated ARVN corps headquarters, and major South Vietnamese positions.

Under the U.S. regional assistance commander in each region, there were two types of advisory teams: province advisory teams and division advisory teams. Each province in each military region was headed by a South Vietnamese colonel. His American counterpart was the province senior adviser, who was either military or civilian, depending on the security situation of the respective province. The province (also known as sector) advisory team was responsible for advising the province chief in both civil and military aspects of the South Vietnamese pacification and development programs. Additionally, the province team advised the Regional and Popular Forces (RF/PF), which were essentially provincial militia. As part of the province advisory group, there were also small teams of advisers with each of the districts (also known as subsectors) of the province. Figure 2 depicts the makeup of the province advisory team.

In addition to the province advisory teams, there was a division combat assistance team (DCAT) with each South Vietnamese infantry division. This advisory team's mission was to advise and assist the ARVN division commander and his staff in command, administration, training, tactical operations, intelligence, security, logistics, and certain elements of political warfare.[7] The division senior adviser was usually an army colonel, who exercised control over the staff advisers as well as the regimental and battalion advisory teams.

The advisers on the DCAT were located with both the division staff and the major subordinate commands. The regimental advisory teams

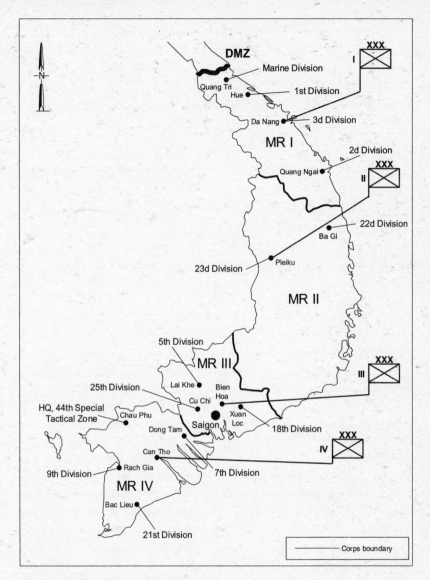

Map 1. Republic of Vietnam Military Regions and Major South Vietnamese Units, 1971

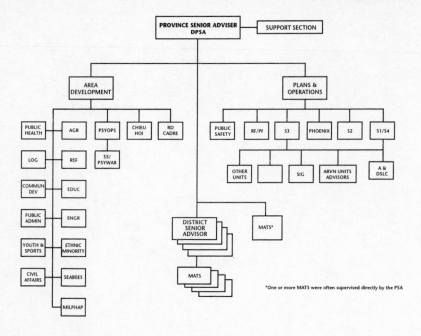

Figure 2. Province Advisory Team, 1968

Source: Ngo Quang Truong, *RVNAF and U.S. Operational Cooperation and Coordination,* Indochina Monographs (Washington, D.C.: U.S. Army Center of Military History, 1980), p. 154.

Note: By 1972, the size of the province advisory teams had been reduced due to the continuing U.S. troop withdrawals.

with the artillery and infantry regiments were normally composed of from three to five U.S. Army personnel (they had been larger, but by 1972 the drawdown of U.S. forces in country had gradually reduced the size of the American teams with the ARVN units). The regimental teams were usually headed by an army lieutenant colonel and included various mixes of officers and noncommissioned officers. There were also advisers with the separate battalions within the division. These advisory teams usually consisted of one or two specialists who advised the South Vietnamese in their respective functional areas: for example, cavalry, intelligence, logistics, or engineering. Figure 3 depicts the makeup of the division combat assistance team.

As the senior U.S. military commander in the region, each regional assistance commander was responsible for both province advisory teams

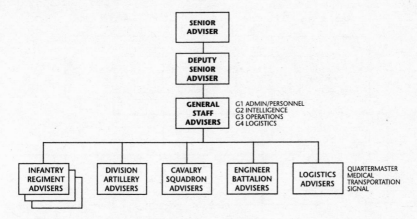

Figure 3. Division Combat Assistance Team (DCAT)

Note: Initially, the division combat assistance teams had been very robust, but because of the continuing U.S. troops withdrawals, the number of advisers was drawn down as well. By 1972, there were only two to three advisers with the infantry regiments, division artillery, cavalry squadron, engineer battalion, and logistics units.

and the division combat assistance teams with the ARVN divisions assigned to the military region. Figure 4 illustrates this command and control relationship.

Elite units, such as the airborne, rangers, and marines, were organized generally along the same lines as regular ARVN units. Each of these organizations was accompanied by an American advisory team, which was headed by a colonel and similar to those found with the regular ARVN units, but was somewhat larger because they still had advisers down to the battalion level.

U.S. Army advisers did not command, nor did they exercise any operational control over any part of the South Vietnamese forces. Their mission was to provide professional military advice and assistance to their counterpart ARVN commanders and staffs in personnel management, training, combat operations, intelligence, security, logistics, and psychological/civil affairs operations. As more and more U.S. combat forces withdrew from South Vietnam, the army advisers increasingly became the focal point for liaison and coordination between ARVN units and the U.S. Air Force, as well as other elements of U.S. combat support forces still left in country. The professional relationship between the advisers and their South Vietnamese counterparts depended on a number of factors, not the least of

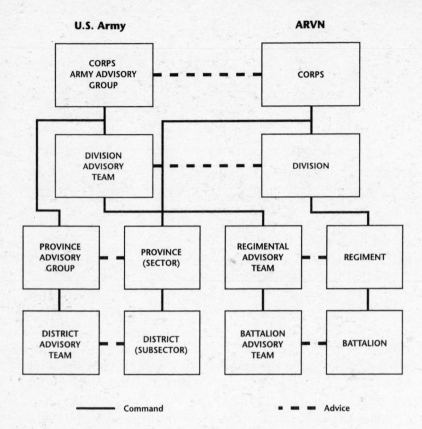

Figure 4. Advisory Command Relationships

Source: General Cao Van Vien, Lieutenant General Ngo Quang Truong, Lieutenant General Dong Van Khuyen, Major General Nguyen Duy Hinh, Brigadier General Tran Dinh Tho, Colonel Hoang Ngoc Lung, and Lieutenant Colonel Chu Xuan Vien, *The U.S. Adviser,* Indochina Monographs (Washington, D.C.: U.S. Army Center of Military History, 1980).

which were cultural and military backgrounds, language skills, unit SOPs, and individual personalities.

Testing Vietnamization

The Vietnamization program had its first real test in April 1970 when South Vietnamese forces joined U.S. units in the limited incursion into the Parrot's Beak and Fishhook areas of Cambodia. During the operation, the South Vietnamese forces accompanied by their advisers fought alongside their U.S. allies. By most accounts, the ARVN forces comported themselves very well, gaining much confidence in the process. U.S. military officials were pleased with the progress demonstrated by the South Vietnamese in these operations.

This good feeling was short-lived, unfortunately, because subsequent operations aimed at Communist sanctuaries in Laos in early 1971 revealed many shortcomings that continued to haunt the South Vietnamese forces. Unlike with the Cambodian incursion, when the South Vietnamese attacked into Laos during Operation LAM SON 719, they went without U.S. ground troops and without their American advisers. The attack along Highway 9 into Laos went fairly well initially, but the ARVN soon became bogged down along the road as the North Vietnamese Army 70B Corps rushed three divisions to the area to block the South Vietnamese thrust toward Tchepone, a key transportation hub along the Ho Chi Minh Trail.[8] In fierce fighting, the South Vietnamese took heavy casualties and withdrew in disarray back into South Vietnam.

Without their American advisers the South Vietnamese had done poorly, and their confidence was badly shaken. So, too, was the confidence of senior American military leaders in the ability of the South Vietnamese to deal with the North Vietnamese once all U.S. troops were gone. Efforts were intensified to address the critical South Vietnamese weaknesses revealed by the debacle in Laos.

Situation at the Beginning of 1972

By early 1972, the RVNAF had rebounded somewhat from the setback in Laos. Units that had suffered serious casualties during LAM SON 719 had been given replacements that brought them back to full strength.

The training program continued and began to show modest success. The South Vietnamese forces went back into Cambodia in late 1971 and were relatively successful, regaining some of the composure lost in Laos earlier that year.

As the Vietnamization effort continued, so did the U.S. troop withdrawals, with 177,000 Americans leaving South Vietnam in 1971. By January 1972, there were only 158,000 American personnel left in country. That month, President Nixon announced that he would withdraw an additional 70,000 troops by 1 May. Between February and April, 58,000 troops returned to the United States. It was the single largest troop reduction of the war, and it came precisely when the NVA was building up for the Easter Offensive. As historian Dale Andradé notes, "As the North Vietnamese built up for the Easter Offensive, the Americans built down."[9]

By March 1972, all U.S. ground combat troops had been withdrawn from South Vietnam except two brigades, one in MR I and one in MR III. The latter, the 3rd Brigade, 1st Cavalry, had become a separate brigade upon departure of the bulk of the division from Vietnam in early 1971. Headquartered at Bien Hoa, the brigade was commanded by Brigadier General James F. Hamlet and consisted of four cavalry battalions (which were actually airmobile infantry), supporting artillery, and several aviation units such as the 229th Assault Helicopter Battalion with F Troop, 9th Cavalry, and F Battery, 79th Aerial Rocket Artillery attached. The only other ground element left in Vietnam at this time was the 196th Light Infantry Brigade, conducting security operations in the Da Nang area. Figure 5 shows the organization of 3rd Brigade, 1st Cavalry Division, at the start of the 1972 NVA offensive.

Aside from these remaining U.S. combat units, the only American soldiers in the field were advisers. However, as previously stated, with the increasing U.S. troop withdrawals, the number of advisers had been steadily reduced in strength. The battalion advisory teams were closed out by 30 June 1971, and the regimental teams had been drastically reduced beginning in September. Therefore, by early 1972, there were only 5,416 U.S. tactical advisers in the whole of Vietnam.[10] Most of these were located at the division staff, and only a small fraction of this number were actually involved in advising units conducting combat operations.

Although there were few American forces operating on the ground in combat roles in Vietnam, U.S. airpower was still very much in evidence throughout the theater of operations. Despite three years of Vietnamization and U.S. troop withdrawals, the U.S. Air Force was still very much

Figure 5. 3rd Brigade, 1st Cavalry Division (Separate), March 1972

Cavalry Battalions (Airmobile Infantry)
  2nd Battalion, 5th Cavalry*
  1st Battalion, 7th Cavalry
  2nd Battalion, 8th Cavalry
  1st Battalion, 12th Cavalry

Brigade Artillery
  1st Battalion, 21st Artillery (105mm)
  Battery F, 26th Artillery (105mm)
  Battery F, 77th Artillery (Aviation)

Brigade Aviation
  229th Aviation Battalion
  (Assault Helicopter)**
    Troop F, 9th Cavalry (Air)
    Battery F, 79th Artillery (Aerial Rocket)
    362nd Aviation Company
    (Assault Helicopter)
    Detachment 1

Brigade Support
  215th Support Battalion
  501st Engineer Company
  525th Signal Company
  26th Chemical Detachment
  14th Military History Detachment

Other Units on Temporary Duty
  2nd Squadron, 11th Armored Cavalry***

*Departed Vietnam, 1 April 1972
**Organic units included Companies A, B, and D Troop (air cavalry)
***Departed Vietnam, 6 April 1972

engaged in the war. At the height of the war, more than 350 USAF jet fighter bombers were based in South Vietnam. With the drawdown, many of these aircraft had been redeployed. However, over 100 air force fighters remained in South Vietnam in early 1972. The workhorse was the F-4 Phantom, which could carry as many as 19 750-pound bombs or a variety of other ordnance, such as cluster bomb units (CBU) and napalm.[11] In addition to the F-4, there were also slower-moving aircraft more suited to close-in work, including the A-1 and A-37. The A-1 Skyraider was a Korean War–vintage propeller-driven aircraft that could carry a massive bomb load and remain on station for extended periods of time. The A-37 Dragonfly was a converted USAF trainer that was modified for close air support; it could carry six 500-pound bombs or a mixed load of other ordnance. The in-country air assets also included a number of AC-119 Stinger gunships, which were jet-assisted, propeller-driven, two-engine cargo aircraft converted to serve as fixed-wing gun platforms; they were armed with 7.62mm miniguns and 20mm Vulcan cannons.

Supplementing the in-country air fleet were a number of strike aircraft, including the AC-130 Spectre gunships based in Thailand. The AC-130, like the AC-119, was a converted cargo aircraft armed with 7.62mm miniguns, 20mm Vulcans, and 40mm Bofors automatic guns, and, on the PAVE AEGIS model, a 105mm gun. Before the 1972 NVA offensive, the Spectres were used primarily to interdict traffic along the Ho Chi Minh Trail in Cambodia and Laos. During the coming NVA offensive, these aircraft would play a major role in supporting the besieged defenders at An Loc.

Adding to this formidable air armada was the venerable Boeing B-52 Stratofortress. The B-52 force, which had proved so critical in the battle of Khe Sanh in 1968, had been reinforced. There were 52 heavy bombers at U Tapao Royal Thai Air Base, Thailand, and 31 at Andersen Air Force Base, Guam. Originally designed as a long-range strategic bomber, B-52s were deployed to Southeast Asia in 1965 and used primarily against enemy troop concentrations. The B-52 could carry a 38,000-pound bomb load internally, and the B-52D with the "Big Belly" modification could carry 24 additional 500- or 700-pound bombs on underwing racks. Figure 6 shows the strike aircraft assets in Southeast Asia as of March 1972.

In addition to the strike aircraft and B-52s, the air force also had C-130 tactical airlift aircraft in Vietnam. By 1968, the airlift effort in Vietnam had consisted of a full air division, controlling three in-country airlift wings and supported by three C-130 wings from elsewhere. By the spring of 1972, the numbers of airlift aircraft and units had been reduced because of the U.S. troop withdrawal. With the exception of a single squadron in the Philippines, the only airlift unit left in the region was the 374th Tactical Airlift Wing based at Ching Chuan Kang (CCK) Air Base in Taiwan. This wing and its four squadrons provided all tactical airlift for Southeast Asia. The 374th had 27 aircraft, 43 crews, and 260 maintenance personnel deployed to Vietnam at the start of 1972. These aircraft would play a major role in supporting the South Vietnamese at An Loc in the coming siege.

Although U.S. forces had been greatly reduced since 1969, the U.S. Navy and Marine Corps were still actively engaged in supporting the war in Vietnam in 1972. Operating off the coast of South Vietnam were two U.S. Navy attack carriers, *Hancock* and *Coral Sea*, each with an air wing of some 90 naval and marine aircraft. Before the beginning of the 1972 NVA invasion, these aircraft, primarily F-4 and other attack aircraft, were used chiefly against targets in North Vietnam, Cambodia, and Laos. During the NVA offensive, these aircraft would join the air force in providing critical close air support to the South Vietnamese forces.

Figure 6. USAF Order of Battle—South Vietnam and Thailand*
Strike Aircraft, 31 March 1972

Bien Hoa, RVN	Da Nang, RVN	Korat RTAB
23 A-37	60 F-4	30 F-4
	5 AC-119	16 F-105

Nakhon Phanom (NKP)	Ubon RTAB	Udorn RTAB
RTAB	10 B-57	52 F-4
10 AC-119	70 F-4	
15 A-1	13 AC-130	
4 F-4		U-Tapao RTAB
		52 B-52

*31 B-52 at Guam

Source: Major A. J. C. Lavalle, ed., *Airpower and the 1972 Spring Offensive*, United States Air Force Southeast Asia Monograph Series (Washington, D.C.: U.S. Government Printing Office, 1976), p. 14.

The Enemy Situation

In November 1971, the consensus among both U.S. and South Vietnamese intelligence had been that the North Vietnamese were not planning anything big for 1972. One Pentagon analyst insisted, "The enemy shows no sign of building up for anything big right now"; another predicted, "They're probably waiting for us to leave, or maybe for election time."[12] However, less than a month later, everything changed. A large tank park just north of the DMZ (demilitarized zone) was identified by photo reconnaissance. Additionally, new NVA units were detected moving south. Other intelligence reports indicated a large North Vietnamese buildup in Laos adjacent to MR I. General Abrams at MACV sensed that the North Vietnamese were making plans for a major offensive.[13] His suspicions proved prescient when revised intelligence estimates predicted a new North Vietnamese offensive in early 1972. Some analysts thought that it would come during the Tet Lunar New Year's celebration in February, but others believed that the enemy assault would come in March. Regardless of the timing, most intelligence analysts agreed that the main enemy effort, when it came, would occur in MRs I and II, with limited supporting activity in the western part of MR III.[14]

CHAPTER TWO

THE NGUYEN HUE CAMPAIGN

Deciding to Launch the Offensive

THE NORTH VIETNAMESE in Hanoi had been considering a general offensive in South Vietnam since the 19th Plenum in late 1970, but the leadership in the Politburo was split over the question. General Vo Nguyen Giap, the hero of Dien Bien Phu, and Le Duan, First Secretary of the Party, were the most vocal advocates of an all-out offensive in the south, but others like Truong Chinh, president of the National Assembly, wished to focus efforts more on rebuilding the North while postponing an attempt to force reunification with the South by conventional military means.

A number of factors motivated Giap and Le Duan to call for a new offensive. The military situation in South Vietnam was at best a stalemate. The Cambodian incursion in April 1970 had severely damaged the logistic apparatus supporting the Communist troops in the southern half of South Vietnam. Additionally, Nixon's Vietnamization and pacification programs were making gains. In the South Vietnamese countryside, the Viet Cong, nearly wiped out militarily during the 1968 Tet Offensive, could gain little momentum as the Saigon government continued to attack the VC infrastructure.

There were, however, positive developments on the political front. Antiwar sentiment within the United States was increasingly impeding Nixon's prosecution of the war. He had all but been forced to begin U.S. troop withdrawals shortly after taking office, and these reductions had continued unabated since the fall of 1969. Giap and Le Duan argued that these factors dictated the need for a new attempt to break the stalemate on the ground in South Vietnam.

No firm decision was made at the 19th Plenum, but several events in 1971 would cause a renewal of the debate. The first of these was Operation LAM SON 719. Giap and Le Duan pointed to the less-than-stellar performance of the South Vietnamese forces in Laos as justification for launching a major effort to overthrow the Saigon government once and for all. Additionally, they maintained that the continued U.S. troop withdrawals meant that the Americans would not be able to react militarily to save the South Vietnamese if Hanoi launched a major invasion. It was also thought that a new offensive would offset the gains made by South Vietnam in the pacification program.

The second event that added weight to Giap's case was Nixon's announcement in the summer of 1971 that he would travel to China during the first half of 1972. The American president was also making overtures toward the Soviet Union. These moves had several effects. First, they convinced many in the North Vietnamese leadership that the international situation was working against them, that in effect they were running out of time and might lose their primary patrons, both of which had supplied massive amounts of military aid that permitted the North Vietnamese to sustain their war in the south. Second, as historian Dale Andradé suggests, the thawing relations between the United States and the two Communist nations had an unintended effect in that the situation "forced Moscow and Beijing to prove their revolutionary credentials by giving increased support to Hanoi without corresponding conditions."[1] This situation would work nicely for Giap and Le Duan as they tried to convince their colleagues of the wisdom of a new offensive.

In May 1971, the Party Central Committee met in Hanoi to discuss how the lessons of LAM SON 719 could be used in the future. During this meeting, Giap and Le Duan once again presented their case for a new general offensive. They acknowledged that the potential reaction of President Nixon was a concern, but made a persuasive case that the political situation in the United States would not permit the American president to commit any new troops to assist the South Vietnamese once the offensive was launched. Additionally, they argued that Nixon was so committed to seeking détente with the Soviets that he would not do anything to upset the ongoing strategic arms control talks. Therefore, Giap and Le Duan reasoned, they could attack South Vietnam with little or no significant interference from the United States. Moreover, if a defeat could be inflicted on South Vietnam while U.S. forces were still in country, North Vietnam could claim a military victory against the Americans as well as the South Vietnamese. This victory, or even partial success, would humiliate Nixon and destroy his war politics and perhaps his bid for reelection in November.

These arguments were very persuasive, and the Party Central Committee decided to forgo the evolutionary phases of their protracted war of liberation and take the calculated risk of launching a decisive, all-out offensive in 1972.[2] According to the official history of the People's Army of Vietnam, the goals for this offensive were "to annihilate a number of enemy regimental task forces and brigades; to render entire puppet regular divisions combat ineffective; to liberate a number of areas; to expand . . . base areas; to move . . . main force units into the various battlefields of South Vietnam and provide them a firm foothold there; and to provide direct support for mass popular movements that would conduct attacks and uprisings to destroy the pacification program in the rural lowlands."[3] The Party Central Committee confirmed this decision at the 20th Plenum, where the Communists proclaimed that "in order to achieve total victory, we must mobilize, coordinate and unify our forces . . . to defeat the 'Vietnamization' policy and Nixon doctrine."[4]

Planning for the Offensive

Once the decision was made by the Politburo to launch the offensive, General Giap had to come up with a plan. While he and his military planners devised a complex campaign designed to strike a knockout blow against the South Vietnamese government and its armed forces, the Politburo initiated a "logistics offensive." Le Duan went to Moscow to request assistance in the form of new weapons and equipment.[5] An appeal was also made to Beijing.[6] Subsequently, the North Vietnamese received massive quantities of modern weapons from the Soviet Union and China, including MiG-21 jet fighters, surface-to-air missiles (SAMs, which would be key to the defense of North Vietnam should the United States step up bombing), T-54 tanks, BTR50-PK armored personnel carriers, Molotova trucks, 122mm howitzers, 130mm guns, 160mm mortars, 57mm antiaircraft guns, and, for the first time, AT-3 Sagger wire-guided antitank missiles and shoulder-fired, heat-seeking SA-7 Strela antiaircraft missiles.[7] All of this matériel enabled the NVA to outfit 12–14 divisions plus a number of independent regiments with new equipment. The North Vietnamese also began stockpiling spare parts, ammunition, and fuel in much greater amounts than ever before reported.[8] Divisions of the NVA general reserves were ordered to move south to position themselves for the invasion.

Giap's campaign plan included a massive, three-pronged invasion of South Vietnam aimed at three critical areas. The first thrust would be made against the provincial capital of Quang Tri in MR I; the second at An Loc in Binh Long Province, northwest of Saigon, MR III; and the third at Kontum in the Central Highlands, MR II.[9] In each attack, the North Vietnamese would use three to four infantry divisions supported by tanks and artillery.

Giap's strategy was audacious and somewhat risky, but he counted on the simultaneous attack on three major fronts to disorganize the RVNAF and thus prevent Saigon from decisively committing its national reserves. Any of the three prongs of the attack, if successful, could have a major impact on the course of the war. The northern prong could sever the two northern provinces and capture the old imperial capital at Hue, which no doubt would have a devastating effect on South Vietnamese morale. The attack in the Central Highlands could cut South Vietnam in two, putting the northernmost provinces also in peril. The southern attack might eventually propel North Vietnamese forces into the capital city itself. Success on any of the fronts would have severe repercussions on the staying power of the Thieu regime in Saigon. However, if all three prongs were successful, the war would be over and the South Vietnamese would be defeated.

According to captured documents and information obtained from NVA prisoners of war, the campaign was designed to destroy as many ARVN forces as possible, thus permitting the North Vietnamese to occupy key South Vietnamese cities, putting the Communist forces in a posture to threaten the Thieu government. Giap hoped to discredit Nixon's Vietnamization and pacification programs, cause the remaining American forces to be withdrawn more quickly, and ultimately to seize control of South Vietnam.[10]

A subset of Giap's strategy called for a Communist Provisional Revolutionary Government to be established in An Loc as a precursor to the assault on Saigon.[11] Although the North Vietnamese hoped to achieve a knockout blow, a corresponding objective was to seize as much terrain as possible to strengthen their position in any subsequent negotiations.[12] Therefore, the North Vietnamese stood to gain one way or the other. As a Communist B-5 Front (northern South Vietnam) communiqué stated before the attack, "regardless of whether the war is ended soon . . . or not, we will have the capability of gaining a decisive victory."[13] As designed, the campaign appeared to be a win-win situation for the North Vietnamese.

The exact timing of the offensive depended on the weather; dry conditions would be imperative for such large-scale operations. Vietnam is dominated by two monsoon seasons. Those areas of South Vietnam subject to the southwest monsoon, generally those in the lower two-thirds of the country, can usually expect dry weather from mid-October until the end of May. Those subject to the northeast monsoon, generally the northern third of the country including Quang Tri and Hue, are dry from about the first of February until the first of September. Therefore, the only common period of dry weather is between 1 February and 31 May. The decision was made to launch the offensive on 30 March to take advantage of these common dry conditions before the wet season and seasonal rains made movement and resupply too difficult.

The North Vietnamese dubbed the invasion the "Nguyen Hue Campaign." It was named in honor of Nguyen Hue, the birth name of Emperor Quang Trung, a Vietnamese national hero, who in 1789 dealt invading Chinese troops a resounding defeat just outside Hanoi. In the United States, the North Vietnamese invasion would become known as the "Easter Offensive," since the opening attack was launched on Good Friday.

D Day

The offensive began as planned on 30 March 1972, when three NVA divisions attacked south across the Demilitarized Zone (DMZ) that separated North and South Vietnam toward Quang Tri and Hue in MR I. Three days later, three more divisions moved from sanctuaries in Cambodia and pushed into Binh Long Province, the capital of which was only 65 miles from the South Vietnamese capital in Saigon. Additional North Vietnamese forces attacked across the Cambodian border in the Central Highlands toward Kontum. A total of 14 NVA infantry divisions and 26 separate regiments—the equivalent of 20 divisions—would take part in the offensive. This included more than 130,000 troops and approximately 1,200 tanks and other armored vehicles.[14] This was virtually every combat unit in the North Vietnamese Army with the exception of the 316th Division, which continued to operate in Laos for the duration of the offensive. Map 2 depicts the three major North Vietnamese thrusts.

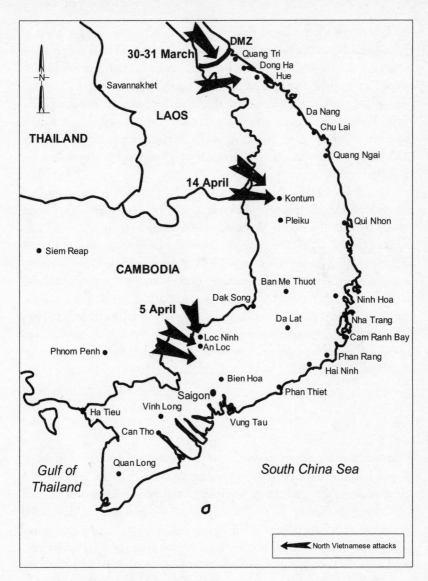

Map 2. The Nguyen Hue Campaign, 1972

The North Vietnamese invasion was characterized by large-scale conventional infantry tactics, accompanied by tanks and massive artillery support, a drastic departure from the methods of warfare previously used by the Communists in their attempts to conquer the South. One *Newsweek* journalist described the offensive in the following manner: "It was a classic World War II–style assault with Russian-made arms—long-range artillery that rained thousands of screaming shells on the Army of South Vietnam (ARVN) and Soviet tanks that churned through the hastily abandoned fire bases and country-side."[15]

The initial enemy thrust into Quang Tri Province by an estimated 39,000 North Vietnamese regulars was highly successful. The NVA forces rapidly overran the South Vietnamese defenders in a string of firebases south of the DMZ as they pushed toward the province capital at Quang Tri City. Within 72 hours, the entire ARVN defensive line in the northern part of Quang Tri Province crumbled. In Saigon, the South Vietnamese Joint General Staff and MACV were stunned at the rapid advance of the North Vietnamese and the collapse of the ARVN forces in MR I. They were soon to find out that these were only the opening shots of a massive countrywide campaign. The next blows would fall in the Central Highlands and MR III.

Nixon Responds

With the South Vietnamese forces on the ropes in Quang Tri and major attacks looming farther south, President Nixon's response to the NVA offensive was threefold. First, he ordered the reinforcement of air and naval assets in theater. Secondly, he ordered the bombing of Hanoi and Haiphong. Thirdly, he instituted an air interdiction campaign against North Vietnam. This was done incrementally, but in a fairly rapid fashion. On 6 April, Nixon ordered Operation FREEDOM TRAIN, which involved intensive bombing in North Vietnam south of the 20th parallel. On 16 April, Nixon extended the target area farther north when 18 B-52s and more than 100 U.S. Navy and USAF fighter bombers hit supply dumps near Haiphong's harbor at the same time that 60 fighter bombers hit petroleum storage facilities near Hanoi. This was the first time that B-52s had been used north of the DMZ. On 8 May, Nixon ordered commencement of Operation POCKET MONEY, the mining of Haiphong harbor. Over the next few days, attack aircraft from the carrier *Coral Sea* emplaced more than

11,000 mines in North Vietnamese waters. On 10 May, Nixon ordered the commencement of Operation LINEBACKER, a comprehensive and extended interdiction campaign designed to reduce the flow of supplies into North Vietnam, to destroy existing stockpiles, and to reduce the flow of men and matériel from North Vietnam south. "The President," said an administration official, was "going all out with air power to help the ARVN stop the Communist offensive."[16] These operations went on simultaneously with the heavy fighting in the south and would continue until 23 October. They would take some time to have the greatest effect, but eventually this interdiction campaign would take its toll on the North Vietnamese capability to sustain the offensive.

The most immediate impact on the situation in the South was the decision to increase the air support assets in theater. The in-theater forces put on a maximum effort once the battle started, but more aircraft were needed to blunt the three-pronged offensive. The orders went out for a worldwide mobilization of USAF units to return to Southeast Asia to support the South Vietnamese and their American advisers. Aircraft deployed from U.S. airbases in Korea, Japan, the Philippines, and the United States. The return of the tactical fighters went by the code name CONSTANT GUARD. The number of fighter aircraft in theater doubled to almost 400. A good example of this operation can be seen with the 49th Tactical Fighter Wing from Holloman AFB in New Mexico, which deployed 72 F-4s to Takhli in Thailand. The first squadron to depart, the 417th, landed in Thailand and less than 24 hours later flew 27 missions in support of the defenders at An Loc.[17]

Concurrent with beefing up the number of attack aircraft in theater, Operation BULLET SHOT involved the reinforcement of the B-52 fleets in Guam and Thailand. During April, three groups of B-52s deployed to Andersen AFB in Guam. In some cases, B-52s were flying bombing missions over South Vietnam less than 72 hours after receiving deployment alert in their stateside bases. Three more groups of bombers arrived in May, bringing the total number of B-52s in Southeast Asia to 171.[18] During the same period, the number of airborne tankers, required to support the B-52s on their long-range missions, rose to 168 in theater. Figure 7 shows the status of strike aircraft in Southeast Asia by 20 May 1972.

The navy and marines also responded rapidly. The carrier force quickly grew from two to six with the arrival in early April of the *Kitty Hawk, Constellation, Midway,* and *Saratoga.* Each of the new carriers brought approximately 90 aircraft that greatly increased the air armada available to blunt

Figure 7. USAF Order of Battle—South Vietnam and Thailand*
Strike Aircraft, 30 May 1972

Bien Hoa, RVN	Da Nang, RVN	Korat RTAB
20 A-37	60 F-4	34 F-4
2 A-1	5 AC-119	31 F-105
5 AC-119	2 A-1	
Nakhon Phanom (NKP)	Ubon RTAB	Udorn RTAB
RTAB	92 F-4	86 F-4
4 AC-119	14 AC-130	
16 A-1		
4 F-4	Takhli RTAB	U Tapao RTAB
	72 F-4	54 B-52

*117 B-52 at Guam

Source: Major A. J. C. Lavalle, ed., *Airpower and the 1972 Spring Offensive*, United States Air Force Southeast Asia Monograph Series (Washington, D.C.: U.S. Government Printing Office, 1976), p. 30.

the NVA offensive. The marines also moved two F-4 squadrons to Da Nang from Iwakuni Air Station in Japan; a third marine squadron arrived at Da Nang from Kaneohe Air Station, Hawaii. Finally, in mid-May, the marines moved two squadrons of A-4 Skyhawk attack aircraft from Iwakuni to Bien Hoa Air Base, where they would join daily in the defense of An Loc.

There was a lot riding on the outcome of the Communist offensive. President Nixon told a press conference that he was confident that "the South Vietnamese lines may bend, [but] not break. If this proves to be the case, it will be the final proof that Vietnamization has succeeded."[19] The man charged with ensuring that the South Vietnamese did not fail, General Creighton Abrams, fully realized the stakes involved in the coming battle. He told the Joint Chiefs of Staff: "If it [the defense of South Vietnam] is skillfully fought by the Republic of Vietnam, supported by all available U.S. air, the outcome will be a major defeat for the enemy, leaving him in a weakened condition and gaining decisive time for the consolidation of the Vietnamization effort. . . . In the final analysis . . . the issue will be whether Vietnamization has been a success or a failure."[20] This statement would be particularly true with regard to the desperate battle that was about to unfold in Binh Long Province.

CHAPTER THREE

THE AREA OF OPERATIONS

Military Region III

BEFORE DISCUSSING THE desperate battle that developed in MR III, it is first appropriate to discuss the nature of the area of operations and the situation on the ground at the start of the fighting. MR III, comprising the 11 provinces that surrounded Saigon, was located between the Central Highlands and the Mekong Delta. The region contained a number of areas, such as the Iron Triangle, the Ho Bo Woods, and War Zones C and D, which had seen heavy fighting during the earlier years of the war. During the height of the U.S. involvement in the war, III Corps Tactical Zone (as MR III was known prior to 1971) was home to the 1st Infantry Division, 25th Infantry Division, two brigades of the 1st Cavalry Division, 199th Light Infantry Brigade, and the 11th Armored Cavalry Regiment. By 1972, all of these forces had departed Vietnam with the exception of the reinforced 3rd Brigade, 1st Cavalry, and elements of the 1st Aviation Brigade.[1] Map 3 depicts MR III.

The senior South Vietnamese headquarters in MR III was III Corps, located in Bien Hoa, arguably one of the most important cities in the region. In addition to holding the ARVN corps headquarters, Bien Hoa was also the site of a large air base from which both USAF and VNAF aircraft operated. The commander of III Corps in 1972 was Lieutenant General Nguyen Van Minh. He had been in the military since 1950, serving initially as an airborne officer with the French. He had assumed command of the corps in February 1971 upon the death of his predecessor, Lieutenant

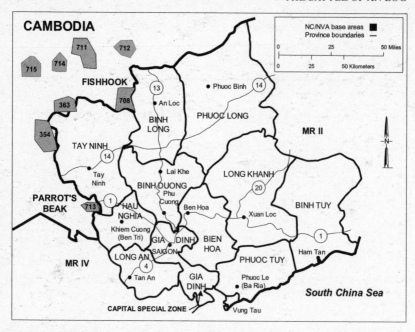

Map 3. Military Region III

General Do Cao Tri, who was killed in a helicopter crash in Cambodia in February 1971. Minh had previously commanded the 21st Infantry Division in the Mekong Delta and was a member of what was known as the "Delta Clan," which had close political ties with Nguyen Van Thieu, president of South Vietnam.

General Minh's counterpart was Major General James F. Hollings-worth, commander of the Third Regional Assistance Command (TRAC), who had assumed that position in December 1971. During World War II, Hollingsworth, a 1940 graduate of Texas A&M University, was wounded five times and recognized by General George S. Patton Jr. as one of the two best armor battalion commanders in the war.[2] Also a veteran of the Korean War, "Holly," as he was known by many of his admirers, had served one previous tour in Vietnam as the assistant division commander of the 1st Infantry Division in 1966–67. He had returned to Vietnam in mid-1971 to serve as deputy commander of the U.S. XXIV Corps at Da Nang. When that headquarters deactivated later that year because of the continuing U.S. troop drawdown, Hollingsworth went to Long Binh to take command of TRAC, which was "the distilled remains of II Field Force and III Corps

Advisory Group."[3] Whereas II Field Force had focused on controlling the combat operations of U.S. units in the region, TRAC focused on the advisory effort and Vietnamization.

The recipient of three Distinguished Service Crosses and four Silver Stars, Hollingsworth was aggressive, brash, and profane; he was described by one adviser as "hell-bent for leather" and one who "loved the smell of smoke." Despite his gruff exterior, the general had a "genuine and deep-seated" concern for the welfare of his officers and men.[4] As TRAC commander, Hollingsworth, whose radio call sign was "Danger 79er," a holdover from his days in the 1st Infantry Division, was responsible for all the U.S. advisers in MR III, both those on the province teams and those with the three ARVN divisions in III Corps. TRAC headquarters, located on a compound called "the Plantation" in Long Binh, had a normal general staff with each staff officer serving as an adviser to his counterpart on the III Corps staff.

Given his reputation as a hands-on combat commander, he may have been miscast in what was originally designed as an essentially managerial and advisory position. Additionally, he was ordered by his old World War II friend, General Abrams, to continue the troop drawdown while not unnecessarily endangering American lives. However, when the battle for Binh Long Province started, Hollingsworth proved to be the perfect man for the task. During the battle he strengthened the resolve of the ARVN corps commander when the situation looked grim. He flew over the city daily during the worst of the shelling and encouraged both the ARVN troops and their American advisers defending the city. He had a great rapport with General Abrams and would be able to convince the MACV commander to divert B-52 strikes from MR I and MR II to An Loc when the city was most seriously threatened. It was Hollingsworth and his deputy, Brigadier General John R. McGiffert, an artillery officer who had also served in the 1st Infantry Division in 1966–67, who would play key roles in planning the B-52 and tactical air strikes that would save the city.

Under command of III Corps were three ARVN Divisions: the 18th, the 25th, and the 5th. The 18th, headquartered at Xuan Loc, was responsible for the provinces of Bien Hoa, Long Khanh, Phuoc Tuy, and Binh Tuy. The 25th, headquartered at Cu Chi, was responsible for the area of operations encompassing the provinces of Tay Ninh, Hau Nghia, and Long An. The 5th ARVN Division, headquartered at Lai Khe, was responsible for Binh Duong, Binh Long, and Phuoc Long Provinces. With these three divisions were three division combat assistance teams made up of American advisers. Additionally, there were 11 province advisory teams in the region. All of these advisers fell under General Hollingsworth's command.

Binh Long Province

Binh Long ("Peaceful Dragon") Province is located in the northwestern portion of MR III and is bordered on the west by Cambodia and on the south by Binh Duong Province. In 1972, the population of the province was about 60,000. The three main populated areas in the province were Loc Ninh, An Loc, and Chon Thanh. Map 4 shows Binh Long Province.

Loc Ninh was a district town that sat on Highway 13 at the edge of a small valley along the Rung Cam River 14 kilometers from the Cambodian border.[5] It consisted of a small dusty town of about 4,000 (mostly Montagnards), with an all-weather airfield about a half mile west of the highway. Arrayed along the airfield were three small compounds. At the north end of the runway was the district compound; at the opposite end was the headquarters compound of the 9th ARVN Regiment. The middle compound housed the regiment's artillery. The area around the town was generally level and fairly open to the south. To the west the vegetation had been bulldozed back about 300 meters.

Chon Thanh was the southernmost town of any size in the province and sat just north of the provincial boundary with Binh Duong. About 25 kilometers from An Loc, it was only a small town but had an airstrip.

Between Loc Ninh and Chon Thanh lay An Loc, the province capital, which was only 65 miles north of Saigon. It was a city of about 15,000, with an additional 5,000 people living in the six major hamlets in the surrounding area. It was a thriving and relatively prosperous city surrounded by vast rubber plantations totaling more than 100,000 acres. An Loc district included a total of 12 villages, 7 of which were populated by Vietnamese and 5 of which were made up of Montagnard tribesmen.

Because of its proximity to Cambodia and the accompanying Communist base areas, Binh Long Province had endured the rigors of war since the early 1960s, witnessing significant fighting in 1967. Because of its strategic location between Cambodia and Saigon, An Loc figured prominently in the North Vietnamese strategy for the 1972 offensive. Militarily, there was no intrinsic value to the city. It was not fortified and really presented no obstacle to the attackers. However, it sat astride Highway 13, a paved highway that wound out of Cambodia to Loc Ninh and then followed an

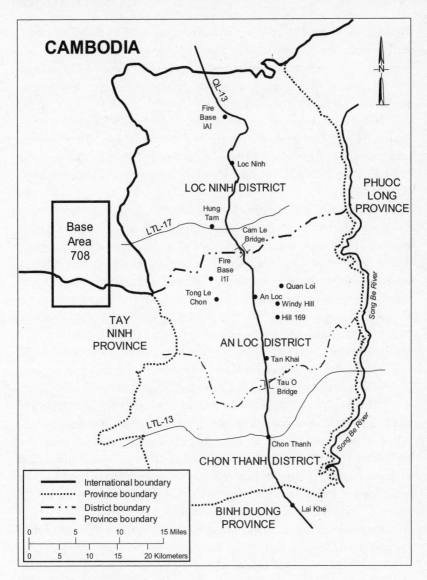

Map 4. Binh Long Province

abandoned railroad bed into An Loc before running south for 76 kilometers to the South Vietnamese capital. This highway was the main high-speed avenue of approach leading from major Communist staging areas in Cambodia to the South Vietnamese capital city. From the South Vietnamese perspective, it effectively provided the only ground link between the 5th ARVN Division headquarters at Lai Khe and the ARVN defensive positions along the Cambodian border in the Loc Ninh area. Thus, An Loc and the highway south would have to be secured by the NVA to facilitate follow-on attacks threatening President Thieu's seat of government in Saigon.

The city itself was just short of two kilometers long and one kilometer wide, encompassing an area 11 blocks long and 6 wide. The entire town consisted of 10 main streets, which were all wide and paved with asphalt. Three of the streets ran north-south, paralleling Highway 13, and seven were cross streets running east-west. The city was made up of two distinct areas. The northern part was the civilian area, while the southern part of the city housed military units and the local government administrative offices. The houses and public buildings were mostly one story high, but there were some two- and three-story buildings as well. Most of the dwellings, shops, and government buildings were solidly constructed of a wide variety of materials, including brick, stone, stucco, and wood.

The town was encircled by a series of earthen berms, bunkers, and fighting positions that formed the defensive perimeter of the town. These positions were normally secured by provincial (usually referred to as "sector") forces. At the southwest center of the city was a standard soccer field marked by typical "An Loc red dirt," a red laterite clay that became embedded in everything. At the southern end of the town was the RF/PF military camp. To the northeast of the town was a short airstrip that was used primarily for light aircraft. Also in this area was the main ammunition dump for the RF/PF forces.

Seven kilometers to the northeast of An Loc was Quan Loi. Located there was the French rubber plantation manager's villa and an airfield built by the U.S. 1st Infantry Division in 1966. The South Vietnamese had a small firebase there secured by two companies from the 7th Regiment of the 5th ARVN Division.

An Loc was bisected by the highway, which ran through the rubber plantation that surrounded the city from the south through the center of town and exited out the north side toward Loc Ninh. To the east was a slight valley between the city and gradually rising ground that ran to the south from Quan Loi to Hill 169, the point of highest elevation in the area. This hill was at the end of a ridgeline that provided good observation of the city. To the north of the town was a small knob, Hill 128, that was slightly higher than the surrounding terrain. From this location, the entire city could be fully observed as well as the highway north for a considerable distance. Hills 169 and 128 would figure prominently in the fighting to come. To the west of the town, the ground was not very uniform and was characterized by slight ups and downs, but generally, with the exception of the aforementioned high ground to the southeast, the terrain in Binh Long Province in the vicinity of An Loc was relatively flat.

Sixteen kilometers to the east of An Loc runs the Song Be River, about 50 meters wide and flowing from north to south. About 15 kilometers to the west of the city runs the Saigon River, which is about 60 meters wide and also flows from north to south. Therefore, An Loc was squeezed in between two rivers, making Highway 13 a very important road linking the areas near the Cambodian border with the provinces to the south.

As previously noted, the terrain in Binh Long Province was primarily covered by rubber plantations, but there were also areas of jungle, open fields, and marshy grassland. In the mature rubber stands, the trees were 10 to 15 feet apart, sufficient to allow the free movement of tanks and other vehicles. The plantations, whose trees provided about one-third of South Vietnam's total exports, contained numerous ditches built to inhibit erosion but that could readily be converted into bunkers. The jungle areas, though relatively thin, provided excellent concealment.

In addition to Highway 13, there were a number of roads in Binh Long, most of them used in connection with the cultivation and harvest of the rubber plantations. Among the other roads in the area were Route 303, which connected An Loc and Quan Loi, and Route 246, which ran west from the southwest corner of An Loc. The quality of these roads varied. The only paved, high-speed avenue was Highway 13. Earlier in the war, U.S. Rome plow "jungle removers" had pushed the jungle back from the highway on both sides to reduce the possibility of ambush.

The overall responsibility for the defense of Binh Long Province lay with the province chief, Colonel Tran Van Nhut, a former marine regimental commander and considered one of the most able South Vietnamese officers (he would later be promoted to general and command an ARVN division). Nhut had also formerly commanded both the 43rd and 48th Regiments of the 18th ARVN Division and was a superb leader and administrator.

Co-located with the Binh Long Province headquarters was Advisory Team 47, which consisted of about 20 advisers under Lieutenant Colonel Robert Corley. This team was responsible for providing advice and assistance to Colonel Nhut and his staff. Colonel Corley, an engineer officer, was a very effective adviser and had an excellent rapport with Colonel Nhut. Together, they had aggressively moved forward with the government pacification program in the province.

For security of the province, Colonel Nhut had at his disposal a mix of Territorial Forces. These included the PSDF and the RF/PF. The PSDF were part-time militia responsible for the defense of their hamlets and villages. The RF/PFs, known as "Ruff Puffs," conducted operations throughout the province. Under the prevailing system, the RF/PFs would do all that was possible on their own, but then the ARVN division located in or near the province would take over the action when the enemy's capabilities outstripped those of the regional and sector forces. Nhut's forces numbered about 2,000 soldiers, including RF and PF units, PSDF forces, a platoon of V-100 armored cars, and one 105mm howitzer platoon.

The 5th ARVN Division

As previously stated, at the beginning of the North Vietnamese offensive in MR III, the Saigon government had only a single division, the 5th ARVN, operating in the critical area that included Binh Long Province. A regular South Vietnamese infantry division, the 5th ARVN was headquartered at Lai Khe, but the division area of responsibility included Phuoc Long and Binh Duong Provinces as well as Binh Long. By March 1972, most divisional units were dispersed throughout Binh Long Province. Elements of the 9th Regiment (less one battalion that was located at Bu Dop in Phuoc Long Province), supported by two batteries of artillery, were located at Loc Ninh. Two companies from the 2nd Battalion, 9th Regiment, supported by two 155mm and four 105mm howitzers, were located at the Cam Le Bridge along Highway 13 between Loc Ninh and An Loc. The 1st Armored Cavalry Squadron, with two attached infantry companies from the 9th Regiment and a mixed artillery battery of 105mm and 155mm howitzers, was located at Fire Support Base Alpha on Highway 13, a few kilometers south of the Cambodian border northwest of Loc Ninh. Also at this location was the 74th Border Ranger Battalion, which had been placed under the operational control of the cavalry squadron.[6] This force was collectively known as Task Force (TF) 1-5.

The 7th Regiment, minus one battalion located at Phuoc Binh in Phuoc Long Province, was operating in an area about six kilometers west of An Loc at Fire Support Base 1. They were supported by two 155mm and four 105mm howitzers. Two companies from the 1st Battalion supported by two 105mm howitzers were located at Quan Loi just east of An Loc.

The remaining regiment from the 5th ARVN, the 8th, was located in Binh Duong Province. However, one of its battalions was out of the immediate area at the national training center in Phuoc Tuy Province.

Also attached to the 5th ARVN was TF 52, commanded by Lieutenant Colonel Nguyen Ba Thinh. The task force was conducting operations from two small firebases (named "FSB North" and "FSB South," and collectively known as Hung Tam Base) located 10–12 kilometers north of An Loc and 2 kilometers west of the junction of Route 17 (a provincial road) and Highway 13. This task force had been formed from the 2nd Battalion of Thinh's own 52nd Regiment and the 1st Battalion from the 48th Regiment, both originally from the 18th ARVN Division; the task force also included the division Intelligence and Reconnaissance (I&R) Company; C Battery, 182nd Artillery (105mm howitzer); a platoon of 155mm howitzers; and B Company, 18th Engineers. The task force, numbering about 1,000 soldiers, had been moved from the 18th Division base in Xuan Loc (Long Khanh Province) in late March and placed under the operational command of the 5th ARVN Division.

In addition to the 5th ARVN Division forces, there were several other units in the area. The 92nd Ranger Battalion was located at Tong Le Chon, southeast of An Loc. This unit was a border ranger battalion and not part of the 5th ARVN Division; it reported directly to III Corps. There were also several artillery tubes at this location.

The 5th ARVN headquarters was at Lai Khe, but the division maintained a very light forward command post at An Loc. The 5th ARVN Division was commanded by Brigadier General Le Van Hung, who as province chief of Phong Dinh (headquartered at Can Tho in MR IV) had been a member of the "Delta Clan" and had been only recently appointed to command of the division by Lieutenant General Minh, who had relieved the previous division commander because of the 5th Division's poor showing in operations in Cambodia during late 1971.

General Hung and the 5th ARVN Division were assisted by the members of Advisory Team 70, a small division combat assistance team, consisting of 15–20 advisers that were co-located with the 5th ARVN headquarters at Lai Khe. The team consisted of several advisers who worked with the G-2, G-3, G-4, and signal sections. In addition to the advisers who worked

with the division staff, there were smaller teams of two to five persons who
worked with each of the three infantry regiments (as previously stated, battalion advisers were no longer authorized by this time), the artillery, and
the armored cavalry squadron.

The division senior adviser when the North Vietnamese offensive
began was Colonel William H. Miller. A veteran of World War II and
Korea (including 10 years as an enlisted man), Colonel Miller was on his
third tour in Vietnam. His first tour in 1963 had also been as an adviser
with the 5th ARVN Division, commanded at that time by then Colonel
Nguyen Van Thieu. On his second tour, Miller commanded a battalion in
the 25th Infantry Division in 1966–67. Miller had seen the ARVN operate
"up close and personal" during his two earlier tours, and he was somewhat
skeptical of their abilities. General Hung appeared to be equally skeptical
about the role of U.S. advisers. He told Miller early on in their relationship that he had already had many advisers and that none of them knew
as much about war as he did. Hung did not often ask for Miller's advice
and frequently did not even inform his counterpart of tactical decisions.[7]
Miller and Hung would have a rocky relationship during the battle to
come.

In addition to Colonel Miller's division team and Lieutenant Colonel
Corley's province team, other American advisers accompanied the ARVN
reinforcements that would be brought in during the course of the battle.
These few Americans (never numbering more than 25 during the course
of the battle) would find themselves in the thick of the combat action once
the North Vietnamese attack began in earnest.

The NVA Plan in Military Region III

The focus of the North Vietnamese effort in MR III was on seizing An
Loc; the campaign would be directed by Lieutenant General Tran Van Tra,
commander of the B-2 Front, whose headquarters was probably located
somewhere in the vicinity of Snoul or Memot in Cambodia.[8] At Tra's disposal were more than 33 battalions. Once An Loc was captured, the path
would be clear for a thrust down Highway 13 to Saigon and vulnerable
areas throughout the northern Mekong Delta. It is unclear whether the
North Vietnamese ever intended to attack Saigon directly, but An Loc
would certainly provide a useful base for subsequent operations to threaten
the South Vietnamese capital.

Figure 8. Estimated NVA Troop Strength, MR III, March 1972

5th VC Division		69th Artillery Division	
HQ & Support	4,680	HQ & Support	1,395
E6 Regiment	1,500	42nd Artillery Regiment	800
174th Regiment	1,500	208th Rocket Regiment	835
275th Regiment	1,500	271st Anti-Aircraft Regiment	800
Total	9,180	Total	3,830

7th NVA Division		Other Forces	
HQ & Support	4,100	205th NVA Regiment	1,250
141st Regiment	1,500	101st NVA Regiment	760
165th Regiment	1,500	203rd Tank Regiment	800
209th Regiment	1,500	Incl 202nd Special Weapons Regiment	
Total	8,600	429th Sapper Group (–)	320
		Total	3,130

9th VC Division	
HQ & Support	4,680
271st Regiment	2,000
272nd Regiment	2,000
95C Regiment	2,000
Total	10,680

Note: The total estimated North Vietnamese forces committed to the Binh Long campaign in late March was approximately 35,500. Additionally, intelligence projections estimated that the committed units received more than 15,000 replacements during the course of the fighting in Binh Long. For a detailed outline of how and when these forces were committed, see appendix 1.

Source: Major General James F. Hollingsworth, "Communist Invasion in Military Region III," unpublished narrative, 1972, in Robert Lester, ed., Records of the Military Assistance Command, Part 1: The War in Vietnam, 1954–1973 (Bethesda, Md.: University Publications of America, 1988), MACV Historical Office Documentary Collection, microfilm reel 44.

The plan for taking An Loc involved the use of three NVA divisions and supporting forces. By this time in the war, although some of the North Vietnamese formations still carried the traditional Viet Cong designations, they were organized and equipped as mainforce NVA units manned primarily by North Vietnamese soldiers who had come down the Ho Chi Minh Trail from the north. Figure 8 shows the units that would participate in the battles in Binh Long Province.

Prior to the launch of the main attack into Loc Ninh, two independent NVA regiments would attack outposts in Tay Ninh Province to the south of Binh Long. This was the traditional Communist attack route toward Saigon. These attacks were meant to focus the allies' attention in that direction while the North Vietnamese launched their main attack against Binh Long Province.

After the diversionary attacks were launched, the 5th VC Division, commanded by Colonel Bui Thanh Van, was to initiate the offensive campaign in Binh Long by capturing Loc Ninh, the northernmost town in the province. After securing this foothold, the North Vietnamese forces would move on An Loc. The 9th VC Division, commanded by Colonel Nguyen Thoi Bung, would then take An Loc itself. This was expected to be accomplished in 5–10 days, and then the new capital of the Provisional Revolutionary Government would be established in An Loc on 20 April. The 7th NVA Division, commanded by Colonel Dam Van Nguy, was tasked to interdict supplies and reinforcements from reaching An Loc from Saigon by cutting Highway 13 south of An Loc, between Chon Thanh and Lai Khe.[9] The attackers would have at their disposal 27 maneuver battalions in the 5th, 7th, and 9th Divisions, plus 6 more in the 24th and 271st independent regiments, which would launch the diversionary attacks against Tay Ninh. Map 5 illustrates the North Vietnamese campaign plan for Binh Long Province.

In support would be the 69th Artillery Division, the 429th Sapper Group, and two tank formations, including two battalions from the 203rd Tank Regiment and elements of the 202nd Special Weapons Tank Regiment. These formations were equipped with T-54s of two types, one of Russian manufacture and one a Chinese copy, the T-59; both types of tanks were equipped with 100mm main guns.[10] There were also amphibious PT-76 light tanks that mounted a 76mm gun. In addition to the tanks, there were other mechanized vehicles, including BTR50-PK armored personnel carriers and the ZSU-57/2, a T-54 tank chassis fitted with twin 57mm antiaircraft guns.

The 69th Artillery Division, famous for the critical role it played in the Battle of Dien Bien Phu 18 years earlier, consisted of three regiments: the 42nd Artillery, the 208th Rocket, and the 271st Anti-Aircraft. These units were equipped with a variety of weapons, including 122mm howitzers, 107mm and 122mm rockets, as well as 82mm and 120mm mortars. There is also some evidence (never confirmed) that the North Vietnamese may have used long-range Soviet 130mm guns at An Loc; this was an impressive

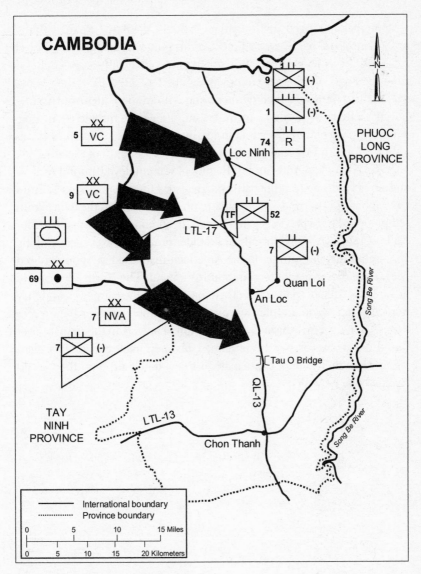

Map 5. NVA Plan in Binh Long Province

weapon that outranged anything that the South Vietnamese had, with the exception of the wildly inaccurate 175mm gun. Augmenting the Soviet weapons, the NVA gunners also had 105mm and 155mm guns captured from the South Vietnamese forces in Cambodia during 1971; they would eventually have more allied weapons and ammunition after overrunning South Vietnamese positions in Binh Long Province en route to An Loc. This firepower played a key role in the intensive barrage of ARVN forces at Loc Ninh, An Loc, and along Highway 13 to the south of the city.

The NVA 271st Anti-Aircraft Regiment was employed around An Loc and along Highway 13 as the battle progressed. This unit possessed 12.7mm (.51 caliber), 23mm, and 37mm antiaircraft guns, as well as the twin 57mm self-propelled guns previously mentioned. In addition, during the battle for An Loc, the NVA would introduce shoulder-fired SA-7 Strela heat-seeking antiaircraft missiles, similar to the American-made Redeye shoulder-fired heat seeker, never before seen in South Vietnam. The North Vietnamese fully realized the need to protect their forces from allied airpower, and they were able to fashion an intensive air-defense "umbrella" over their forces that made it extremely hazardous for aircraft to operate in the airspace over Binh Long. However, North Vietnamese planners made a major miscalculation when they failed to anticipate just how much airpower they would have to contend with.

CHAPTER FOUR

THE BATTLE OF LOC NINH

The Enemy Buildup

FROM NOVEMBER 1971 to January 1972, the 5th ARVN Division conducted cross-border operations into eastern Cambodia. These incursions were limited in depth, being within 105mm howitzer range from fire support bases located along the border across from the Fishhook area, which had long been used as a sanctuary for VC and NVA troops. No significant contacts were made or caches uncovered in spite of considerable indications of intensifying enemy activity in the area.[1] In late January, there were scattered contacts with the enemy along the Cambodian border. In February and early March of 1972, intelligence sources identified two NVA divisions, the 7th and 9th, in the Cambodian Krek-Chup plantation areas across the border from Tay Ninh and Binh Long Provinces. In early March, ARVN intelligence reported the presence of the 5th VC Division in Base Area 712, near the Cambodian town of Snoul, about 30 kilometers northwest of Loc Ninh on Highway 13. Additionally, the 24th and 271st Regiments were reported operating in Cambodia in an area just adjacent to Tan Ninh.

During this period, the focus of TRAC intelligence analysts was on Tay Ninh Province. There was good reason for this. Tay Ninh Province, and not Binh Long, had always been the traditional avenue for enemy attacks on Saigon from Cambodia. On numerous occasions in the past, Communist forces had launched attacks toward Saigon from their Cambodian sanctuaries northwest of Tay Ninh Province. Accordingly, in February,

U.S. intelligence determined that Tay Ninh was the most likely target for any North Vietnamese offensive in the region. "Within MR 3, the level of enemy activity is expected to increase during the period 19–25 Feb. 72 probably focalized in the Tay Ninh area," concluded one report.[2]

On 16 March, ARVN soldiers ambushed an NVA patrol in northern Tay Ninh Province, capturing three Communist soldiers. One of them turned out to be the executive officer of the 272nd Regiment. He indicated that the 9th VC Division was moving east of the Saigon River west of An Loc. On 17 and 18 March, a patrol from the 7th Regiment captured a signal officer and two sergeants from the 69th Artillery Division on Highway 13 adjacent to the Cambodian border. These prisoners indicated that they were a reconnaissance team looking for firing positions.[3]

An enemy document captured in late March further confirmed that something unusual was afoot in Binh Long. It indicated that the 9th VC Division was planning to move to Base Area 708 in the Fishhook, and the 272nd Regiment would move into an area west of Binh Long. The document also mentioned that the 7th NVA and 9th VC Divisions were to coordinate actions for future campaigns and that cadres of the 9th Division had received training in urban warfare.[4] On 27 March, a soldier from the 7th NVA Division's reconnaissance element surrendered to the ARVN, reporting that his unit had been given the mission to reconnoiter routes from Tay Ninh to Binh Long for the division's next movement.[5]

In March, Colonel Miller, senior adviser to the 5th ARVN Division, tried desperately to get General Hung to launch a preemptive strike against the forces massing against Binh Long, but the ARVN commander replied that he could do nothing without orders from III Corps, implying that it went against Vietnamese culture and tradition for him to even suggest such an operation to his higher commander. Given what Miller clearly saw as the enemy buildup in Binh Long, he was very frustrated with Hung and became increasingly concerned that the South Vietnamese general might not possess the ability to visualize and respond to the major NVA attack that appeared to be looming.

Despite the signs that the enemy was massing in the area adjacent to Binh Long, Lieutenant General Minh, Major General Hollingsworth, and their intelligence staffs remained convinced that the enemy's main attack would be in Tay Ninh Province when it came. In reality, the diversionary attacks in Tay Ninh effectively masked the movements of the three Communist divisions preparing to launch the main attack in Binh Long Province.

The South Vietnamese Joint General Staff also discounted the possibility of a major attack in the Binh Long area. However, JGS intelligence
broadcast an alarm about a possible general offensive in the Central Highlands area. On 30 March the NVA forces streamed across the DMZ. All
eyes at JGS and MACV in Saigon naturally focused on I Corps as the 3rd
ARVN Division crumbled in the face of the North Vietnamese onslaught.
However, the JGS was about to be presented with another threat, one that
would put Saigon itself at peril.

Launching the Binh Long Campaign

As part of the deception plan, the NVA tried to nurture allied preconceived
notions that the main attack in MR III would come in Tay Ninh by mounting a major attack by the NVA 24th Regiment (Separate) on the morning
of 2 April against an ARVN fire support base at Lac Long along Route 20,
about 35 kilometers northwest of Tay Ninh City in the Dog's Head area of
the Cambodian-Vietnamese border. The firebase was defended by the 49th
Regiment of the 25th ARVN Division. A 600-round rocket and mortar barrage was followed by a regimental-size ground assault. This attack marked
the first use of enemy armor in MR III and included M-41 tanks, possibly
captured from earlier ARVN operations in Snoul and Dambe, Cambodia.
By noon, the NVA had overwhelmed the defenders, who lost 10 killed, 44
wounded, and 22 missing.

The attack on Lac Long prompted III Corps to order the withdrawal
of the small ARVN outposts located along the Cambodian border. It was
felt that it was better to pull these forces back to more defendable terrain
rather than leave them "hanging out there by themselves" where they
would quickly fall prey to the NVA attackers. The only exception to the
order was the small ranger outpost at Tong Le Chon, whose commander
requested to stay where he was rather than pull back.[6]

Most of the border outposts withdrew with only scattered contacts with
the NVA. However, when the ARVN tried to withdraw from a firebase
at Thien Ngon on Highway 22 near the Cambodian border, they were
ambushed by elements of the 271st NVA Regiment (Independent). The
North Vietnamese attacked once again with infantry and tanks, supported
by heavy mortar and rocket fire. The South Vietnamese suffered heavy
casualties and lost most of their vehicles and artillery. The firebase had
protected the approaches to Tay Ninh City, and with it taken the NVA had

a clear path to continue the attack. However, when ARVN reinforcements arrived the next day, they were surprised to find that the abandoned South Vietnamese vehicles and tanks were still there; the enemy had withdrawn without taking the weapons and equipment with them. This mystery would be solved when it became known that the attacks in Tay Ninh were only diversions.

As stated previously, there had been earlier intelligence reports that the North Vietnamese were making preparations for offensive operations in III Corps, but the South Vietnamese and their advisers were totally surprised by the ferocity of the enemy attacks and the use of tanks by the NVA.[7] The attacks on Lac Long and Thien Ngon served to confirm the opinion of observers at both III Corps and TRAC headquarters that the main enemy effort would be made in Tay Ninh Province. However, it did not appear that the NVA were making preparations to exploit their success in Tay Ninh.

A captured North Vietnamese soldier revealed that the main enemy element in the Tay Ninh area was the 7th NVA Division.[8] The real question for intelligence analysts had to do with the current location and activity of the other two previously identified NVA divisions (5th VC and 9th VC) that were known to be operating in Cambodia in the area adjacent to western MR III. As time passed and the North Vietnamese did not press their advantage in Tay Ninh, General Hollingsworth would come to the conclusion that the enemy's main effort would come in Binh Long Province and not in Tay Ninh.

However, what appeared to be a developing situation in Tay Ninh initially took attention away from Binh Long despite the continued intelligence reports of NVA units in that province. On 2 April, U.S. intelligence reported that a radio intercept indicated that the 5th VC Division was operating 10–12 kilometers west of Loc Ninh. There were other reports of VC and NVA troops sighted in squad, platoon, and company formations in Binh Long close to the Cambodian border.[9]

The attacks in Tay Ninh served as a screening action to enable the 9th VC Division to move undetected into Base Area 708, northwest of An Loc, putting the NVA within easy striking distance of any point within Binh Long Province. Having already infiltrated into Binh Long from the region in Cambodia directly north, the 5th VC Division maneuvered its troops into attack positions for an assault on Loc Ninh. Further to the south of An Loc, the elements of the 7th NVA Division positioned forces to interdict Highway 13.[10]

In Saigon, intelligence analysts could determine no clear pattern indicating the role Binh Long Province was to play in the overall NVA campaign plan. The primary focus of JGS attention was still on Quang Tri, where things continued to go badly for the South Vietnamese. On 4 April, the JGS ordered the redeployment of three ranger groups from Tay Ninh to Phu Bai in MR I, indicating that most observers at MACV and the JGS continued to believe that the main enemy thrust was in I Corps and that incidents occurring in MR III were only NVA attempts to tie down government forces and thus prevent reinforcement of more critical areas.

One man was unfooled by the early NVA moves. At the 5th ARVN Division headquarters, Colonel Miller, convinced that the NVA were planning to hit Binh Long in force, urged General Hung to do something to prepare for the battle he was sure was coming, but Hung still maintained that he could do nothing without orders from III Corps. Miller was certain that Hung's forces, basically static and vulnerable, would be the next NVA objective. To Miller, the attacks in Tay Ninh did not match the growing buildup of forces just across the border in Cambodia from Binh Long. Additionally, he reasoned that the enemy would use Highway 13 as an avenue of approach toward Saigon rather than try to traffic the more difficult terrain in Tay Ninh Province. With this in mind, he predicted that the first attack would come at Loc Ninh.

Always an advocate of the offensive, Miller strongly urged Hung to seize the initiative by reinforcing Loc Ninh and maneuvering his forces to block the coming NVA onslaught. He thought if the 5th ARVN could mass their forces at Loc Ninh, the South Vietnamese could defeat the NVA there and preclude a battle farther south at An Loc.

Believing that the NVA would try to take Loc Ninh, Miller strongly recommended that Hung remove Colonel Nguyen Cong Vinh, commander of the 9th Regiment there. Vinh was a weak officer who Miller thought had a defeatist attitude. Hung adamantly refused on all counts and launched into a tirade about advisers meddling in South Vietnamese affairs. Miller later reported that Hung at first appeared to be relieved that the enemy forces were concentrating on Tay Ninh Province, rather than Binh Long. However, when it became apparent that the North Vietnamese were instead headed straight for him, he became almost paralyzed, according to Miller. Nevertheless, Miller continued his efforts to get the division commander to reposition his forces. On the night of 3 April, Hung told Miller that he had ordered TF 1-5 back to Loc Ninh from FSB Alpha.

It was later revealed that he had not given such an order, and the task force remained at the firebase.

Miller was also worried about the advisers in Loc Ninh. There were a total of seven Americans in the town. Lieutenant Colonel Richard S. Schott, who had just transferred from a desk job in Saigon, was the regimental senior adviser with the 9th ARVN. He was assisted by Major Albert E. Carlson, Captain Mark A. Smith, and two enlisted communications specialists, Sergeant First Class Howard B. Lull and Sergeant Kenneth Wallingford. They were normally co-located with the 9th Regimental headquarters in the southernmost compound. At the other end of the airfield were two officers at the Loc Ninh district compound. Captain George Wanat was the acting district senior adviser while his boss, Major Robert Blair, was on leave. The other American in the district compound was Major Thomas Davidson, who had been sent from An Loc to Loc Ninh to gather information on the situation there for Lieutenant Colonel Corley, the province senior adviser. Map 6 depicts the Loc Ninh defenses.

Earlier on 3 April, the advisers to the 9th Regiment, Major Carlson, Captain Smith, and Sergeant Wallingford, accompanied by French freelance photographer Michel Dumond, were returning by jeep from a supply run to Lai Khe when they observed numerous overloaded vehicles moving south along Highway 13. One such vehicle was driven by the French plantation manager from Loc Ninh who urged them to go back to Lai Khe because "the communists were coming." Nevertheless, the advisers continued on to Loc Ninh, where they found the village virtually deserted. They finally found some ARVN soldiers drunk in a bar. Smith, fluent in Vietnamese, asked them what they were doing drunk during the duty day; they fatalistically replied that they were drinking because they were doomed and expected to die soon.[11] The advisers rejoined the 9th Regiment at its command post in the compound near the south end of the airstrip. Map 6 depicts the ARVN positions in and around Loc Ninh.

The Battle of Loc Ninh

On 4 April very late in the afternoon, the 9th Reconnaissance Company operating west of Loc Ninh made contact with an NVA element and was nearly wiped out. This proved to be the opening shots of the battle for Binh Long Province. That evening, a patrol from 3rd Battalion, 9th Regiment, located on a hill due south of Loc Ninh airstrip, ambushed a five-man NVA

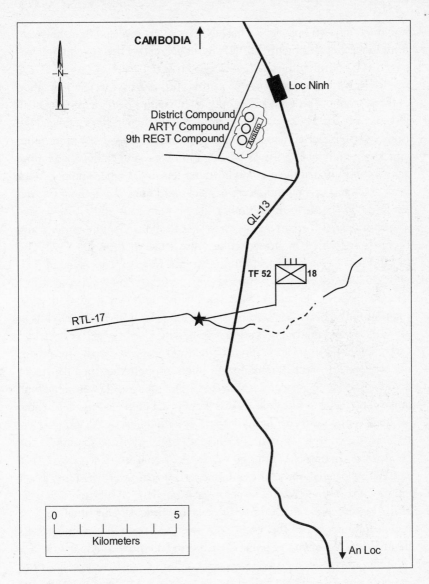

CAMBODIA ↑

Loc Ninh

District Compound
ARTY Compound
9th REGT Compound

AIRSTRIP

QL-13

TF 52 ⊠ 18

RTL-17

0   5
Kilometers

↓ An Loc

Map 6. Loc Ninh

squad, taking two prisoners. These NVA soldiers revealed that they were from the 272nd Regiment, 9th VC Division, and that their parent unit was passing Loc Ninh to the south to attack An Loc.

In the early morning hours of 5 April, the NVA gave a clear indication of their intentions in Binh Long, opening up with a heavy barrage of artillery, mortars, and rockets on the headquarters of the 9th Regiment and the Loc Ninh District compound. Almost simultaneously, there were other attacks throughout the 5th ARVN Division area of operations, including a few rounds fired at the division headquarters in Lai Khe, a sapper attack against Quan Loi, and indirect fire attacks on Phuoc Vinh, Song Be, and Bo Duc. The battle for Binh Long had started in earnest.

Shortly after the barrage began at Loc Ninh, two NVA regiments and 25 tanks supported by heavy artillery fire attacked from the west. The North Vietnamese attackers from the 5th VC Division concentrated their efforts on the regimental command post at the south end of the airstrip.[12] The defenders beat back the first attack with tactical air support, destroying one of the tanks, but around 0600 there was a 30-40-minute lull in aircraft support and the tanks broke through the ARVN lines.[13] Fortunately, more fighter-bombers arrived on station, and the tanks were driven back once again. The South Vietnamese soldiers, supported by their American advisers, acquitted themselves well and stood up against the enemy tank and infantry attack. The fighting was desperate, but the South Vietnamese soldiers for the most part hung in there and fought hard; ARVN gunners lowered the muzzles of their 105mm howitzers and fired directly at the NVA infantry advancing through the rubber trees.

With the battle now raging at Loc Ninh, Hollingsworth and his ARVN counterpart, General Minh, operating from III Corps headquarters in Bien Hoa, quickly realized the seriousness of the developing situation. The increasing intensity of the attack convinced the two senior commanders that this was the opening shot of the expected offensive and that an attack of major proportions was now focused on Binh Long and not Tay Ninh. Accordingly, they directed all available tactical air support north to Loc Ninh, and more aircraft began arriving in the area almost immediately, including USAF A-37s from 8th Special Operations Squadron at Bien Hoa, naval attack aircraft from the carrier *Constellation*, VNAF F-5s and A-1s, and USAF F-4s and AC-130s from Thailand. These aircraft provided almost continual air cover over Loc Ninh as the battle unfolded.

More help arrived after a dramatic radio call went out from the area flight-following control station over the channel monitored by all helicopters in the area: "Attention all aircraft, this is Paris, on Guard. Loc Ninh is under tank and infantry attack. I say again, Loc Ninh is under tank and infantry attack. Any aircraft with armament, please respond."[14] Among the first to respond to this plea was F Troop, 9th Cavalry, with six AH-1G Cobra gunships and their three OH-6 scouts. Also responding were Cobras from F Battery, 79th Aerial Rocket Artillery, otherwise known as the "Blue Max."

The Bell AH-1G Huey Cobra was a two-person attack helicopter armed with various configurations of weapons systems, including 7.62mm miniguns, 40mm grenade launcher, and rocket launchers. The Cobra, which came into service in 1967, had been designed to take the place of the slower UH-1B Huey gunship. During the coming battle, it would prove itself against North Vietnamese tanks and armored personnel carriers.

On arrival in the Loc Ninh area, the Cobras made radio contact with the advisers on the ground and began immediately to engage the NVA tanks and infantry. Working in close under some of the most intense anti-aircraft fire any of the pilots had ever seen, the army helicopters did everything within their power to support the advisers and the South Vietnamese troops. The situation was very confused because the NVA and ARVN were so closely intertwined; from the air, the pilots had a difficult time separating friend from foe. Nevertheless, they managed to unravel the situation and knocked out several tanks that were threatening the advisers.

Time and again, the Cobras rolled in on the attackers against horrendous antiaircraft fire from the ground. In one instance, a Cobra made a rocket run on a tank, destroyed it with his rockets, but was taking heavy antiaircraft fire in exiting the target area. An alert forward air controller directed a flight of F-4 Phantoms right in behind the helicopter, helping the Cobra pilot to escape the devastating fire.

As the fighting intensified at Loc Ninh, Colonel Miller and General Hung boarded a command and control helicopter and headed north from Lai Khe. As they approached Chon Thanh, they were able to monitor the advisers' radios inside the perimeter at Loc Ninh. Miller spoke with Captain Smith, whose call sign was "Zippo." Smith, a seasoned veteran on his fifth tour in Vietnam, told Miller to keep the air support coming as he directed strike after strike into the attackers. The situation was critical, with the ARVN taking significant casualties from the continuing artillery and mortar barrage. As Smith directed the close air support, Major Carlson and Sergeant Wallingford attended to directing the ARVN artillery. In the other compound, Major Davidson and Captain Wanat, the district advisers, relayed their requests for air support through Captain Smith to hit the NVA attacking their perimeter.

Colonel Nguyen Cong Vinh, commander of the 9th Regiment, shaken by the ferocity and scope of the enemy attack, ordered TF 1-5 to withdraw from FSB Alpha to reinforce Loc Ninh. The commander of TF 1-5 refused, saying that he was going to surrender his unit to the NVA. Vinh said he understood. Smith then snapped and berated the regimental commander for allowing the cavalry squadron commander to surrender without a fight. Colonel Miller had long been worried about Vinh's reliability, and now it was clear that he was not up to the demands of the growing battle. From that point on, it appears that Smith was virtually in command of the ARVN troops as they attempted to repel the NVA attack. Lieutenant Colonel Schott, recognizing Smith's combat experience and knowledge of the Vietnamese language, allowed Smith to take the lead role in handling the situation.[15] Smith called the commander of TF 1-5 on the radio and warned him not to surrender without a fight, saying he would call in an air strike on the task force if they did not fight. A short time later, before Smith could make good on his threat, the rangers and the two infantry companies from 2nd Battalion, 9th Regiment, notified the regimental command post that they had broken out and were fighting their way back to Loc Ninh, but that the cavalry squadron had already surrendered to the NVA and was moving west with the enemy, willingly driving their tanks and APCs toward the Cambodian border. The survivors of TF 1-5 made their way south but ran into an ambush a few kilometers south of the junction of Highway 13 and Route 14. They called for instructions and Colonel Vinh told them to return to FSB Alpha, but Smith grabbed the microphone and told them to continue south. They made their way toward Loc Ninh, arriving there the next day and joining the defenders against the continuing attack.

While the rangers and infantrymen fought their way back to Loc Ninh, the ARVN defenders inside the town and their seven American advisers fought desperately against the North Vietnamese onslaught. Smith and the other American advisers coordinated and directed U.S. tactical air support from Bien Hoa Air Base, aircraft carriers in the South China Sea, and other attack aircraft flying from bases in Thailand, including AC-130 Spectre gunships. The volume of well-placed air strikes and AC-130 fire would enable the advisers and a rapidly dwindling number of South Vietnamese defenders to hold the NVA at bay for two days, fighting off at least three mass attacks in the process.

Around noon on 5 April, the NVA reinforced their forces to the south-west of the town and launched another major ground assault. When the NVA tried to get through the defenses of the southern compound, an AC-130 gunship, according to Major General Hollingsworth, "slaughtered" them in the wire and "destroyed the better part of a regiment."[16] The four-engine propeller-driven aircraft was originally designed as a transport, but it had been armed and modified earlier in the war to carry out interdiction missions against North Vietnamese men and matériel moving down the Ho Chi Minh Trail into South Vietnam. In addition to its armament, it was equipped with a variety of tracking equipment, including Black Crow radar used to pick up vehicle ignitions, a low-light-level television camera, an infrared detector, ground target radar, and a strong searchlight. These well-armed, versatile aircraft would prove crucial in the coming battle for An Loc.

Another attempt was made by the enemy to cross the runway from the west, but it was stopped cold by well-placed air strikes using CBUs. Yet another enemy assault succeeded in getting into the wire on the east side of the 9th Regiment's command post, but it was stopped by Cobra gunships. However, during the course of this battle, the first Blue Max Cobra was lost. On a rocket run at almost 4,000 feet just south of Loc Ninh, the Cobra flown by Warrant Officer Charles Windeler and Captain Henry Spengler was hit. Told by his wingman that he was on fire, Windeler tried to get the aircraft safely to the ground, but it appeared that the controls burned through at about 1,500 feet and the helicopter hit the ground and exploded. Another Cobra from Blue Max confirmed that the two pilots did not survive the crash.[17]

During the fight, the enemy artillery and rocket bombardment of Loc Ninh continued without letup. In addition, the defenders in both compounds were taking direct fire from tanks and recoilless rifles. One of the recoilless rifle rounds made a direct hit on the regimental command bunker near Smith and Schott, wounding them both. While Smith was attending to his wounds, Major Carlson took over in directing the air effort. At one point during this part of the battle, Smith and Schott, although wounded, manned a 106mm recoilless rifle and engaged tanks attacking from the tree line to the west.

As the advisers in Loc Ninh fought for their lives, Colonel Miller tried to convince General Hung that the NVA's main objective was An Loc and urged him to withdraw the 7th Regiment from FSB 1 back into An Loc; the

7th had just come under attack and was in danger of being overwhelmed if something was not done. Pulling these forces back to An Loc was a prudent move, because the town was virtually undefended at this point, with nothing manning the perimeter but RF/PF soldiers. The attack at FSB 1 probably meant that this was the lead element of the 9th VC Division headed for An Loc. After a contentious exchange, Hung grudgingly gave the order to pull the 7th Regiment back. Miller was also worried about the mounting vulnerability of TF 52 at Hung Tam and the small force at Cam Le Bridge, but Hung's plate was obviously too full at this point to deal with anything but the worsening situation at Loc Ninh.

Meanwhile, in Loc Ninh the South Vietnamese and their advisers continued to maintain a tenuous hold on their compounds. Having blunted the initial attacks, the advisers employed the Spectre gunships and attack helicopters close to their positions while directing the fighter-bombers further out to break up enemy formations. Still, the artillery, rockets, and mortar shells continued to fall on the defenders. Later on the afternoon of 5 April, Captain Smith radioed Colonel Miller, now at the 5th ARVN forward command post at An Loc, that he thought the enemy was preparing for another major push. However, things quieted down a bit as night began to fall, and the situation was stabilized for the time being.

Later that evening, two T-54 tanks rolled through the perimeter until they were engaged by ARVN 106mm fire, killing one and forcing the other one back. Captain Smith later reported that around 2200 hours that night, the regimental commander, Colonel Vinh, ordered two soldiers to open the compound gates, explaining that it would make things easier when it came time to "run out." It appeared that the South Vietnamese commander was planning to surrender or desert.

Smith continued to work close-in targets during the night with the Spectre gunships, on several occasions calling for fire within his own compound. General Hollingsworth reported to General Abrams that the town would have fallen on 5 April had it not been for the "magnificent support of the 7th Air Force and the brilliant direction of a young Army captain, Smith."[18]

At An Loc, Miller and Hung continued to argue about the situation at Loc Ninh. Miller wanted to send reinforcements, at least from TF 52 still located at Hung Tam south of Loc Ninh, but Hung refused. Since Hung would not order more troops to Loc Ninh, Miller wanted to use B-52s to help the beleaguered defenders, but Hung was not clear on where all the friendly troops were located, so it was too dangerous to bring in the big bombers.

Early on the morning of 6 April, Colonel Miller and General Hung boarded the general's command and control ship and flew to Lai Khe to confer with Hung's staff and the commander of the 8th Regiment. After a brief discussion, they took off again and headed north. Just north of Chon Thanh, they saw a column of vehicles halted on the road. A closer look revealed that the vehicles were North Vietnamese. Miller quickly surmised that this was the heretofore unlocated NVA division, the 7th; shortly thereafter the North Vietnamese established a road block across the highway. It was now clear that the enemy planned to cut An Loc off from the south. General Hung was stunned. The situation was falling apart: Loc Ninh was under siege, TF 52 had reported contact at Hung Tam, Quan Loi was being probed, the 7th Regiment was in contact, and the North Vietnamese were cutting Highway 13 south of An Loc. Miller again urged Hung to give the order to reposition his forces, but Hung was not responsive. By this time, Miller felt the battle was rapidly escalating out of Hung's control.

Meanwhile, the tactical situation at Loc Ninh had once again reached a critical point. The shelling had continued sporadically throughout the night as the NVA maneuvered their forces in preparation for another major push. In the early morning hours, the advisers heard tanks in the vicinity of the southern end of the runway. At first light, the NVA began probing the ARVN positions. Smith continued to put air strikes on suspected enemy positions. Shortly thereafter, the NVA infantry succeeded in getting into the wire, and tanks joined the attack from the northwest and southeast. The battle seesawed back and forth for the next three hours.

About noon, the advisers observed a group of civilians being driven forward by NVA soldiers from the nearby village. Smith fired a burst of rifle fire over their heads, scattering them. Meanwhile, he and Schott, assisted by the regimental surgeon and two soldiers, had set up claymore mines and white phosphorus grenades in the wire along the western perimeter. In the late afternoon, the NVA launched their next attempt to capture the ARVN positions. One company from the E-6 Regiment rushed the front gate and made it inside the compound. Captain Smith called in U.S. Air Force fighters, who stopped the attack in its tracks with CBUs and napalm. As the North Vietnamese troops massed for yet another wave of attacks on the remaining ARVN positions, the repeated tactical air strikes and accurate AC-130 fire wrought terrible damage on them. A Spectre gunship orbiting the area blunted one tank attack, killing one tank and forcing the others to withdraw. However, the flyers did not have it easy. The NVA had ringed the town with .51-caliber Soviet- and Chinese-made machine guns, and this antiaircraft fire became so intense that resupply and medevac missions could not be flown into the town.[19] The defenders were cut off from outside help.

Complicating things for everyone in the air was the sheer number of aircraft working the area. The forward air controllers (FACs) had to try to sort it all out in order to provide the most effective support to the troops on the ground. Attack helicopters and AC-130s had to be waved off in order to employ the "fast movers," leading to some control issues that would presage more command and control problems in the air over An Loc in the major battle yet to come.

During the early evening, Lieutenant Colonel Schott and Captain Smith, both wounded several times by this point in the battle, toured the bunker line. The 9th Regiment was down to 50 defenders, with over 150 wounded in the hospital bunker. The regimental surgeon, who stuck it out with the Americans for the whole battle, said that some of the wounded were well enough to go back on the perimeter, and they did so without complaining. By this time, some of the survivors of FSB Alpha who had refused to surrender with the cavalry squadron had made it into the compound. A few others from 3rd Battalion, 9th Regiment, which had been virtually wiped out on the hill to the south of the town, had also made it in.

General Hollingsworth was pleased with the advisers and their day's work. In his daily situation report to General Abrams, he said, "I estimate that the better part of a regiment operating southwest and west of Loc Ninh has been blown away by tac air strikes."[20] Although Hollingsworth was outwardly positive about the day's fighting, he knew that the eventual outcome of the battle was very much in question. So, too, did the defenders in Loc Ninh. Colonel Vinh apparently thought that the situation was hopeless; stripping down to his T-shirt and undershorts, he told his men in the command bunker that they would all have to surrender soon.

Things got much worse during the night when a volley of huge 240mm rockets hit the hospital bunker, killing a large number of the wounded. Rockets also hit the artillery compound, causing considerable damage to the guns, killing and wounding a number of the gunners, and also blowing up the ammo storage area. To add to the confusion, the NVA launched another ground attack from the east across the airfield. The ARVN defenders repulsed the attack, but in so doing expended the last of the 106mm recoilless ammunition.

As dawn broke on 7 April, Captain Smith reported that Loc Ninh was strangely quiet except for some incoming mortar and artillery rounds. The lull was short-lived. At 0700, the NVA launched a major ground attack from the west and north supported by 75mm recoilless rifles, 122mm rockets, armored personnel carriers, and tanks. What was left of the ARVN defense all but disintegrated under this onslaught. When tanks breached the perimeter, Captain Smith killed one with an M72 LAW (light antitank weapon). It was apparent to all observers that the situation was all but hopeless. It appeared to the crew of the AC-130 overhead that if someone did not "get the men out before nightfall," they would be "overrun for sure."[21]

At around 0800, Colonel Vinh showed his true colors when he and his bodyguard ran through the open gate and surrendered to the enemy. Inside the compound, his executive officer took down the South Vietnamese flag and ran a white T-shirt up the flagpole as a sign of surrender. Smith subdued the ARVN officer and ran the South Vietnamese flag back up the pole. Several ARVN soldiers had begun to strip off their shirts, indicating that they too intended to surrender, but when Smith put the South Vietnamese flag back up, they put their shirts back on and returned to their defensive positions on the perimeter.

While all of this transpired, the battle continued to rage. At 0930, the NVA launched another wave of attacks. Smith later reported that at this point the defense fell apart. When two M-113 APCs entered the perimeter, the defenders thought they were being joined by their comrades from the cavalry squadron, but the ramps dropped and NVA soldiers piled out of the troop compartments. The NVA apparently captured these APCs when the cavalry squadron at FSB Alpha surrendered. Miller, at An Loc, lost communications with Major Carlson and the other advisers with him (Sergeant First Class Lull and Sergeant Wallingford, plus Michel Dumond, the French photographer, who had remained with them throughout the battle). The situation was chaotic. At 1000 hours, B-52s delivered a strike just west of Loc Ninh, requiring the suspension of tactical air support until the bomber strike was over.[22] This disruption of air support played a key role in the ultimate outcome of the battle, taking the pressure from the close air support off the attackers. With the situation all but out of control and the NVA in the process of overrunning the ARVN positions, Smith called for air strikes on both compounds.

"They're on top of us," radioed Smith from the ground. "Drop your stuff on us. They're in the bunker and we want to get rid of them. Tear the damn thing down!"[23] By this time, only about 50 soldiers remained in the southern compound and fewer than 20 RF/PF in the northern compound.

That afternoon, an OH-6 scout helicopter flown by First Lieutenant Richard Dey from F Troop, 9th Cavalry, contacted Smith about landing to extract him. Smith refused to leave his post. Nevertheless, an attempt was made to pick up the advisers in Loc Ninh. After air force fighters delivered an incapacitating riot control agent on the NVA positions, Dey flew into the compound. The gas did not work as anticipated, and Dey was driven off by heavy .51-caliber fire from several directions.

Late that afternoon as Smith again called in air strikes on his own bunker, the NVA mounted a tower on the inner perimeter and took a shot at him. The round struck Smith's radio, the back pack, and penetrated his back, lodging in his lung. He patched himself up and continued to fight, but without a radio he could only organize the walking wounded and used them to secure two bunkers on the original perimeter. By this time, Lieutenant Colonel Schott, who had sustained a severe head injury earlier in the battle, had begun to deteriorate. Smith and his small band held out against the NVA until around 1830, when Smith determined that it was time to make a run for it. Smith related later that Schott told the others to leave him and then heroically took his own life with his pistol, sacrificing himself for the others.[24] Smith, Lull, and the ARVN surgeon escaped through the surrounding minefield to the southwest. Captain Mike Brown of Blue Max was orbiting overhead in his Cobra and heard the last radio transmission from unidentified advisers in Loc Ninh. He never learned who made the call, but recalled later that he could hear a baby crying in the background as the NVA captured the command bunker.[25]

The district compound just north of the artillery position was still holding out and would continue to hold out for several more hours. This compound had originally been manned by about 225 RF/PF and their two American advisers, but by this time, only a handful of South Vietnamese and advisers remained. During the first two days of the battle, Captain Wanat and Major Davidson called for air support through Captain Smith, but when the 9th Regiment compound fell and Smith was without an operable radio, they began to talk directly with the FACs to call in fire support for the remainder of the battle. On the night of 6 April, Davidson was on the verge of calling in air strikes on his own bunker when he got a call from an AC-130 Spectre gunship orbiting the area. The Spectre was prepared to provide fire support, but was unsure where the advisers were located in the compound. The pilot asked Davidson, but he was unable to sufficiently pinpoint his location. The Spectre pilot told Davidson to start up a vehicle near his location; the sophisticated target acquisition gear on the aircraft picked up the heat signature of the engine and the Spectre's guns were able to engage without endangering the advisers.

The Spectre strike provided only a brief respite. The next morning the attacking NVA made another push to take the northern compound. Davidson called in an air strike on his compound, driving away many of the attackers. Still, the NVA kept coming. The advisers and the surviving RF/PF soldiers held out as long as they could and then were forced to break out and run across the airstrip toward the town. Another attempt was made by air elements of the 1st Cavalry Division to rescue the advisers and the ARVN survivors, but the antiaircraft fire was just too intense. At around 1830, General Hollingsworth, orbiting the area, lost contact will all advisers in Loc Ninh.

Davidson, Wanat, the district chief Major Thinh, and a small group of RF/PF soldiers ran into several patrols; after several firefights, they turned south toward An Loc. Somewhere in the process of eluding the enemy patrols, Davidson and his interpreter became separated from the others. The two continued to the south for the next four days, barely avoiding capture on numerous occasions and finally reaching an ARVN ranger battalion in the northern part of An Loc.[26]

After becoming separated from Davidson, Captain Wanat continued on with the district chief, who told him he planned to move from friendly hamlet to friendly hamlet until they reached An Loc. However, on the second day, Thinh left Wanat waiting in one of the hamlets while he supposedly went forward to check out a village they had approached. Thinh never returned. After waiting some time for the district chief, Wanat, realizing that he had been abandoned, set out on his own. Over the next 29 days, Wanat, moving alone, attempted to escape and evade to An Loc. On the 31st day after leaving the compound in Loc Ninh, he was captured by an NVA patrol. Major Thinh made it into An Loc, where Colonel Miller berated him for abandoning Wanat.

Things were going no better for the other advisers. Smith, Lull, and the surgeon, plus about a dozen ARVN soldiers made their way south from the original perimeter. They ran into a group of NVA soldiers and a brisk firefight ensued, in which Smith was shot in the groin and took shrapnel in the lower abdomen. Lull and the South Vietnamese continued to move south, while the regimental surgeon and an ARVN corporal stayed with Smith. The trio tried to make their way south, observing along the way a number of dead enemy soldiers apparently killed by air strikes. The surgeon did what he could to keep Smith moving. The following day, 8 April, while still moving to the south, a blast occurred in their midst, knocking Smith unconscious. When he regained consciousness, he found that he was in the hands of the 272nd Regiment, 9th VC Division. The NVA had shot the corporal, but Smith pleaded for the life of the surgeon and the enemy spared him. Smith would later receive the Distinguished Service Cross, the nation's second-highest award for valor, for his actions during the defense of Loc Ninh.[27]

By the time that Loc Ninh fell, all seven Americans were listed as missing in action. In fact, Major Carlson, Sergeant Wallingford, and Michel Dumond had also been captured. Soon Smith, Carlson, Wallingford, and Dumond were brought together and moved to a prisoner of war camp at Kratie, Cambodia. About a month later, they were joined by Captain Wanat. With the exception of Dumond, who was released on 13 July "in honor of Bastille Day," the captured advisers would be held in Cambodia until released at Loc Ninh on 12 February 1973 as part of the provisions of the Paris Peace Accords. Schott died in Loc Ninh, and Lull and the South Vietnamese he was last seen with were never heard from again. Schott and Lull were both eventually listed as Killed in Action, Bodies Not Recovered. More than a thousand South Vietnamese were taken prisoner, and only about 50 South Vietnamese survivors of the battle at Loc Ninh escaped to An Loc.[28]

Colonel Miller was distraught. He had threatened to pull the advisers out of Loc Ninh and now it was too late. He later said, "I will have that on my conscience for the rest of my life."[29] Hollingsworth also was deeply saddened by the loss of the advisers. He reported to General Abrams, "Those on the ground at Loc Ninh fought gallantly against insurmountable odds. . . . Dauntless and remarkable courage kept them going." However, Hollingsworth told him, "the camp appears to have been overrun. Some fighting continues, I have no estimate of the extent of friendly casualties within the Loc Ninh complex. I feel it must be heavy."[30]

Task Force 52

As the attack on Loc Ninh unfolded, TF 52, accompanied by three U.S. Army advisers—Lieutenant Colonel Walter D. Ginger, Captain Marvin C. Zumwalt, and Sergeant First Class Floyd Winland—realized that they would be next. Since 28 March, the task force had conducted operations in the vicinity of the two fire support bases. There had been only sporadic contact with small enemy units, and friendly casualties were light. However, beginning on 1 April, the task force began to sustain an increasing amount of indirect fire from enemy mortars and 122mm rockets. In the early morning hours of 4 April, an unknown enemy element walked into a mechanical ambush set up by the 1st Battalion, 48th Regiment. The action resulted in one ARVN killed and two lightly wounded. Fifteen enemy soldiers were killed, and after the fighting subsided, it was determined that they were NVA troops. This was the first inkling Colonel Thinh and his advisers had that they were up against the North Vietnamese Army and not Viet Cong.[31] Map 7 depicts the withdrawal of TF 52.

On 5 April, General Hung ordered Lieutenant Colonel Thinh to mount an attack with one battalion to reinforce the beleaguered Loc Ninh garrison. Thinh directed his northernmost unit, 2nd Battalion, 52nd Regiment, to carry out the assigned task, but they ran into a strong enemy ambush near the road junction of Route 17 and Highway 13. Tac air was not available since all air support was being diverted to Loc Ninh. Despite firing 600 rounds of artillery and mortar fire, the ARVN were unable to dislodge the NVA, and they returned to FSB North. As the 2nd Battalion withdrew to its original position, both firebases came under heavy enemy attack from several directions. The NVA unleashed an artillery barrage, pouring down more than 150 rounds of 82mm mortar, 105mm howitzer fire, and 122mm rockets from the south and northwest.[32] This action continued into 6 April. U.S. medevac helicopters, painted a brilliant white, made several runs under enemy fire on 5 and 6 April to evacuate the ARVN wounded.[33]

As the NVA attacks on TF 52 increased in intensity, it became apparent to all observers that Loc Ninh could not hold out much longer, and it looked like Thinh's forces would soon be lost as well. Lieutenant Colonel Ginger radioed to Colonel Miller that the NVA forces had nearly completed the encirclement of TF 52 and that they were in dire need of resupply. Colonel Miller was very frustrated with General Hung, who failed to see the urgency in the worsening situation with TF 52 and did not react

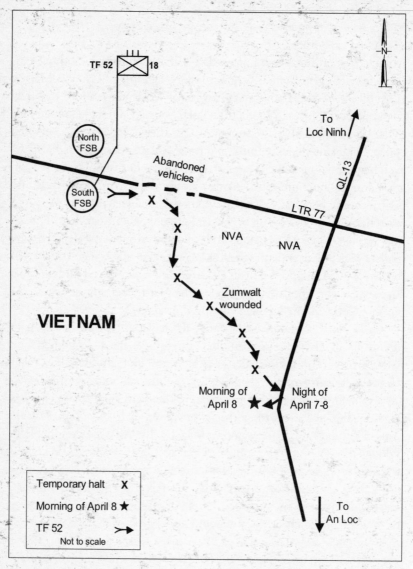

TF 52

18

North
FSB

South
FSB

Abandoned
vehicles

X

X

X

X

Zumwalt
wounded

X

X

X

NVA

NVA

VIETNAM

To
Loc Ninh

QL-13

LTR 77

Morning of
April 8

Night of
April 7-8

Temporary halt   X

Morning of April 8   ★

TF 52   →

Not to scale

To
An Loc

Map 7. Task Force 52

to their resupply problems or the rapidly deteriorating tactical situation. Miller believed that Hung was all but overcome with the ever-growing complexity and urgency of the tactical situation developing in northern Binh Long.

Part of the problem was that the resupply mission would have to be flown by VNAF helicopters. Unlike the U.S. system, South Vietnamese helicopters belonged to the air force and not the army; the ARVN and VNAF had a long tradition of not getting along, and, for that reason, Miller felt that Hung would not ask for the needed help. Nevertheless, Miller pressed Hung to do something about the task force before they were completely surrounded and incapable of breaking out.

Hung refused to order a night move, but finally on the morning of 7 April he directed Colonel Thinh to withdraw to An Loc.[34] Accordingly, at 0830, as enemy shells continued to fall, the task force attempted to break out, but the effort, hastily organized, with trucks towing artillery pieces and water trailers leading the way, looked more like an administrative move than an attack to break out from encirclement. The convoy had not gone more than 300–400 meters down the road when they encountered heavy fire from an enemy ambush. Unable to advance, the rear of the convoy withdrew back to the firebase from which they had come, but not before the NVA captured three 105mm howitzers and the trucks that towed them. As the ARVN returned to their original positions, the NVA gunners once again increased the volume of artillery into both firebases. One ARVN solider was wounded by incoming artillery; blinded and bleeding heavily, he crawled aimlessly in a continually exposed position. Despite the heavy incoming fire, Sergeant First Class Winland left a secure position and ran toward the wounded soldier. An incoming mortar round knocked him off his feet, wounding him slightly, but he proceeded to the soldier and administered first aid.

Another attempt to break out was made, but the ARVN forces almost immediately ran into intense direct and indirect fire from strong NVA ambush positions. At 0900, General Hung ordered Colonel Thinh to destroy all equipment and move south on foot as best he could. According to Captain Zumwalt, the "order was put out [by the regimental commander] to abandon everything."[35] Leaving most of the vehicles and the rest of the artillery, Thinh ordered the 1st Battalion, 48th, to lead the march, while 2nd Battalion, 52nd, would hold FSB North as long as it could and then follow, forming the rear guard. An attempt was made to disable the remaining artillery and vehicles, but not all of them were destroyed by the ARVN. So they were hit 20 minutes later by an air strike ordered by General Hollingsworth.[36]

Colonel Thinh and his advisers moved out behind the lead battalion as the column headed east along Route 17 toward the intersection with Highway 13, the same route the earlier convoy had tried. Around noon, they ran into a large North Vietnamese ambush from three sides and were unable to go forward. Lieutenant Colonel Ginger convinced Thinh to leave the road about 800 meters from the intersection with Highway 13 in an attempt to maneuver his elements around the ambush sites, but they were unable to skirt the NVA positions. Meanwhile, the trailing battalion, which had also sustained a ground attack, had departed FSB North under enemy pressure, but in their haste to get away from the NVA, they ran into the back of the lead battalion. The ARVN forces began to bunch up. Ginger pleaded with Thinh to spread his troops out and provide flank security, but this did little good and unit integrity began to break down.

Ginger requested air support from 5th ARVN Division, but did not get what he thought was a quick response. Hollingsworth had told all advisers in III Corps that if they were ever in "deep shit" and failed to ask for help, "I'm going to blister your ass."[37] Frustrated with the lack of air support and taking the general at his word, Ginger switched frequencies and contacted Hollingsworth directly, telling the general that the task force would be lost if support was not forthcoming. Hollingsworth told Ginger to "hang in there" and then transmitted a message to Colonel Miller to "get someone off their dead ass and get that boy some help up there."[38]

The situation began to deteriorate rapidly as all semblance of control broke down. To make matters worse, the NVA artillery opened up, the rounds striking in the trees overhead and exploding in air bursts, peppering the fleeing South Vietnamese. Around 1300 hours, air support arrived in the area as Colonel Thinh and his advisers, now just north of the Cam Le Bridge, tried to move to the southeast against heavy enemy fire. However, to get there, they had to cross a large open area. As the command party began to cross, the NVA opened up with everything they had. Captain Zumwalt was talking on the radio to a forward air controller when a B-40 rocket exploded nearby, killing one ARVN soldier. Zumwalt was thrown to the ground and seriously wounded in the face, breaking his jaw and making breathing difficult. The regimental commander Lieutenant Colonel Ginger and Sergeant First Class Winland were also slightly wounded, the second time for Winland. Ginger determined that Zumwalt was too badly injured to continue, and he requested immediate evacuation by helicopter.

Brigadier General McGiffert, Hollingsworth's deputy, who was in a helicopter over the battlefield, broke in on Ginger's radio frequency and told him that he would get a medevac for all the advisers. Ginger asked, "What about my counterpart?"[39] McGiffert replied that Thinh was to remain with his unit and fight on to An Loc. Ginger explained this to his counterpart, who only looked at his adviser without saying anything. Back in An Loc, Miller thought Ginger and his group should have stayed with the regimental commander, but Ginger acceded to General McGiffert's directions. Colonel Thinh waited for several hours, but soon realized that what was left of his unit would not escape if they did not get moving. Leaving several wounded ARVN soldiers with the Americans, the colonel and the remnants of the task force, utilizing support provided by two A-1E Skyraiders, pressed on for An Loc.

Ginger and his party, joined by a handful of ARVN soldiers, took up a position in a deadfall and waited for the promised medevac helicopter. Later that afternoon, two attempts were made to get a medevac helicopter in to pick up Captain Zumwalt. On the first attempt, a Huey "slick" was accompanied by Cobra gunships. As the pilot flared the helicopter, the NVA soldiers opened up with small arms and automatic fire from every direction. The aircraft was able to escape the fire but one of the crewmen was wounded. On the next attempt, which was also aborted, the pilot, Warrant Officer Robert L. Horst of the 156th Medical Detachment, was killed by ground fire. Brigadier General McGiffert radioed Ginger to stay put until they could get them out. As they waited to be picked up, they fought off continual enemy attacks at very close range and employed all available tactical air support as they continued to take incoming indirect fire.

After the first two costly attempts had been made to rescue the advisers, a brief thought was given to trying to rescue the advisers with an air force Jolly Green Giant (CH-53 search and rescue helicopter). But after it was determined that it would take almost three hours for the helicopter to arrive in the area, that idea was abandoned. The advisers were informed that since night was falling no more attempts would be made until the next morning.

That meant that the advisers had a long night ahead of them. The tactical air support had worked exceedingly well during the day, but with nightfall, they relied on the Spectre gunship that had arrived in the area and was orbiting overhead. The gunship flew continuous cover throughout the night to keep the NVA off the advisers with 20mm and 40mm rounds, some placed within 25 meters of the advisers below. When the first aircraft had to leave station because of low fuel, another was there to relieve it so there was no gap in the covering fire. The next day, it was estimated that over 100 NVA bodies littered the area around the Americans' position.

Ginger had been in contact with the 5th ARVN Division advisory team back at An Loc. He found out during the night that Loc Ninh had fallen and that all the U.S. advisers there were presumed lost. With the dawning of the new day, Ginger was understandably anxious to find out what was being done to evacuate him and his fellow advisers. When Lieutenant Colonel Ed Benedit, the deputy senior adviser in An Loc, could not respond sufficiently to his queries, Ginger lost his temper, asking angrily, "Is everyone afraid to wake up one of the generals?"[40]

Unknown to Ginger, the previous evening General McGiffert, back at TRAC headquarters in Long Binh, tasked the 3rd Brigade, 1st Cavalry, to conduct the evacuation mission. Colonel George Casey, deputy commander of the 3rd Brigade, pulled the mission together and the army aviators prepared to launch the mission the next morning.

The mission to extract the advisers was a complex army–air force operation. Air force fighter-bombers and army Cobra attack helicopters would suppress enemy fire in the area around the advisers, and then army OH-6 light observation helicopters would swoop in and pick up the Americans. Beginning at 0630, the air force began bombing and strafing the enemy around the advisers' position. For the next three hours, the jets dropped 500-pound bombs, CBU, and napalm, while pouring rockets, 20mm and 40mm cannon, and machine-gun fire into the NVA. At 1000, a voice calling himself "Thunder Six" came on the air and told the advisers that he had a surprise for them. A lone A-37 Dragonfly swept over the treeline dropping a nontoxic chemical agent meant to immobilize the surviving NVA. Shortly thereafter, two OH-6s came in from the east under withering enemy fire from a machine gun that had survived the air attack.

The first helicopter, piloted by Captain John B. Whitehead, a scout pilot from D Company, 229th Assault Helicopter Battalion, with Sergeant Raymond F. Waite as crew chief/gunner, went in to pick up the Ginger party.[41] The aircraft was mobbed by desperate ARVN soldiers seeking to escape the NVA. While Waite tried to hold off the mob, Ginger and the other Americans clambered aboard the aircraft, but four ARVN soldiers clung to the skids and anywhere else they could get a handhold. Ginger was only partly in the helicopter, sitting in the door with his feet on the skids. As the helicopter lifted off, one of the ARVN grabbed his ankle and held on for dear life. Through sheer force of will and some unbelievable flying,

Whitehead managed to skip, bounce, and force the overloaded helicopter into the air with a total of nine personnel on board an aircraft designed to carry four. The second OH-6, piloted by First Lieutenant David E. Ripley, picked up a number of ARVN soldiers, some of whom were hanging on the skids. The extraction was accomplished in the face of intense enemy fire. In Whitehead's aircraft, Sergeant First Class Winland was hit in the hand by an AK-47 bullet as the aircraft lifted off; the aircraft took additional hits on the main rotor, fuel cells, and tail boom. NVA fire also hit the second aircraft, causing three Vietnamese hanging onto the skids to fall. The two helicopters sped to the airstrip at Chon Thanh, about 25 kilometers south of An Loc, where the wounded ARVN were evacuated further south by ambulance. Ginger, Zumwalt, and Winland were flown by another helicopter to the 3rd Brigade, 1st Cavalry Division, aid station, where they were treated and evacuated to 3rd Field Hospital in Saigon. Back at Chon Thanh, Whitehead and Ripley checked their aircraft for damage; both aircraft were found to be full of bullet holes. While checking the aircraft for damage, an ARVN soldier ran up to Whitehead, fell on his knees, and kept bowing down in a sign of thanks.[42] Whitehead was embarrassed, but he should not have been. What he and Ripley had accomplished in rescuing the American advisers under withering fire was nothing less than miraculous.

Captain Whitehead and Sergeant Waite each received the Distinguished Service Cross for braving intense ground fire to effect the rescue, and General Hamlet nominated Whitehead for the Congressional Medal of Honor.[43] Dave Ripley received the Silver Star for his part in the rescue. Sergeant First Class Winland would also later receive the Distinguished Service Cross for his valorous actions during the withdrawal operations and subsequent evacuation attempts.

As the successful rescue effort transpired, Colonel Thinh and the remainder of the battered and disorganized TF 52, only about 600 of the original 1,000 soldiers, continued on to An Loc, where they joined the defenders girding themselves for the coming attack.

The beginning of the Easter Offensive in Binh Long Province had been a disaster for the South Vietnamese and their American advisers. In a matter of just a few days, the ARVN had lost the equivalent of four maneuver battalions (one armor, one ranger, and two infantry), more than one-third of TF 52, a sizable number of RF/PF soldiers, nearly two artillery battalions, and over 100 vehicles, including 12 tanks, 35 APCs, and 30 tubes of artillery. As Colonel Miller noted after the battle, the North

Vietnamese did not have to worry a lot about logistics initially because they had captured such a vast quantity of equipment and weapons from the South Vietnamese in the first week of the fighting in Binh Long.

In An Loc, General Hung was a demoralized man. Everything had happened very quickly, and the enemy had definitely seized the initiative. Hung fully expected to be relieved for the debacle at Loc Ninh as the allies got ready for the NVA onslaught headed right for them. Miller had urged him to either reinforce his forces at Loc Ninh and fight the decisive battle there or to pull all his forces back to An Loc and prepare to make a stand there. Hung had vacillated as the enemy attacked and in the end did neither. When he finally decided to pull his forces back to An Loc, it was too late; the result was that he lost most of his artillery and more than a regiment of troops. The battle as it unfolded in Loc Ninh further strained the relationship between Hung and his American adviser. Miller saw Hung as totally indecisive and unable to handle the stress of high-intensity combat; Hung no doubt deeply resented Miller's pushing, feeling that the American was overstepping his bounds and meddling in South Vietnamese affairs. The relationship would not get better.

As Loc Ninh fell, refugees were pouring into An Loc from the villages and hamlets to the north. A journalist in An Loc reported: "The most pitiful sights were two columns of civilian refugees coming in from nearby villages. Each time one of these processions came near the edge of town, it came under shell fire. Old people, women and children, would scramble for cover. The shell fire would die down. They would pick themselves up and run, the children screaming in terror, to some other place that might offer food, water, shelter. In An Loc, this week, there is no such place."[44]

The only bright spot for the allies as Loc Ninh fell was the arrival back in An Loc of Colonel Tran Van Nhut, the Binh Long province chief. He had been in Vung Tau when the NVA launched their attack against Loc Ninh. Arriving at Lai Khe, he grabbed a jeep and drove 48 kilometers up the already dangerous Highway 13 to An Loc. Always calm and confident under fire, Nhut was a very impressive officer who played a key role in the defense of An Loc.

With the fall of Loc Ninh, General Hollingsworth reported to Abrams: "Situation in Binh Long has taken a turn for the worse."[45] He predicted that the enemy would continue his momentum south astride Highway 13 and eventually make a move on Saigon. Having provided an update to MACV, he then placed the entire region on alert, saying, "All US elements and personnel in Military Region 3 will immediately check and improve defensive positions to insure that they are in best possible condition to withstand heavy attacks-by-fire from 76mm tank guns." Additionally, he continued, "commanders will secure all possible antitank weapons, insure that people are assigned to operate them and that those assigned know how to fire them properly."[46]

At the time, I was at the 18th ARVN Division headquarters some distance away at Xuan Loc in Long Khanh Province. Because of some atmospheric abnormality, we had been able to monitor the radio traffic as Loc Ninh fell. It was apparent to everyone listening that the attack on Loc Ninh was just the beginning.

CHAPTER FIVE

THE OPENING BATTLE FOR AN LOC

Preparing for the Coming Storm

THE ATTACKS ON Loc Ninh and TF 52 confirmed for General Minh and General Hollingsworth that the enemy's main effort in MR III was not to be in Tay Ninh, but rather in Binh Long Province; they correctly surmised that An Loc would be the primary objective of the main enemy attack.[1] They also realized that if An Loc fell, the North Vietnamese would have very little standing between them and Saigon. Accordingly, the decision was made to hold An Loc at all costs.

On 7 April, there was a meeting at Independence Palace in Saigon between President Thieu and his senior generals to discuss the military crisis developing all over the country. General Minh, reporting the equivalent of four NVA divisions in MR III, pleaded for more troops to defend An Loc. He argued that the enemy attacks in MR I and II were diversionary and that Saigon was the real target. However, the situation had worsened in I Corps, so most of Thieu's attention continued to be focused there. Lieutenant General Dang Van Quang, Thieu's assistant for national security, agreed with Minh about the threat to Saigon and made a strong case for reinforcing III Corps. Finally, Thieu agreed and gave Minh the remaining airborne brigade and ordered an infantry division to redeploy from IV Corps to reinforce Minh's troops. Some consideration was given to sending the 9th Infantry Division, but it was finally decided to send the

21st Division, which was currently conducting operations in the U Minh Forest. The 21st was considered to be effective in mobile operations, and, as it had once been commanded by General Minh, it was thought the division would work better for him.[2]

South Vietnamese President Thieu radioed the senior ARVN officers in An Loc that the city would be defended to the death.[3] This had a psychological impact on the enemy, as well as the defenders. Colonel Miller later commented that for Thieu, An Loc was "a Bastogne, a place where a stand or die defense would decide the fate of the enemy offensive closest to the national capital."[4] By directing that the city be held "at all costs," Thieu all but challenged the North Vietnamese to take it. In the weeks that followed, they became virtually obsessed with the desire to overrun An Loc, even long after it had ceased to hold any real military significance.[5]

On the American side, some advisers had been pulled out of Quang Tri when the enemy offensive had started in MR I, and this had had disastrous effects on the morale of the South Vietnamese forces there. They subsequently fell apart in the face of the NVA attack. General Hollingsworth determined that the stakes were too high to risk a recurrence so close to Saigon; he believed that the presence of the American advisers on the ground was necessary to the survival of An Loc. Still, he directed Colonel Miller and Lieutenant Colonel Corley to evacuate all nonessential American personnel from An Loc. Miller kept his deputy, Lieutenant Colonel Edward B. Benedit, and Major Allan Borstaff, his operations officer, to assist him in the 5th ARVN command bunker. In addition to Miller's crew and the small number of advisers that remained with Corley, there were a handful of other advisers with the other units now inside the city. Hollingsworth notified the remaining advisers that they were there for the duration.[6] Thus, the American advisers prepared to share the fate of their ARVN counterparts in the coming battle. This proved to be a crucial factor in convincing the South Vietnamese defenders that they would not be abandoned to face the repeated North Vietnamese attacks alone. The presence of the advisers meant that the South Vietnamese would have access to U.S. air support. The advisers ensured that there would be a quick channel of communication between air and ground forces and allowed for on-the-spot adjustments of close air strikes.

While concerned about the welfare of his advisers, General Hollingsworth was excited about the opportunity to get the NVA to stand and fight. He later said, "Once the Communists decided to take An Loc, and I could get a handful of soldiers to hold and a lot of American advisers to keep them from running off, that's all I needed." He told the advisers in An Loc, "Hold them and I'll kill them with airpower; give me something to bomb and I'll win."[7] General Abrams chastised Hollingsworth for this statement because he thought Hollingsworth had given the impression that he was taking over what should have been a South Vietnamese–run show. In fact, he would do just that because the ARVN corps commander was not prepared to handle a battle of this magnitude. It was just what the American general had prepared for his whole life. Hollingsworth would play a deciding role in the desperate battle that would soon unfold.

By this time, the NVA held most of Binh Long Province from Chon Thanh north to the Cambodian border, with the exception of the town of An Loc. It was clear that An Loc would be the focus of the next major North Vietnamese effort. A lot was at stake. Not only were the lives of the South Vietnamese soldiers and their American advisers on the line, but so too was the prestige of the South Vietnamese government. The loss of a province so close to Saigon would be a disastrous loss of face for President Thieu and his administration. From the American perspective, the battle would be the supreme test of Vietnamization and President Nixon's policies in Vietnam. More than that, however, was the fact that very little stood between the North Vietnamese and Saigon except the forces at An Loc.

When the battle for Loc Ninh started, An Loc was only lightly defended by RF/PF soldiers. General Minh, III Corps commander, ordered the 3rd Ranger Group and two of its battalions, the 36th and 52nd, which had previously been conducting operations in the Parrot's Beak area along the Cambodian border, to deploy by helicopter to An Loc to bolster the ARVN defenders. The rangers were among the best South Vietnamese troops; the North Vietnamese called the ARVN rangers the "Cat soldiers" for their distinctive panther-headed shoulder patches. The 3rd Ranger Group commander, Lieutenant Colonel Nguyen Van Biet, and his troops boarded helicopters on the morning of 7 April and headed for the city. Artillery was already falling on the city when the helicopters approached the landing zone, and several of the rangers, including the group commander, were lightly wounded.[8] Two of Biet's staff officers and several of the troops were more seriously injured and were evacuated from An Loc on the helicopter that carried the last element of the 52nd Ranger Battalion into the city.

Even with the addition of the rangers, An Loc was still only lightly defended. Therefore, General Hollingsworth urged General Minh to send the 1st Airborne Brigade, now under the operational control of III Corps, to An Loc immediately. Instead Minh decided to employ them along Highway 13 with the mission of breaking the North Vietnamese roadblock and securing An Loc's lifeline to Lai Khe and ultimately Saigon. Responding to these orders, the 1st Airborne Brigade, consisting of the 5th, 6th, and 8th Airborne Battalions and the 81st Airborne Ranger Battalion, began moving from Saigon by road to Lai Khe; the whole brigade had closed by 8 April. The next day, the brigade, with the 5th Battalion in the lead, struck out up Highway 13 to Chon Thanh, advancing to the village without incident. At 1730 hours on 10 April, reaching a point only six kilometers north of Chon Thanh and still 15 kilometers short of An Loc, the paratroopers came under heavy enemy attack by a regiment from the 7th NVA Division. The level of fighting along Highway 13 was extremely intense. One adviser told a reporter, "I've been over here for years and I've never seen anything like this and I was at the Khe Sanh siege."[9] It was apparent that the North Vietnamese were determined to dominate this road and interdict any attempt to reinforce or resupply An Loc by ground.[10]

As the airborne brigade was attempting to force the roadblock on Highway 13, chaos reigned in An Loc as preparations were made for the coming NVA assault. VNAF C-123 aircraft were flying low over the city dropping supplies by parachute. Helicopters, mostly VNAF Chinooks and Hueys, were also bringing in supplies. Miller was gratified to see the arrival of supplies for the defenders, but he was concerned that no artillery or mortars had been sent. There were only eight 105mm howitzers in An Loc at this time; Miller knew more artillery was needed to counter the 69th NVA Artillery Division, which appeared to be headed for An Loc. Miller later said that he thought the South Vietnamese did not send any more artillery because they were "afraid they might lose it." This did not bode well for the defenders in the coming battle.

Miller's relationship with General Hung had deteriorated to a new low. Miller tried to get Hung to make preparations for the attack on An Loc that was certain to come soon, but the losses at Loc Ninh and Hung Tam had stunned the South Vietnamese general. Miller suggested to the clearly demoralized Hung that he relinquish command to Colonel Nhut, the province chief. When Hung did not respond, Miller took a different tact, urging the general to bring the rest of division to An Loc. Hung demurred and asked Miller to request the two U.S. battalions from the 1st Cavalry task force at Bien Hoa. Miller responded angrily, "It's ARVN's war now, General."[11] Faced with that reality, the question was how to get ready to deal with the NVA.

At the province level, Colonel Nhut was very busy. His staff worked feverishly to provide temporary housing, food, and medicine to the refugees from Loc Ninh and outlying villages and hamlets who were streaming into the city. He also directed that M72 LAWs be issued to the PSDF soldiers and began training them on their use. The LAW would play a significant role in the battles to come. The antitank rocket system employed a warhead with an explosive charge shaped to direct a jet of high-velocity molten copper capable of burning through inches of steel plate. The ARVN had an earlier model in Laos in 1971 that was less powerful. The new model, the M72A2, would prove much more effective.

Nhut, who had a lot of combat experience, tried to prepare his troops for what was coming. He knew that the enemy would begin the assault with a massive artillery bombardment, so he told his troops to stay in their bunkers until that had passed. When the artillery was lifted, he told them, they were to stand up, get into firing position, and shoot anything that was headed their way. Nhut was very active in visiting his forces deployed along the perimeter defenses in these final hours; he realized that he had very little time to get his troops ready for the coming battle.

The North Vietnamese Turn on An Loc

As the final moments of the battles at Loc Ninh and Hung Tam raged, the North Vietnamese realized that they had the advantage. A postwar review of the battle by the North Vietnamese said that the senior officers at COSVN headquarters in Cambodia had concluded at the time that the attack on Loc Ninh could be considered "a solid victory" and that the problem was now "to 'steal time' by quickly taking the Binh Long Province capital."[12] The Communist high command hoped to capture An Loc by 9 April. Accordingly, they had already moved forces south to make the main assault on the city. Under cover of darkness and moving stealthily through the jungle and rubber plantations, the NVA troops, according to a unit history released after the war, began to take up positions "to encircle the city as the prelude to an attack to annihilate all enemy defenders and to liberate An Loc city."[13]

As previously stated, the North Vietnamese had already begun to shell An Loc on 5 April. These were only the preliminary shots in the coming battle for the city. For the next 48 hours, there was only sporadic contact at Quan Loi, just seven kilometers northeast of An Loc, where the next blow would fall. It was defended by two rifle companies from 1st Battalion, 7th Regiment, and two 105mm howitzers. The North Vietnamese made a strong probe of the ARVN positions in the afternoon of 6 April. During this action, the South Vietnamese troops were supported by Cobras from F Troop, 9th Cavalry.

On the evening of 7 April, North Vietnamese forces from the elite 9th VC Division attacked the Quan Loi airstrip. The NVA attack was characterized by repeated human wave attacks and the use of tear and nausea gas by the attackers. The two companies defending the airfield were unable to hold against the NVA attacks, and they were ordered to destroy their equipment and withdraw to An Loc. They did so, and the survivors would close into An Loc by 9 April. The loss of Quan Loi airstrip and the blocking of Highway 13 by the 7th NVA Division south of An Loc meant that the city had been surrounded by Communist troops and cut off from the outside. Thus began a siege that would last for almost three months.

With the seizure of the Quan Loi area, the NVA gained control of the high ground overlooking An Loc, from which they could direct accurate artillery fire and rockets into the city. Still, the NVA made no move to launch ground attacks on the city for several days. North Vietnamese documents later revealed that the ARVN's rapid withdrawal from Loc Ninh and the other border outposts surprised the NVA and upset their planning timetable.[14] They had expected the securing of Loc Ninh and the outlying positions to take more time, during which they would continue to build up their logistics base in Binh Long Province in preparation for the attack on An Loc. Following their rapid success in the initial attacks on Loc Ninh and TF 52, they needed time to regroup and continue the buildup for the main thrust on the provincial capital. They did, however, launch a number of small ground probes on 8 April while increasing the rockets and artillery.

The temporary lull in the enemy advance was put to good use by the South Vietnamese. With the cutting of Highway 13 to the south and the loss of the airfield at Quan Loi, the only way to resupply An Loc with food and ammunition was by helicopters and fixed-wing aircraft, whose pilots had to risk flying though the increasingly intense antiaircraft fire ringing the city. With a population of 15,000, the resupply required would be 200 tons a day, including 140 tons of ammunition, 36 tons of rice and other rations, and 20 tons of water. This requirement would increase and reach critical levels very quickly once the battle for An Loc began and refugees began to pour into the city from the outlying areas.

On the 8th of April, the remnants of TF 52 began to drift into An Loc. What had started out as a two-battalion task force was now about the size of one battalion; they had lost over 400 men, much of their heavy equipment, and all of their artillery. General Hung told the task force commander, Lieutenant Colonel Thinh, to position his troops in the center of the town around the artillery pieces already located there. Hung also ordered the 7th Regiment (two battalions) and the ARVN contingent at Cam Le Bridge to pull their forces back into the town. The handful of South Vietnamese soldiers who had escaped capture at Loc Ninh also began to make their way into the city.

At 0530 hours on the morning of 9 April, An Loc received strong ground probes from the west, east, and north. The contacts lasted until around 0900. Four enemy prisoners were captured during this action; they were from the 95C, 271st, and 272nd Regiments of the 9th VC Division. The 271st was located to the west of the city, the 272nd to the north, and 95C on the east. On 10 April, the NVA attacked again at 0530 hours, but following the earlier pattern, backed off at 0715 hours.

Colonel Miller said later that the loss of Loc Ninh and the airfield at Quan Loi, coupled with the increase of enemy activity, made it pretty clear to the defenders in An Loc what was in store for them; "the message was written on all the faces of the civilians and the military."[15] The survivors of the battles at Loch Ninh and Hung Tam were particularly frightened because they had barely survived the first NVA onslaught.

On 10 and 11 April, the 8th Regiment (less one battalion) was brought into An Loc by helicopter from the Tri Tam–Dau Tieng area in Binh Duong Province by the 229th Aviation Battalion, 1st Cavalry Division. Additionally, the 1st Cavalry provided CH-47 helicopters from the 362nd Aviation Company to transport supplies and evacuate wounded and civilian personnel. One of the UH-1H Huey pilots, former Warrant Officer Mike Wheeler from A/229th Aviation, recalled that the runs into the LZ on the soccer field at An Loc were "hot" and that the helicopters received small-arms and machine-gun fire going into and out of An Loc. He also said that mortar rounds and rockets were falling on the city as the helicopters landed on the soccer field. On the last run of the day into the LZ, having flown continuously for nearly 10 hours, Wheeler's aircraft was struck by ground fire from a .51-caliber machine gun, and he was wounded in the leg when a round shattered the cyclic control.[16] For the army aviators, this was merely a portent of what was to come.

On 12 April, about 1,000 soldiers from the 7th Regiment finished pulling back into the town. So as the NVA made final preparations for the coming attack, the defenders in An Loc included a mixture of regular ARVN infantrymen from elements of two divisions, border rangers, sector artillery, and Territorial Forces.

Over the next several months, these forces would undergo a protracted attack, marked by repeated human wave assaults and heavy shelling at levels seldom seen during the conduct of the entire Vietnamese War. The intensity of this prolonged level of combat would demand almost superhuman endurance on the part of the defenders and their advisers. Additionally, the absence of friendly artillery support and surface resupply would demand the utmost from American air support.[17] On the morning of 12 April, intense antiaircraft fire downed a Vietnamese Air Force CH-47 helicopter attempting to bring supplies into the city. The amount and types of antiaircraft fire indicated that the NVA were going to do their utmost to isolate An Loc from outside support.

Concurrent with the intensifying antiaircraft situation, the enemy artillery and rocket bombardment began to increase in intensity and frequency. Late on the afternoon of 12 April, Major Raymond Haney and the author, both from the 18th ARVN Division, arrived in An Loc by helicopter to replace the evacuated advisory team with TF 52. As the helicopter approached the landing zone on the city soccer field, the enemy began shelling the city. Once the helicopter had lifted off and the incoming artillery stopped, we found the 5th ARVN Division bunker, reported in to Colonel Miller and inquired as to the location of Lieutenant Colonel Thinh's command post, and then departed to join up with the task force.

Major Haney and I immediately determined that the situation was not good. A feeling of near panic seemed to lurk just under the surface among the soldiers and civilians we encountered; everyone realized that the North Vietnamese were preparing to hit An Loc hard. The South Vietnamese, still reeling from the defeats at Loc Ninh and Hung Tam, were trying to deal with what they knew was coming next. Artillery, mortar, and rocket fire continued to increase, and patrols outside the defensive perimeter encountered stiffening resistance from enemy forces toward the northeast and southwest of the city. Refugees streaming into An Loc from the north reported sighting tanks, artillery, and other heavy equipment, all headed south. An ARVN officer who was captured by the NVA at Loc Ninh, but escaped and made his way to An Loc, reported that his captors told him that they were going to take An Loc at "any" cost.[18] This and other intelligence indicated that the enemy was preparing for an all-out assault on the city.

By this time the forces in An Loc, now numbering around 3,000, had "circled the wagons." The 8th Regiment (–) defended the northwestern corner of the perimeter, TF 52 the center, the 3rd Rangers the northeast corner, and the 7th Regiment (–) held down the southwestern corner.[19]

Apparently General Hung did not get along very well with Colonel Nhut, and Hung chose to deploy his assets with little regard for Nhut's RF/PF soldiers.[20] Nevertheless, the RF/PFs occupied the southeast corner of the perimeter. Map 8 shows the positions of the defenders as of 12 April 1972.

Meanwhile, the 21st ARVN Division under command of Major General Nguyen Vin Nghi had been given orders to redeploy to MR III. The soldiers from the Delta began to arrive in Lai Khe on 11 April. Once employed, the 21st would fight a bloody battle to open the lifeline to An Loc. The story of their fight will be told in a later chapter.

At TRAC headquarters in Long Binh, General Hollingsworth and his deputy, Brigadier General McGiffert, read the intelligence reports and determined that the enemy's main attack on An Loc was about to begin. They met with air force representatives at Lai Khe and planned B-52 missions and tactical air strikes on suspected enemy positions around An Loc for the next day. The B-52 strikes, known as ARC LIGHT, would play a critical role in the coming battle for An Loc.

Hollingsworth flew to MACV to confer with General Abrams. The TRAC commander made a strong case that the enemy was preparing to make an all-out push for An Loc and requested additional B-52 sorties. Abrams agreed with Hollingsworth's assessment and gave the order to divert ARC LIGHT missions from I and II Corps for the next day.[21]

The Battle for An Loc Begins

During the early hours of 13 April, enemy artillery increased dramatically in volume all over An Loc. A total of 7,000 shells and rockets would fall on the city during the next 15 hours, a rate of one round every 8 seconds.[22] About 0400 hours, an ARVN reconnaissance patrol from the 7th Regiment reported that they heard sounds of tanks and trucks moving around in the darkness. Trip flares and claymore mines began to go off as the NVA probed the ARVN lines. An AC-130 Spectre gunship arrived on station and fired on three trucks in the rubber trees to the west. At 0530, the indirect fire increased; incoming rounds touched off the ammunition dump and POL storage areas.

At 0600, the NVA forces launched their attack on An Loc with tank and infantry assaults from the west and northeast. The Soviet-made T-54 and PT-76 tanks from the 6th Company of the 20th Tank Battalion moved down the main north-south street toward the 5th ARVN Division

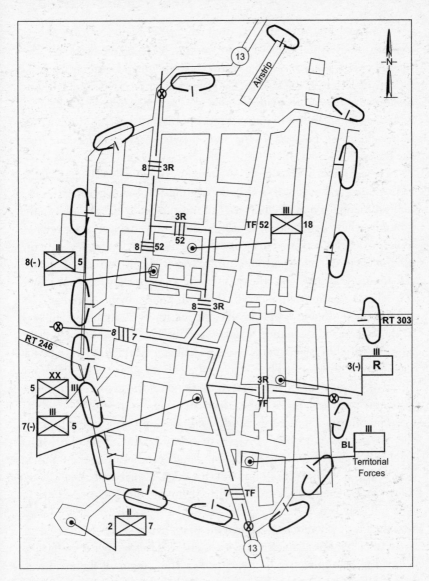

Map 8. Initial ARVN Dispositions, 12 April 1972

command post in the southern central section of the city. The South Vietnamese troops, who had never faced tanks in battle before, were terrified; the forces in the north of the city that took the initial brunt of the attack quickly withdrew in the face of the advancing tanks. TF 52 had left most of their heavy weapons at Hung Tam and were armed only with individual weapons and a handful of machine guns. Still in shock from their earlier pummeling by the North Vietnamese, they fell back in near panic from the tanks.

The reaction of the South Vietnamese troops was understandable. One of the great advantages of tanks in combat is their shock effect; it is really difficult to comprehend what this means until you have been on the ground as these behemoths are bearing down on you. Near chaos reigned as the ARVN soldiers tried to escape the enemy tanks. Colonel Thinh, the task force commander, with the help of Major Haney and myself, finally rallied his troops in the southeastern corner of the city, where they joined the defensive positions manned by the Binh Long provincial soldiers.

On the north and northeast side, the 3rd Ranger Group also fell back in the face of the combined attack. Captain Harold Moffett, one of the advisers with the rangers, called Colonel Miller to alert him to the fact that they were pulling back. The ranger group commander and his staff were able to get them stopped and formed into a new defensive line at a point a little north of where Route 303 entered An Loc from the east.

The 8th Regiment on the north and northwest also pulled back. At the 5th ARVN command post, it was unclear what was happening. Miller wanted to plug the holes left when the rangers and 8th Regiment pulled back with TF 52, but soon found out that the task force had already withdrawn under enemy pressure. The 7th Regiment to the south and southwest held up against the initial attack, but were eventually pushed back into the town, where they occupied the berm line.

Miller became concerned with General Hung and his staff, who seemed to be completely overwhelmed by the ferocity of the enemy attack. Rather than react to the dire situation, they appeared to be resigned to defeat. Miller, however, had determined to go down fighting if he had to go down. He was really worried about the hole left in the center of the defense when TF 52 fell back in disarray. He prodded the general until he ordered the rangers to bend their forces around from the east to try to cover the gap in the line.

The appearance of the tanks also surprised the III Corps commander, General Minh. It is unclear why tanks at An Loc should have been such a shock; ARVN intelligence from late the previous year had indicated the presence of Communist tanks in the Kratie-Dambe-Chup area of Cambodia. In December 1971, the Intelligence Section of the Royal Khmer Armed Forces General Staff also reported approximately 30 NVA tanks in Base Area 361 near Snoul. These reports did not receive much credence at the time, because they were not confirmed by aerial photo reconnaissance missions.[23]

Such photographic confirmation was not needed now, because the North Vietnamese T-54s were rolling down the main street of the city. The situation was rapidly falling apart when Colonel Miller, maintaining a sense of humor, albeit of the gallows variety, in the face of the enemy attack, radioed "Send me some Stukas!" He was referring to the Junkers JU-87 Stuka that was used so successfully by Germany for precision dive-bombing and close air support during the early years of World War II. In response, Miller received a call on his radio from an unknown party, saying "This is Serpent Six [his call sign] with a flight of Cobras." The caller was Major Larry McKay, commander of F Battery, 79th Aerial Rocket Artillery, 1st Cavalry Division, otherwise known as the "Blue Max." By this time, Miller was virtually looking down the barrel of a T-54 tank, but he did not think that helicopters would have any effect on the tanks. Worried about the aviators' survival, he warned off McKay telling him that if they rolled in they would not roll out because of the intense antiaircraft fire in the area. McKay replied, "Negative! Negative! Sir, I've got HEAT!"[24] This meant that his Cobra attack helicopters were armed with 2.75-inch rockets with high-explosive antitank warheads. The rocket-equipped AH-1G Cobras were the only weapon system accurate enough to attack tanks in the midst of the friendly troops and civilians near the heart of the city.

The first Cobra turned nose-down, diving at a steeper angle than usual to ensure accuracy because of the close proximity of the enemy tanks to the friendly troops. The Cobra destroyed the lead North Vietnamese tank just two blocks north of the 5th ARVN Division command post. Miller called the FAC orbiting above and asked that tac air be placed on the antiaircraft sites that ringed the city so he could get the Cobras in closer to take out the rest of the tanks inside the city. The FAC skillfully orchestrated the air strikes with the Cobra rocket runs.

As the Cobras took on the tanks from the air, the key event for the South Vietnamese forces on the ground in this early attack occurred as the tanks moved through the center of the city. One of the tanks made it all the way down the main street to the southern gate, where it was destroyed by three soldiers from the local Territorial Forces with M72 LAWs. At about the same time, another tank was destroyed by ground troops on the eastern side of the perimeter. Captain Harold Moffett, an adviser with the ARVN rangers, described the impact of the first destruction of a tank by the rangers: "This little guy goes out to hunt a 40-ton piece of metal with a light antitank weapon on his back weighing two to three pounds. That's beyond belief and it inspired me. How do you describe a little ARVN soldier fighting tanks?" He later recalled, "I was pretty well frightened like everyone else till it was determined we could knock them out with the weapons we had."[25]

The destruction of these two tanks demonstrated that the shoulder-fired antitank weapons could stop the T-54s. This galvanized the confidence of the badly shaken defenders. Word spread quickly, and the ARVN soldiers overcame their fear and began to emerge from their holes to fire at the tanks with their own LAWs.

Several other factors contributed to ARVN efforts to stabilize their defensive lines. First, the NVA were extremely inept in their coordination of armor and infantry in the attack. Although most of the tank crews had recently returned from tank training in the Soviet Union, they quickly demonstrated that they did not understand the use of combined arms tactics—the coordination of tanks, infantry, and artillery.[26] The tanks routinely attacked without infantry, persisted in advancing along roads when cross-country movement would have been safer, and proceeded slowly and indecisively when speed and initiative were called for.[27] This failure to apply the most basic tenets of combined arms tactics left the North Vietnamese tanks unprotected against the ARVN defenders, who found them easy prey for their LAWs, once they overcame the initial shock of the armored attack. In a postwar account, the North Vietnamese acknowledged that this was the first time that the 9th VC Division had ever fought a combined arms battle with tank support, acknowledging that "the command skills of their cadre at all levels were deficient in many areas."[28]

During the confusion of the initial attack, one North Vietnamese tank crew demonstrated that even the NVA had that small percentage of people who "don't get the word." Thinking that the city had been secured by the NVA infantry, they rolled down Ngo Quyen Street, the main north-south avenue in the city, with all hatches open, completely oblivious to the fact that the soldiers in the fighting positions were ARVN, not NVA. Thus, they soon found themselves isolated inside the South Vietnamese defenses and fell prey to the ARVN soldiers with LAWs. Three more enemy tanks were knocked out, and one surrendered when its crew ran out of ammunition.

One of the captured tankers said he was from the 203rd Tank Regiment and had come down the Ho Chi Minh Trail from North Vietnam.[29]

Contributing to the chaos for the NVA tankers was the fact that they did not have any guides and in many cases were not sure where they were going. The NVA had planned on using agents in place and sympathizers to direct the tanks once they were in the city, but Colonel Nhut's police and intelligence agencies had rounded up most of these individuals before the battle started.[30] Additionally, the enemy tankers had been told that the local people would greet them with open arms. That such was not the case became apparent fairly quickly to the enemy tankers.

Adding to the problem for the enemy tanks was that COSVN had decided to centralize control of the armor, since the 9th VC Division did not have any experience with combined arms tactics. Therefore, the tanks and infantry that attacked the city were working under separate chains of command. For all of these reasons, the tank attacks were handled so poorly that the North Vietnamese missed a golden opportunity.

The enemy was not the only one confused. Miller and Hung had trouble sorting out where all the friendly units were. Adding to the chaos was the arrival of all kinds of air support in the skies over An Loc. The support was much needed because the city was in imminent danger of falling to the enemy, but the sheer volume of aircraft in the area was initially difficult to control. Making matters worse for the airmen, there were now nine enemy antiaircraft battalions ringing the city, creating one of the most intense antiaircraft situations of the war.

The A-6s, A-7s, F-4s, A-37s, and VNAF A-1s dropped their bombs well forward of the city on the NVA forces massing for the attack. The army Cobra attack helicopters and air force AC-119K Stinger and AC-130 Spectre gunships worked targets in close proximity to friendly troops. With all this support, the ARVN troops were able to defend against the reduced number of NVA infantry and tanks that escaped the air strikes and assaulted the city.

The A-37s from the 8th Special Operations Squadron were particularly effective. A converted trainer, the Dragonfly was able to fly "low and slow" and put bombs and other ordnance on targets extremely accurately. The aircraft was fitted with a Gatling gun, 14 rockets, and 4 bombs. Because of their relatively low speed, they were very accurate and, thus, were able to work very close to friendly troops.

However, the really close work fell to the Cobra attack helicopters from F/79th Aerial Rocket Artillery and F/9th Cavalry. They were particularly effective in hitting the tanks in the close confines of the city streets.

During the battle for An Loc, the highly maneuverable Cobras would use 17-pound high-explosive armor-piercing 2.75-inch rockets very effectively against the North Vietnamese attackers. During the initial NVA assault, the Cobras from Blue Max caught one tank column attacking south near the 8th ARVN Regiment's command post. They knocked out the lead tank, one in the middle, and the last tank in the column, effectively stopping the attack in its tracks. Another Cobra, flown by Captain Bill Causey with Lieutenant Steve Shields as gunner, was eventually credited with killing or disabling five tanks during the first week of the battle for An Loc.[31] The extremely high degree of accuracy attained for an unguided rocket system demonstrated both skill and extraordinary courage. The Cobra dove close enough to the target to assure a hit while reducing the amount of possible collateral damage to the friendly troops on the ground. Over the course of the battle for An Loc, the Blue Max would be credited with destroying 20 NVA tanks, but at a terrible cost; five Cobras were shot down on 12 May alone and eight brave Blue Max crewmen (out of 32 engaged) were lost.

The effectiveness of the Cobras would be enhanced on 15 April when they were armed with new rockets that had just arrived from the United States. These were also 17-pounders, but the warhead was high-explosive, dual purpose (HEDP), which employed a shaped charge much like that of the M72 LAW. The warhead was found to be capable of penetrating a T-54 series tank from all directions. On soft targets, it gave the same antipersonnel effects as a normal 10-pound high-explosive warhead, and was thus the perfect compromise to engage armor, vehicles, equipment, and personnel. The new warheads had just been developed at Picatinney Arsenal and were being combat tested for the first time.[32]

On 13 April and successive days, the Cobra pilots would prove again and again that army helicopters could indeed kill tanks in a hostile anti-aircraft environment. Later during the battle when friendly artillery had been captured or destroyed, the Cobras provided the most responsive direct fire support. In many cases, the attack helicopters were decisive in denying the NVA an assured victory. When the proximity of friendly troops and, later, inclement weather inhibited the use of tactical air support, the attack helicopters were the only air support that could be employed. On this day and those that followed, the presence of the Cobras was often the difference between victory and defeat. They repeatedly flew against targets in the face of intense antiaircraft fire. The advisers and their counterparts on the ground were repeatedly heartened as the pilots expended their ordnance, only to promise, "I'll be back as soon as I can re-arm." Colonel

Miller later remarked that "nothing more could have been asked" of the aviators from the 1st Cavalry Division.[33] After the battle, he was even more emphatic, stating unequivocally that "the Cobras were the instruments of our salvation."[34]

At around 1000 hours on 13 April, the North Vietnamese launched a second ground attack from the northwest by infantry and tanks. A half hour later, a T-54 tank wandered aimlessly through the streets of the city. It made it all the way to the southern part of the city, where it tried to breach the defense surrounding the province headquarters. However, it became tangled in the concertina wire and was effectively immobilized. Captain Khai, commander of the sector artillery, utilized the only 105mm howitzer not already destroyed by the enemy artillery barrage. Enemy shrapnel had already shredded the gun's tires and destroyed its gun sight, but with the help of several RF/PF soldiers, Captain Khai pointed the gun directly at the T-54 and fired, hitting the tank and putting it out of commission.[35] For this act, Colonel Nhut promoted Captain Khai to major on the spot. One of the enemy tankers was captured. He told his captors that he was a corporal from the 26th Tank Company and that he and his unit had moved down the Ho Chi Minh Trail from North Vietnam to Cambodia in February. He confirmed that his leaders had told the tankers that the NVA infantry already held the city and that the other defenders would run away when they saw the tanks. He seemed stunned that his reception had been so different from what he had been told to expect.

Despite the destruction of the tank near the province headquarters, the attack went well for the NVA, and by 1130 hours they controlled the airstrip and the northern part of An Loc itself. However, intense air strikes slowed the momentum of the attack and prevented the South Vietnamese defenders from being completely overrun. A postwar PAVN report acknowledged that the battles on 13 April resulted in heavy losses for the 6th Tank Company.[36] The North Vietnamese were very close to success in the initial attack, but failed to realize it because of all the confusion on the ground. Miller later observed, "He [the enemy commander] had An Loc, but the bastard did not know it."[37]

By the middle of the afternoon, the situation had stabilized somewhat. Colonel Miller later recalled, "We had the south side, they had the north side, and it was no-man's land in the middle. There were mistakes on both sides that first day, plenty of them, but we must have made fewer because we were still there when it quieted down, and that meant we were there from then on in my opinion."[38]

For the remainder of the 13th and the next two days, the American advisers directed repeated air strikes against the NVA forces, sometimes as close as 20 meters to friendly troops. At the 5th ARVN command bunker, Colonel Miller tirelessly orchestrated the battle, tracking the situation, coordinating with the forward air controllers, and talking by radio with the other advisers located on the defensive perimeter, who were working with the FACs to put the arriving aircraft on target and get ready for the next round of strikes. Throughout this period, Miller was also repeatedly on the radio to General Hollingsworth, keeping him updated on the situation and requesting more support.

By now, B-52 strikes were being diverted to close tactical support of An Loc. One enemy attack late on 13 April dissolved when the attacking force was caught in a preplanned B-52 strike area. The tenacity of the defenders and the continuous air strikes prevented the enemy from expanding its foothold in the northern part of the city, but the house-to-house fighting continued unabated. Lieutenant Colonel Benedit, Colonel Miller's deputy, later recalled: "The enemy pounded and pounded. He'd hit and take a house, then reinforce at night, and next day take the next house and the next."[39]

A pattern developed in the fighting. Tac air, attack helicopters, and B-52s were used during the day to hold off the attackers. The B-52s struck the enemy staging areas, the tac air "fast movers" were used just over the defensive perimeter, while the attack helicopters and A-37s worked targets inside the city in close proximity to friendly troops. The USAF fixed-wing gunships flew night and day, but they were particularly effective at night; the steady drone of their engines in the nighttime sky was very comforting to the advisers and their counterparts. Both AC-119s and AC-130s flew in support of the defenders. Six AC-119 Stingers moved from Nakhon Phanom, Thailand, to Bien Hoa, establishing a forward operating base that gave them more flying time over the target area. The AC-119 was initially very effective in the early fighting in Binh Long. Working at its normal operational altitude of 3,500 feet over Loc Ninh and An Loc, the Stinger's 7.62mm miniguns and 20mm cannon were very accurate. However, the Stinger required a relatively permissive air environment, and as the anti-aircraft fire over the city intensified, the Stingers were forced up and away from the city. Still they were able to perform area reconnaissance and engage targets of opportunity. In these roles, they proved most effective in impeding the flow of supplies to the NVA forces assembled around the provincial capital.

The AC-130 Spectres from Thailand assumed the majority of the responsibility for gunship missions over the city. They continued to operate from Ubon, landing once or twice at Tan Son Nhut during each mission day to replenish fuel or ammunition. Sometimes crews remained on duty 24 hours or more without rest, fighting fatigue but doing everything they could to make sure that the troops on the ground had all the support they needed. At least one gunship remained on station over An Loc around the clock for the duration of the entire siege.

The early Spectre missions over An Loc were disappointing. FACs were generally inclined to give priority to fighter-bombers, and often held off gunships from targets to permit strikes by the jets. The first AC-130 mission over An Loc returned to base without having fired a shot because they were continually diverted in favor of the "fast movers." However, this situation rapidly changed as both the FACs and the advisers on the ground realized the capabilities of the Spectres. Soon the AC-130s were responding to calls for fire on specific buildings within the city. Their accuracy was such that they could bring fire very close to the friendly troops with little danger of fratricide.

The civilian citizens of An Loc were not immune to the death and destruction going on all around them. One of the NVA T-54 tanks made it into the center of the city, where it rolled into a Catholic church. Huddled inside were old men, women, and children conducting a prayer service. According to Captain Moffett with the 3rd Ranger Group, the tank opened fire with its cannon and machine guns, killing well over 100 of the innocent civilians.[40] Having expended its ammunition, it withdrew to the city square and put a white flag on its antenna. The FAC overhead called the 5th ARVN and asked what to do. The adviser on the radio told him to "blow it away!" The FAC proceeded to do just that, directing several air strikes on the tank.

The fighting on the ground was intense, and the level of combat far exceeded the experience of the South Vietnamese soldiers and most of their advisers. I, for one, had been in country for four months and had already been wounded once, but my experience had been limited to battalion-size search and clear operations in the area around Xuan Loc. During those operations, we had more than our share of enemy contacts and engagements with North Vietnamese regulars, but it had none of the unabating intensity of the fighting we would face for the next two months in An Loc. We were stunned by the enemy tanks and the ferocity of the NVA attack, and it would only get worse.

While the opposing infantry fought house to house and door to door in the northern half of the city, the North Vietnamese tanks roamed the city shooting up any target. The South Vietnamese had no armor of their own; they had to rely on sheer courage and M72 LAWs. The South Vietnamese soon learned how to fight the tanks. Eventually, the ARVN and RF/PFs would form tank-killer teams that proved very effective against the repeated enemy tank attacks. Antitank weapons were set in basements, a level to which the tanks could not lower their gun tubes, or on the second or third stories of buildings, where ARVN M72 gunners tried to find a weak spot on the tank before it could elevate its guns sufficiently to engage the South Vietnamese soldiers. A fifteen-year-old Popular Force soldier, on the second story of a school, knocked out a tank with a LAW. During the first few days of the initial battle for the city, the ARVN defenders had destroyed 18 NVA tanks on the ground and the Cobras had gotten 12. Lieutenant Colonel Le Nguyen Vy, deputy commander of the 5th ARVN, personally destroyed four tanks with M72s.[41]

The North Vietnamese continued to demonstrate difficulties in employing tanks during the battle, feeding the tanks in piecemeal, possibly because of a fear of air strikes on massed columns. They also insisted on repeatedly sending the tanks in without infantry support. Supplying the tanks also proved problematic, and many ran out of fuel before they ran out of ammunition.

As the battle inside the city raged, General Hollingsworth directed B-52 strikes on NVA staging areas around the city. The battle had stabilized somewhat by the evening of the 13th. However, the enemy continued to pour artillery, mortars, and rockets into the city. There were a number of ground probes during the day on the 14th. A number of tanks were observed in the rubber trees to the north and east. Four B-52 strikes were directed against these areas. Each ARC LIGHT mission consisted of three aircraft, each carrying a mixed load of 108 MK-82 500-pound and 750-pound conventional bombs. The devastation wrought by these strikes was immense. No accounts have been found of what it was like for the NVA at An Loc to suffer these attacks, but the description by Truong Nhu Tang, a former Viet Cong, is no doubt representative of the experience. After the war, he wrote about having survived a B-52 strike: "From a kilometer, the shock waves knocked their victims senseless. Any hit within a half kilometer would collapse the walls of an unreinforced bunker, burying alive the people cowering inside. . . . It was not just that things were destroyed; in some awesome way they had ceased to exist."[42]

The North Vietnamese arrayed around An Loc and along the highway to the south would experience the same terror as Truong Nhu Tang did under the repeated ARC LIGHT strikes. During the early days of the battle for An Loc, one B-52 strike caught an entire battalion in the open before it reached the northwest approach to the city. The bombs killed an estimated 100 attackers, destroyed at least three tanks, and broke the back of the NVA attack on that part of the city.[43] These strikes would prove the difference between victory and defeat countless times during the next three months.

The NVA increased the heavy shelling on the city, but the ARVN defenders dug in and used tactical airpower to hold the NVA ground attacks at bay, while the B-52s pounded on the enemy staging areas. General McGiffert later commented on the effectiveness of the B-52 strikes and the preplanned tactical air sorties of 13–15 April: "I really believe that without these the city would have fallen, because I think the infantry would have gotten in with the tanks."[44]

It was not just the B-52s that made the difference. Air support in all its forms had a tremendous impact on the outcome of every engagement. Patrols sent out after the first assault on An Loc confirmed more than 400 enemy dead, half of whom were killed by air. During the first two weeks of the battle for the city, over 2,500 air strikes were flown in support of the ARVN forces in and around An Loc.[45] Hollingsworth would report to General Abrams that "massive air support of all types tipped the scales in our favor."[46]

The South Vietnamese had withstood the initial assault on An Loc, but that day in Paris, Madame Nguyen Thi Binh, the National Liberation Front's representative to the peace talks, boasted that "within the next ten days, An Loc will be proclaimed the capital of the Provisional Revolutionary Government of South Vietnam."[47]

Back in An Loc, the advisers were not sure that Madame Binh would be proven wrong. The ARVN had held, but just barely. The advisers could clearly see how the day's ferocious battle had badly shaken the South Vietnamese soldiers. Panic lay just below the surface. The advisers only hoped that General Hollingsworth could keep the tac air and B-52s coming for it was apparent that the North Vietnamese were going to throw everything they had into taking the city.

The North Vietnamese forces were undeterred by the heavy casualties being inflicted by the continuous air strikes and relentlessly pressed the attack, still leading with tanks. On 14 April, after another intense artillery bombardment, the 8th Tank Company, consisting of nine T-54s and two attached self-propelled antiaircraft guns, attacked the sector held by the 8th ARVN Regiment.[48] This attack, accompanied by small groups of infantry, came within a hundred meters of the 5th Division command post in the center of the city, before it was beaten back by the defenders and Cobra attack helicopters.

During the course of the first two days of the battle, two province officials later reported, six young women were discovered with small radio transmitters concealed in their brassieres. They were apparently relaying information to enemy forces around the town. ARVN soldiers tied them up and left them in an open area where incoming NVA artillery subsequently killed them. "The townspeople," according to the two officials, "who had no love for communist sympathizers or infiltrators, approved of this action."[49]

Even as the desperate battle for the city raged, there was some humor, even if it was of the darker variety. In the evenings, the Communists would break into the province communications frequency and demand to speak to Colonel Nhut. They would then trade insults. On one occasion, an arrogant voice shouted over the radio, "We have located your position. Surrender or die!" Hardly intimidated, Colonel Nhut invited the caller to come on over and that he would arrange for him to fulfill the dream of "being born in the North to die in the South."[50] These exchanges went on every night for several weeks.

While Nhut jousted with the enemy over the radio, the advisers were extremely busy. Since the initial attack, Colonel Miller and his fellow American officers in the 5th ARVN command bunker worked 24 hours a day, stopping only briefly to grab quick naps. Huddled around the plywood map table, they planned and coordinated the battle. The ARVN commander and his staff had very little training or experience in handling operations as complex as those demanded by the NVA onslaught. The American officers acted as General Hung's staff, advising him on troop dispositions, planning air strikes, coordinating support, and processing intelligence. Intelligence to facilitate targeting came from a variety of sources, including local civilians moving into An Loc from outlying areas, U.S. helicopter reconnaissance, flash and sound ranging of enemy indirect fire, crater analysis, on-the-ground observation, Spectre and Stinger electronic capabilities, and continuous surveillance by airborne FACs. Having decided where to use the ever-present airpower, the advisers spoke constantly with the FACs to ensure that the firepower was used where it could do the most good. For B-52 strikes, they forwarded the targeting information through ARVN channels to III Corps and TRAC. The advisers also planned the next day's missions and attempted to coordinate the air resupply drops and medevac helicopters.

The advisers with the regiments and battalions were also busy. They advised their counterparts on defenses and tried to bolster their morale. Their primary function, however, was to coordinate the air strikes that had been allocated to their respective units by Colonel Miller and his "staff" in the 5th ARVN command bunker. This was a full-time job that would go on day and night for the next two months with little pause.

To coordinate the allocated air strikes, the advisers talked directly to the FACs of the 21st Tactical Air Support Squadron (TASS) who were orbiting over the city in Cessna O-2As, small, fixed-wing aircraft with push-pull engines, one in the front and the other in the back. These "good old boys," as one adviser called them, were the true heroes of the air war over An Loc.[51] The advisers on the ground looked on the FACs, answering to the call signs of "Sundog," "Rash," and "Chico," as their saviors. Most of the FACs were young men on their first assignments as pilots, and they daily braved the intense antiaircraft fire over the city to provide the tactical air support that was the difference between victory and defeat. Their job was to fly "low and slow" over the battlefield to coordinate with the ground troops and direct the aircraft, naval and marine air as well as USAF, to their targets. In addition to controlling the air strikes, they also frequently controlled VNAF strike aircraft, flights of Huey Cobras, and AC-130 gunships, while coordinating airspace, performing visual reconnaissance, and coordinating aerial resupply. The FAC aircraft were unarmed, except for smoke rockets that were used to mark the targets, and the pilots orbited over the city every day like sitting ducks in the intense antiaircraft fire that covered the city. Since most of the fighter-bomber aircraft did not have the same kind of tactical radios that the ground soldiers had, the FACs, who had both kinds, acted as the link between those on the ground who needed the ordnance put on target and those aircraft carrying the ordnance. Leon Daniel, a reporter for UPI, flew with Captain Gary Foust, one of the FACs from 21st TASS, in a mission over An Loc in mid-April. Foust repeatedly marked enemy targets for fighter-bomber aircraft in response to radio calls from the advisers on the ground. Daniel described how Foust "worked at a fast pace as he shuffled maps, wrote target coordinates on his windshield with a grease pencil, and fired marking rockets while diving, twisting, and turning to lessen his chances of getting blown out of the air."[52]

The enemy knew that if they knocked out a FAC, they knocked out the eyes of the aircraft that carried the rockets, bombs, and napalm. So the FACs were the target of a lot of antiaircraft fire. Nevertheless, they routinely disregarded their own safety to help the U.S. advisers and their counterparts on the ground.

As had happened earlier in the battle for Loc Ninh, the sheer volume of air assets over An Loc posed a serious problem. As aircraft were rushed to the scene, the airspace became very crowded. VNAF FACs and tactical aircraft also working in the area compounded the problem of command and control. One AC-130 pilot reported that he was engaging a target as directed by the FAC when VNAF A-1s kept flying through his firing orbit.[53] Aircraft were stacked up over the city as the FACs tried to utilize them before they ran out of "station time" and had to return to base without expending their ordnance. There was also the danger of midair collisions.

To remedy the situation, a new system of command and control was devised. VNAF FACs were assigned to a specific sector and they handled VNAF tac air within their area. Three USAF FACs were assigned to control the U.S. assets over the city.[54] One of these, usually the most experienced, flew high above the action and acted as the "King FAC." His job was to control all of the inbound aircraft and parcel them out to the other two FACs, who were given area responsibility for different parts of the city and surrounding area. The normal procedure was for the senior advisers in the 5th ARVN bunker to coordinate requests for air support by talking to the "King FAC," who would then hand off the incoming aircraft to one of the other FACs depending on who would get the support. The designated FAC then talked directly with the advisers on the ground with the South Vietnamese unit to be supported to learn the nature of the target to be struck. He then spoke with the inbound fighter-bombers and directed them to the targets, using smoke rockets and adjustment instructions relayed from the ground.

For the duration of the entire battle, the FACs and advisers, working closely together, were able to make the best use of all available aircraft and munitions to help the outnumbered defenders in very tenuous situations. The constant presence of the small FAC aircraft over the city was reassuring to the advisers and their South Vietnamese counterparts. Not surprisingly, a unique rapport developed between the advisers and the FACs, many of whom came back time and again, instead of rotating to less demanding operations. Thus, the advisers and FACs became accustomed to working together and the FACs' familiarity with the area and the needs of the troops on the ground greatly facilitated timely targeting and coordination.

As the advisers worked hard with the FACs to bring in the crucial air support, they performed another, equally important function. The presence of the American advisers demonstrated to the ARVN soldiers that they were not going to be abandoned. This knowledge helped them to recover from the initial shock of the NVA attack and would bolster their morale and confidence in the dark days to come.

Reinforcing the City under Attack

The ever-present air support greatly bolstered the ARVN morale, which got another boost on 14 April when General Minh ordered the 1st Airborne Brigade, commanded by Colonel Le Quang Luong, to disengage along Highway 13 and move by helicopter to reinforce the 5th ARVN Division forces at An Loc. At 1600 that afternoon, the 6th Battalion conducted the initial combat assault by CH-47 Chinook helicopters from the 362nd Assault Helicopter Company, 229th Aviation, into an area adjacent to Windy Hill and Hill 169, the high ground three kilometers to the southeast of the city. Having achieved surprise, the combat assault was made unopposed, but shortly after landing, the airborne troops made heavy contact with the enemy, sustaining moderate casualties. The American advisers with the unit called in tactical air support and the situation was stabilized.

The next day, the remainder of the brigade was inserted into the same area southeast of the city. The brigade headquarters, along with the 5th and 8th Battalions, occupied positions east of the city. The 81st Ranger Battalion, a superb unit commanded by Lieutenant Colonel Pham Van Huan, assaulted into a landing zone southeast of Hill 169 and began moving toward An Loc. The 6th Battalion began to construct a firebase for the six 105mm howitzers from a battery of the 3rd Artillery Battalion that were airlifted in that morning by CH-47s.

As the paratroopers prepared their positions on the high ground to the southeast of the city, the pressure on the city itself increased. On 15 April, the NVA once again renewed their attempt to take the city. Following the normal pattern, the North Vietnamese began with an intense artillery barrage at 0430 hours, focusing on General Hung's 5th Division headquarters and the Binh Long Province compound. This shelling set portions of the city on fire. At 0600, two separate tank-led thrusts were made from the north and west. During the course of this attack, the enemy pressure forced the 8th Regiment to pull back several streets, where they established a new defensive line; the fighting was bitter and in some cases, hand to hand. The South Vietnamese soldiers had learned some valuable lessons in the fighting on 13 April, but the NVA continued to lead with the tanks, followed by infantry. When the enemy tanks reached Hung Vuong Street, in the center of the city, ARVN soldiers engaged the tanks from the flanks with multiple M72 LAWs, knocking out several of them and forcing the others to withdraw. A determined defense by the ARVN defenders and continuous close air support had enabled the South Vietnamese to stabilize the situation for the time being.

A second attack began at 1000. Along the western perimeter, the 9th VC Division threw the entire 271st Regiment into the battle. Enemy troops reached the wire in the southeast. Overhead, heavy antiaircraft fire, including .51 caliber and 23mm as well as 37mm and 57mm, made "flying most gamey" in the words of General Hollingsworth.[55] Under cover of the air defense umbrella, the NVA attackers once again almost took the 5th ARVN Division command post, with one tank making it to within 100 meters of General Hung's command bunker, firing directly into it and wounding the province S-3 operations officer and two other staff officers.[56] Because the enemy troops were so close, Colonel Miller called for help from Blue Max. Chief Warrant Officer Ron Tusi responded immediately, braving intense ground fire to destroy the tank with his rockets.[57] Tusi and Captain Billy H. Causey would each be credited with five tank kills before the battle was over.

Despite the intense antiaircraft fire, the FACs, attack aircraft, and Cobras continued to press the fight. As the defenders held tenaciously to their small piece of terrain, air support once again provided the difference between victory and defeat. In one attack at 1400 that day, attack aircraft destroyed 9 of 10 attacking tanks. However, the decisive event in turning back the threat from the west was a very timely B-52 strike on the rubber plantation four kilometers west of the city; it was later determined that this strike annihilated an entire battalion from the 271st Regiment.

The outcomes of the battles on 15 April were extremely close, but the South Vietnamese held. Key to the successful defense by the ARVN was the continuous air cover over the city. In the first two and a half weeks of the battle, more than 2,500 air strikes had been flown in MR III, primarily around Loc Ninh and An Loc. Much of this support was readily available because of a 7th Air Force decision to use Bien Hoa as a turnaround base for F-4s flying out of Thailand. On some days, the fighters made two turns at Bien Hoa before returning to Thailand, allowing three sorties over the target during a mission day.

By late on the 16th, the battle inside An Loc had abated somewhat. The enemy shelling was still heavy, but there was a momentary lull in the ground attack. After three days of intense combat, the enemy had lost 23 tanks, most of them T-54s.[58] Still, the NVA forces held almost the entire northern half of the city, the air strip, and most of the territory surrounding the city. In many cases the opposing forces were separated only by the width of a city street. Meanwhile, the NVA attempted to tightened its stranglehold on An Loc. The city had received 25,000 rounds in the previous five days, and it would continue to receive between 1,200 and 2,000 enemy rocket, artillery, and mortar rounds per day.[59]

Major Ray Haney, my fellow adviser with TF 52, had been wounded by an incoming 122mm rocket on 14 April. Several attempts were made to evacuate him by helicopter, but the enemy antiaircraft umbrella was too intense. Finally on 16 April, we carried him on a stretcher to an LZ south of the city where a medevac Huey was finally able to land and pick him up, along with a French Canadian reporter who had also been wounded. However, Haney's troubles were not over. The Dustoff helicopter took ground fire exiting the area and had to make an emergency landing several miles southwest of An Loc. Colonel William Crouch, deputy commander of the 3rd Brigade, 1st Cavalry Division, flying nearby in a command and control UH-1H Huey saw the medevac helicopter go down. He immediately landed and picked up the nine downed personnel—four Dustoff crewmen, Haney, the wounded reporter, and three ARVN soldiers. Even though Crouch's aircraft already had six aboard and carried a heavy command radio console, he was able to take off under fire with 15 people aboard—a weight, theoretically, a Huey could not lift.[60] Haney finally made it to the hospital; he ultimately survived his wounds but would have bled to death had he not gotten out of An Loc when he did.

Later in the afternoon of 16 April, the 5th and 8th Battalions and the 81st Rangers attacked west to relieve An Loc. The 6th Airborne Battalion remained on Hill 169 to secure the firebase that had been established. Initially, there was only light contact. The 8th Battalion reached the southern portion of the city without incident. However, the 5th Battalion made heavy contact with a strong enemy force as the unit moved west toward the city; the battle lasted for six hours until the NVA withdrew. Having driven the enemy off for the time being, the airborne troops took up a defensive position just east of the city. Meanwhile, the 81st Rangers had entered An Loc and occupied a position in the northeastern corner of the city; they would remain under the operational control of 5th ARVN Division for the duration of the battle. That evening, the battalion commander of the 81st called 5th ARVN Division headquarters and requested that no one use any illumination flares; under the cover of darkness, they began to clear their assigned area, one house after another.

Upon returning to Long Binh that night, Hollingsworth reported to General Abrams that "there was a great battle at An Loc yesterday." Continuing, he wrote, "The enemy hit us hard all day long with everything he could muster—and we threw it right back at him. The forces in An Loc realized that they had to fight and they fought well."[61] In truth, the fighting ability of the ARVN during the initial NVA onslaught had been less than uniformly outstanding. Near panic had reigned, and the ARVN had yielded half of the city in the face of heavy ground, armor, and artillery attacks. However, the fact remained that the ARVN had not completely broken despite the repeated ground attacks and the continual artillery and rocket barrage, and at least the southern half of the city was still in South Vietnamese hands.

Earlier, President Thieu, realizing the criticality of holding An Loc to prevent a direct thrust on Saigon, had ordered the 21st ARVN Infantry Division from its base in the Mekong Delta to Lai Khe to reinforce III Corps forces. General Minh directed the new division to attack north to block any further moves to the south by the North Vietnamese. After arriving at Lai Khe, the 21st had moved north and was attacking the heavily entrenched NVA forces at Tau O Bridge on Highway 13 south of the city. With the situation in An Loc somewhat stabilized, the III Corps commander, realizing that there would not be an enemy drive on Saigon until An Loc was taken, changed the mission of the 21st from blocking an NVA move south to clearing the highway from Chon Thanh to An Loc to break the siege.[62] Unfortunately, the mission change meant little, because the 21st was by now dealing with an entrenched enemy, and the fight to open the highway would soon all but consume the division. The 7th NVA Division proved to be a determined and skillful defender. In addition, the enemy, having operated in Binh Long Province for a number of years, was more familiar with the terrain than were the 21st ARVN troops from the Mekong Delta. The effort to root out the NVA along Highway 13 would take more than two months and would be a very bloody affair.

As the 21st Division tried to break the NVA roadblock to the south, the defenders inside An Loc realized that they had only a momentary respite before the NVA attacked once again. On 17 April, Colonel Miller reported to General Hollingsworth that An Loc continued to sustain heavy shelling and that he believed the enemy would "use strangulation and starvation tactics—then attack in force."[63] Although the ARVN troops still held the city, Miller was very pessimistic regarding their capability to carry on: "The division is tired and worn out; supplies minimal, casualties continue to mount, medical supplies are low; wounded a major problem, mass burials for military and civilians, morale at a low ebb. In spite of incurring heavy losses from U.S. air strikes, the enemy continues to persist."[64]

Things were indeed bleak. Intelligence reports indicated that there were at least five enemy regiments in the An Loc area. The ARVN had no artillery, and counterbattery efforts could be made only though the use of tactical air strikes. The U.S. Air Force and the Vietnamese Air Force (VNAF) attempted to resupply the city on a daily basis, but the enemy antiaircraft fire made it increasingly difficult to drop the supplies so that the defenders could recover them. Extremely heavy casualties had been sustained by all ARVN units in the opening battles, and the number of dead and wounded mounted due to the seemingly unending artillery bombardment. Evacuation of the wounded was nearly impossible, because the VNAF evacuation helicopters either refused to fly into the city, or, if they made it into the city, refused to touch down long enough to load the wounded. Those few courageous airmen who did try to pick up the wounded were usually shot down or their aircraft heavily damaged by enemy ground fire.

The situation in the city was grim. The defenders had held out so far, but just barely. The enemy artillery continued to fall day and night. Neither the South Vietnamese nor their American advisers were sure that they could hold against another determined attack by the NVA. A BBC Radio broadcast at the time stated that only a miracle could save the South Vietnamese at An Loc. As far as the advisers were concerned, this was not far from the truth. There was a feeling that the South Vietnamese were on the verge of breaking.

Compounding the problem, as far as Colonel Miller was concerned, was the continued indecisiveness of General Hung. Miller reported to Hollingsworth: "The Division CG [commanding general] is tired—unstable—irrational—irritable—inadvisable—and unapproachable. . . . When the chips are down he looses [sic] all of his composure. . . . Unless the Airborne saves us I believe the enemy can take An Loc any time."[65]

The NVA Change Their Plans

Although the defenders did not know it at the time, the enemy's costly attack on 15 April climaxed the first phase of the battle for An Loc. The enemy's initial plan to seize the city had been thwarted. The main attack conducted by the 9th VC Division, supported by two battalions of the 203rd Tank Regiment, had been unsuccessful, largely due to the continuous pounding by B-52s, fighter-bomber aircraft, AC-130 Spectre gunships, and attack helicopters. Accordingly, the North Vietnamese modified their plan.

The original North Vietnamese plan had called for An Loc to be overrun and occupied by NVA forces no later than 15 April.[66] Due to the defenders' ability to hold out and the devastation wrought by the constant air support, the North Vietnamese timetable was no longer achievable. Accordingly, the NVA headquarters ordered a renewed main attack on An Loc from the east supported by secondary attacks on the airborne brigade south of the city. In an attempt to negate the impact of American airpower, additional antiaircraft weapons were emplaced around An Loc.

By a twist of fate, the revised NVA plan of attack came into ARVN hands on 18 April. On that day, an element from the 92nd Border Ranger Battalion engaged NVA forces near Tong Le Chon Base. One of the enemy killed in the action was discovered to be a North Vietnamese political officer. The rangers found two handwritten letters on his body. One was a letter that addressed the failure of the NVA attack to take An Loc in accordance with the initial plan. Criticizing the 9th VC Division and its commander, General Bung, the letter cited two reasons for the division's inability to capture the city.[67] First, the intervention of American airpower, particularly the B-52s, had been devastating on the attacking forces. Secondly, the lack of coordination between armor and infantry forces in the attack had allowed the ARVN forces to regroup and reorganize their defenses.

The other letter, six pages in length, was from the political officer of the 9th VC Division outlining a new plan to take the city on 19 April. The 9th VC Division, still reinforced by the 203rd Tank Regiment and the 69th Artillery Division, would get another chance to take the city. The 271st Regiment would again attack An Loc from the west, the 272nd would strike from the north, and 95C Regiment from the northeast. The 275th Regiment from the 5th VC Division and the 141st Regiment from the 7th NVA Division with supporting tanks would attack the 6th Airborne and its six 105mm artillery pieces on Windy Hill and Hill 169 east of An Loc.

With this plan, the enemy was very confident that the city could be seized in a matter of days, no more than 5 to 10. In fact, the NVA were so confident of victory that Radio Hanoi broadcast a report that the city would be taken and the People's Revolutionary Government established in An Loc by 20 April.[68]

Captured North Vietnamese soldiers later reported that after the initial attack, their leaders increased efforts to exhort the Communist troops to do their utmost to defeat the ARVN "puppets." There were also reports that North Vietnamese tankers were found chained in their tanks.[69] Gerald Hebert, a freelance photographer from Montreal, Quebec, had spent five days in An Loc before he was wounded and evacuated on the same aircraft with Major Haney. Hebert and Haney reported that they had seen dead NVA tankers chained in their tanks. Whether the tankers were actually chained in their tanks by their commanders or did so merely as a symbolic gesture, it indicated the North Vietnamese commitment to take the city and did not bode well for ARVN defenders in the next round of attacks.[70]

CHAPTER SIX

SECOND ATTACK ON AN LOC

The Second Attack

THE SECOND MAJOR attack on An Loc began as planned in the early morning hours of 19 April with a massive bombardment by rockets and artillery on both the city and the 1st Airborne positions on Windy Hill and Hill 169. Following the heavy artillery preparation, the three regiments of the 9th VC Division conducted the main attack on An Loc itself. Map 9 reflects the disposition of forces on the morning of 19 April 1972.

At the same time, the North Vietnamese launched a supporting ground attack with two NVA regiments on the scattered elements of the 1st Airborne Brigade arrayed southeast of the city. The 6th Battalion came under intense attack from the 275th Regiment of the 5th NVA Division and the 141st Regiment of the 7th NVA Division. Tactical air and B-52 strikes inflicted heavy casualties on the attackers and six enemy tanks were destroyed, but the 6th Airborne Battalion was eventually overcome by the NVA and the paratroopers were forced to abandon their positions. By this time, Lieutenant Colonel Dinh, commander of the 6th Battalion, had all but abdicated command; after having his men dig a foxhole, he jumped in and refused to come out. The battalion operations officer told the American advisers that "Dinh had made his peace with dying."[1]

One airborne company was completely overrun. The other two companies were forced to destroy their 105mm artillery pieces and withdraw. Under cover of B-52 strikes planned by Major Jack Todd, deputy senior

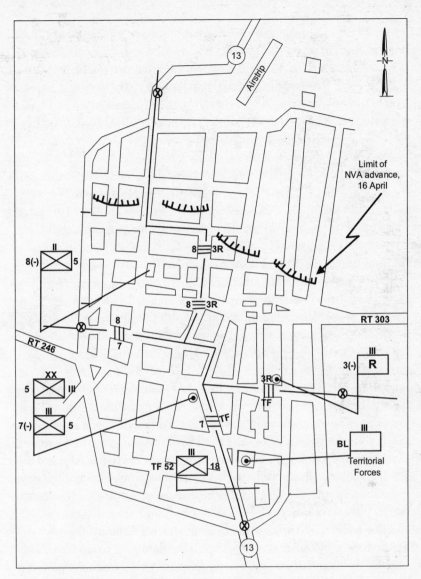

Map 9. ARVN Dispositions, 19 April 1972

adviser to the airborne brigade, a small force of about 80 paratroopers broke out and were later extracted by helicopter. However, stragglers and escaped prisoners from the 6th Airborne Battalion continued to turn up in An Loc and farther to the south in Chon Thanh and Lai Khe for several weeks. The 6th Battalion as a unit was virtually out of the operation until it was reconstituted in late May.[2] One of the U.S. advisers, First Lieutenant Ross Kelly, would receive the Distinguished Service Cross for his role in the breakout of the survivors of the 6th Battalion.

In the process of overrunning the 6th Battalion, the NVA also captured the ARVN artillery. This appeared to be part of an NVA plan to systematically destroy the South Vietnamese artillery capability. They had captured or destroyed virtually every artillery piece available to the ARVN for the defense of the city, severely inhibiting the defenders' ability to launch any meaningful counterattack efforts from inside the city.[3] In addition, most of the artillery ammunition was also destroyed by enemy indirect fire. The NVA even struck the ammunition storage area at Lai Khe on 16 April, resulting in the destruction of 8,000 rounds of ammunition for 105mm and 155mm howitzers as well as damage to the artillery pieces there. This left only 60mm and 81mm mortars for the ARVN defenders in An Loc during the siege.

On 21 April, the 1st Airborne Brigade's command group moved into the southeastern section of An Loc and co-located with the Binh Long Province command post. The 5th and 8th Battalions had already established defensive positions near An Loc. The 8th Battalion was in the rubber plantation just south of the city along the east side of Highway 13, and the 5th Battalion occupied positions just to the east of the city. For the next several weeks, the two airborne battalions remained in their respective positions, beating back daily ground attacks from the south and west.

The addition of the airborne brigade greatly reinforced the city's defenses, but the NVA forces now occupied the dominant terrain previously held by the South Vietnamese paratroopers. These positions provided them unencumbered observation of ARVN defenses throughout the city.

While the supporting attack against the 6th Airborne Battalion had gone well for the NVA, the main enemy attack on the city by the 9th VC Division did not go as well. In An Loc the defenders, surrounded and with no choice but to stand or die, fought off repeated desperate attempts to take the city. As the advisers called in air strikes to within 200 meters of friendly positions, the ARVN soldiers brought devastating fire to bear on enemy massed formations throwing themselves against the South Vietnamese defenses in the southern half of the city. During the day, tac air and B-52s pounded the attackers with wave after wave of aircraft. At night the ever-present droning of the Spectre gunships comforted the advisers as they targeted NVA troops moving around in the darkness.

The fighting had been intense, but the around-the-clock air support had permitted the defenders to beat back the repeated enemy attacks. By 22 April, the ground assaults had abated somewhat, but the artillery and rocket attacks had increased. The situation had stabilized; the NVA still occupied the northern part of the city, while the ARVN held the southern portion.

That night, the ARVN decided to see if they could improve the situation. The 81st Ranger Battalion launched a limited counterattack to eliminate several enemy lodgements in the northern sector of the city. Their aggressive attacks, among the first South Vietnamese offensive actions since the NVA invasion began, were supported by a PAVE AEGIS AC-130, a specially outfitted Spectre gunship with a 105mm cannon. Sergeant First Class Jesse Yerta, light weapons adviser with the 81st, employed the Spectre's fire in the form of a rolling barrage to support the ARVN attack. In order to bring the supporting fire in very close, Sergeant Yerta moved with the lead assault element and repeatedly exposed himself to enemy fire, maintaining radio contact with the Spectre and directing its fire with small handheld pen flares. He was later awarded the Distinguished Service Cross for his actions that night.

The attack by the 81st was mildly successful, but the tactical situation remained virtually unchanged from 22 April to 10 May. Both sides jockeyed for position and the opposing forces remained in contact, but neither side made significant gains. However, the NVA were able to secure a small salient in the western part of the city. Nevertheless, Colonel Miller was greatly encouraged; in a report to TRAC, he wrote that the uninterrupted air support was making the difference: "Indications are we are stacking the little bastards up like cordwood." Buoyed by the outcome of the most recent battles, he even had a charitable word or two for General Hung: "Counterpart ti ti [a little] cooler but worn out. . . . Like whiskey, [he] will improve with age." Still, he realistically observed, "Pucker factor is high. Little ARVN has got to hold, there ain't no place to go." He closed by saying, "We will do it," and signed off with his characteristic, "Hanging in there, Colonel Miller."[4] At this time, the South Vietnamese held an area that measured only about a thousand meters square—the rest of the area in the city and surrounding area in every direction belonged to the enemy.

Conditions in the City

Although the defenders had turned back the most recent North Vietnamese ground attacks, the enemy continued to pour rocket, artillery, and mortar rounds into the city. More than 1,000 rounds fell on An Loc every day. The enemy used a variety of weapons to produce this deadly fire. Some of it was from captured ARVN weapons, but additional artillery and heavy mortars had been hauled in from Cambodia. The FACs tried desperately to locate and knock out these weapons, but it was a difficult task. On 17 April, a FAC spotted four trucks pulling four 155mm howitzers south toward An Loc. Because of poor weather, he could not use fighter aircraft, but he directed a Spectre gunship against the trucks. Shortly thereafter, tac air arrived on the scene and assisted the Spectre in destroying the trucks and the artillery.

While the North Vietnamese may have had trouble with the use of their tanks, their use of artillery was masterful. Throughout the entire siege, they were able to bring deadly observed fire on the city at will. Despite extensive efforts to silence the enemy guns, the NVA continued to pour mortars, rockets, and artillery shells into the city at an almost unbelievable rate. They were able to do this in the face of overwhelming airpower because they organized their artillery in depth, constantly moved the guns, maintained mortars and artillery in reserve to replace those destroyed by B-52s and tactical air strikes, utilized well-camouflaged firing positions, and refrained from firing when FACs were operating in the immediate vicinity of artillery positions.[5] Because virtually all of the ARVN artillery had been captured or destroyed, there was no counterbattery fire. All of these factors contributed to the NVA ability to maintain a constant barrage of the city for the entire length of the siege.

As the enemy shelling continued without letup, the conditions in An Loc deteriorated to a new low. The defenders lived underground, venturing outside only at great risk. The enemy fire was extremely accurate; one adviser put the odds for surviving five minutes outside in the open at "only 50-50."[6] The defenders had been brought to a point where they feared to move or expose themselves in any way.

Most buildings and other structures in the city had been destroyed by the repeated ground attacks, shelling, and air strikes. The city was strewn with mounds of rubble, shattered trees, garbage, and dead domestic animals. Captain Harold Moffett, an adviser with the 3rd Ranger Group, later described the landscape as looking "like Berlin at the end of World War

II."[7] A South Vietnamese soldier who fought at An Loc, writing after the war, said that "the shelling so filled the sky that death was everywhere, the dead bodies scattered like weeds. Death became something natural . . . death was an expected phenomenon. . . . All humanity died in An Loc."[8] A South Vietnamese ranger remembered the agonizing screams of the wounded and dying and "the bodies and body parts blown around the area, even hanging from tree limbs or laying on the roofs of houses."[9] An American journalist described conditions inside the city more succinctly when he said that An Loc was "quite simply hell."[10]

The advisers were not immune to the situation. The sheer destruction of the constant shelling wore on them, just as it did the South Vietnamese. The Americans fully realized what a tenuous position they were in, but they had to put a good face on for their counterparts; they could not allow the South Vietnamese to see their concern. That was a difficult proposition. The advisers, many of whom had never before experienced this level of sustained combat, worked around the clock with little rest and were exhausted.

One of the factors that helped sustain the advisers was the continual presence of General Hollingsworth. Even when things looked the darkest, he was in the air over the city encouraging the advisers and their counterparts. He would be on the radio for long periods of time in detailed conversations with the guys on the ground. One might wonder if these conversations gave the enemy too much information, but the old warrior knew that the men in An Loc needed his personal encouragement, and he exposed himself repeatedly in the deadly air over the city to give it. Even when we were convinced that we could not hold out and were about to be overrun, it was the gruff voice of "Danger 79er" who convinced us that he would give us all the support we needed if we could just hold on. This meant everything to those on the ground in An Loc.

The Civilians

Unlike during the 1968 Tet Offensive in which the Communists tried to promote a "General Uprising" among the South Vietnamese people, in 1972 the North Vietnamese leaders made no effort to win over the people. Refugees from Loc Ninh reported that after taking the town, the NVA rounded up the civilian administrators, other representatives of the Saigon government, and teachers. The refugees said that the Communist cadre invited the people of Loc Ninh to public trials where officials were condemned and executed.[11] In one case, they publicly executed the leader of the local self-defense militia and two of his men in the town square. The rest of the "people's enemies" were trucked off to a camp near Snoul, Cambodia.[12] They were no less harsh with the rest of the civilians in Loc Ninh. In fact, throughout the Easter Offensive, they targeted the civilian populace and tried to use them to stress the South Vietnamese infrastructure. This was particularly true in the battle for An Loc. The NVA actions were not meant to "win the hearts and minds" and engendered hostility rather than sympathy for the attackers and their cause.

The civilian refugees from the fighting in Loc Ninh who had escaped to the "safety" of An Loc earlier in the month now joined the citizens of the provincial capital in the battle for survival amid some of the most intense combat of the Vietnam War. By this time, the civilian populace in An Loc was estimated at between 15,000 and 20,000.[13]

Suffering from lack of food, water, medical supplies, and shelter, they were caught in the cross fire between the defenders and the NVA attackers. During the early stages of the battle, a number of civilians took refuge in the Quoc Hoan School, but the North Vietnamese sent 57mm recoilless rifle fire straight into the three-story building, killing an unknown number of men, women, and children. The civilians, like the ARVN troops, had to go underground for survival. Tan Thang Ung, a civil servant, recalled after the battle: "We lived with the soldiers. We cooked and slept in our bunkers and relieved ourselves in tins and threw them out of the bunkers. No one worried about burying the dead, and the wounded were often left to die."[14]

Even living underground did not guarantee survival. One family of seven, a husband, wife, and five children, took shelter in a bunker built under the foundation of their house. The floor above them was covered with a layer of sandbags, making a roof on the basement several feet thick. Unfortunately this was not enough to negate the destructive power of a heavy artillery shell with a delay fuze. The house was hit with several of these rounds, collapsing the building and the bunker under it. The only one to survive was the father, who was left to collect the remains of his family for burial.[15]

The NVA realized that the civilians complicated the problems of the defenders and made every effort to guide additional refugees into the city and prevent them from leaving. The civilians merely wanted to get away from the fighting, but the North Vietnamese forces had the city encircled.

Still they tried to escape; some were successful, but many suffered the same fate as a group of 200 refugees who made a run for it on 15 April. Led by a Vietnamese Catholic priest, they went through the barbed wire and concertina that surrounded the city and tried to move south down Highway 13 to safety. They made it to the southern edge of the city before the NVA opened fire with rockets and artillery, driving those who survived back into the city. This abortive attempt left dead and wounded "lying in ditches like cordwood" all along the highway.[16] Another attempt led by two Buddhist monks several days later had the same bloody results. Nguyen Quoc Khue, a staff officer with the 3rd Ranger Group headquarters, witnessed both of these atrocities. He was captured by the North Vietnamese in 1975 and spent time in a prison camp in North Vietnam. When he mentioned the incident in a self-criticism class during political "training," the political officer replied: "The revolution shelled this civilian crowd because this was a crowd of puppet civilians, filled with reactionaries and counter-revolutionaries. We could not exempt them, and we had to teach them a lesson."[17]

These were not isolated incidents. Almost every time a large group of refugees tried to escape from the heavy combat, the NVA artillery forward observers targeted the fleeing columns and wrought devastation on these innocents. This pattern also prevailed in MR I and the Central Highlands; President Thieu claimed on 9 May that enemy guns had killed a total of 25,000 refugees trying to escape the three major battlefields.[18]

On 20 April, the International Red Cross requested a 24-hour cease-fire in An Loc so that 2,000 wounded civilians could be evacuated, but in Paris, Madame Nguyen Thi Binh, one of the Communist negotiators, said that there was no possibility of interrupting the offensive by a truce.

The human toll inside the city was ghastly; the streets and rubble were littered with bodies, both military and civilian. Lieutenant Colonel Corley, Binh Long Province senior adviser, reported that "the bodies of men, women, and children are everywhere."[19] The sickening smell of death permeated the air. Under these conditions, innumerable diseases ran rampant through both civilian and soldier ranks; there was even an outbreak of cholera among the Montagnards who had taken refuge in the city. To avoid a full-fledged epidemic, bodies were buried in common mass graves, some containing 300–500 corpses, by soldiers operating bulldozers during the infrequent lulls in the almost constant shelling. Many bodies had to be buried again after exploding shells churned up the original graves. Under such conditions, rats ran rampant through the city streets.

With medical supplies almost exhausted and South Vietnamese casualties running about 50 to 70 per day, the situation grew critical. The NVA forces had shelled the province hospital and its 300 patients on the night of 25 April, destroying the clearly marked building and killing most of the patients and staff.[20] This effectively meant that there was no longer any central surgical treatment available. The few remaining ARVN medical officers were overwhelmed by the rapidly mounting number of casualties. The shortage of medical supplies forced one of the ARVN doctors, Nguyen Van Qui, to take nylon threads from sandbags, boil them to kill any germs, and use them to stitch up the soldiers' wounds.[21]

It remained almost impossible to evacuate the wounded because the few VNAF helicopters that made it even near the city usually refused to do anything but hover for a few minutes before flying away. Many of the wounded, both the civilian refugees trapped in the city and the soldiers who were wounded in the fighting, went unattended; they watched their wounds fester in the heat and turn gangrenous. To sustain a serious head, chest, or stomach wound was tantamount to a death sentence. Obviously, this grim situation had a major impact on the defenders' morale.

The morale was further degraded by several incidents involving what one adviser called "the olympic wounded."[22] On at least two separate occasions, evacuation helicopters braved intense ground fire to land in or near the city to pick up casualties only to have certain "wounded" ARVN soldiers drop their more severely injured compatriots to clamber aboard the departing helicopters.

The performance of VNAF helicopters in general was very poor. They were reluctant to fly in the area and would often refuse to land, even to pick up their own wounded. The VNAF helicopter pilots were not dependable in either medevac or resupply. Ground coordination was at times nonexistent. ARVN ground commanders and their troops alike had no confidence in VNAF helicopter crews. One adviser observed: "They'll [the South Vietnamese] never win this war as long as the Vietnamese let those guys [VNAF] fly choppers. . . . These guys can't fight and won't fight. You'll never catch them in the air after 5 P.M."[23]

The failure of the VNAF to provide the necessary evacuation support drove Lieutenant General Minh to ask General Hollingsworth to put together a joint U.S.–South Vietnamese evacuation mission under the command of a U.S. officer to show the VNAF how it was done. Colonel John Richardson of the 12th Combat Aviation Group personally led the mission on 3 May accompanied by four VNAF Hueys. Coming in fast at treetop level, Richardson in the lead ship was able to pick up a load of wounded. However, the VNAF helicopters were not as successful. Three of the VNAF helicopters were almost overwhelmed and swamped by the walking wounded, who fought to get aboard. The trail VNAF helicopter came down only low enough to kick off supplies and then hovered out of reach of the wounded on the ground. The outcome of the mission left a lot to be desired, but Colonel Richardson had shown that helicopters could land in An Loc. His demonstration set the example for the VNAF pilots, who, despite the continuing intense antiaircraft environment, succeeded in getting three or four ships a day thereafter into and out of An Loc, usually landing to the south of the city along Highway 13.

Aerial Resupply

Having failed to take the city by 20 April as promised, but with the city surrounded and cut off from ground resupply, the North Vietnamese turned to what Colonel Miller described as "strangulation tactics."[24] They hoped to compress the ARVN defenders into as small an area as possible, restrict movement, preclude resupply and medical evacuation, and inflict maximum casualties and destruction with indirect fire.[25] This was not a bad strategy on the part of the NVA. With the city surrounded and cut off from ground access, An Loc could only be resupplied by air, and the North Vietnamese antiaircraft gunners were prepared to make that as difficult as possible.

Initially, the responsibility for aerial resupply lay with the South Vietnamese Air Force, and between 7 and 12 April, the VNAF 237th Helicopter Squadron, assisted by American UH-1H Huey and CH-47 Chinook helicopters from 229th Aviation Battalion, completed 42 sorties bringing in much-needed supply. However, the NVA rushed antiaircraft weapons to the area surrounding the city, and soon enemy antiaircraft fire had increased to the point that it became very risky and difficult to supply the defenders by helicopter. On 12 April, an enemy mortar round scored a direct hit on a VNAF Chinook, which burst into flames and crashed; this effectively ended the Chinook flights into An Loc, and the South Vietnamese turned almost exclusively to fixed-wing aircraft to resupply the city. VNAF C-123s and C-119s began dropping supplies on 12 April, but they encountered a deadly concentration of antiaircraft fire that increased with each passing day. All drops were made during daylight, and the city could be approached from the south only along Highway 13. Some flights were attempted at 700 feet, but the ground fire was so intense that the following flights had to release their loads from 5,000 feet or higher. Drops made from such a high altitude were usually off target and drifted outside the very small defensive perimeter. After 27 drops in 48 hours, only 34 of the 135 tons dropped were recovered by the defenders. On 15 April, a VNAF C-123 was shot down, killing all aboard, including the squadron commander.

On 19 April, another VNAF C-123 laden with ammunition exploded in midair after being hit by ground fire, and the VNAF subsequently halted all low-level C-123 resupply attempts. From that point the U.S. Air Force assumed primary responsibility for aerial resupply. The task proved no easier for the American pilots, as they endured what air force historian Ray Bowers called "the most trying times of the war for Air Force C-130 crews."[26] By this time, the NVA had all avenues of approach covered by a complex array of .51-caliber, 23mm, 37mm, and 57mm antiaircraft guns that ringed the city. They used an early warning network of spotters to notify the firing units when aircraft were inbound. As soon as any aircraft approached the city, the spotters alerted the gunners, who filled the sky with tracers and explosive shells. It was estimated that the North Vietnamese would eventually have more than nine antiaircraft battalions around the city.

The C-130 pilots were no strangers to the An Loc area. The first U.S. Air Force C-130 resupply flights over An Loc had come on 15 April after MACV requested that the U.S. Air Force begin dropping supplies in the city. Three C-130s from the 374th Tactical Airlift Wing at Ton Son Nhut made the initial run into An Loc loaded with pallets of ammunition, rations, and medical supplies. Prior to takeoff, the 374th wing commander, Colonel Andrew P. Iosue, stopped by each aircraft to personally wish the crews luck. Captain William Caldwell, one of the aircraft commanders, realized the seriousness of the situation, because never before had the wing commander done this before a mission.[27]

Using the computerized aerial drop system (CARP) and the low-altitude container-delivery method, the first C-130 piloted by Major Robert F. Wallace of the 776th Tactical Airlift Squadron approached the city from the south. Using the An Loc soccer stadium in the southern part of the city as a drop zone, the C-130 approached at 600 feet. The onboard computer released the supplies at a prearranged point. The NVA opened fire on the aircraft as it climbed to escape the area, but the aircraft sustained only slight damage to the rudder.

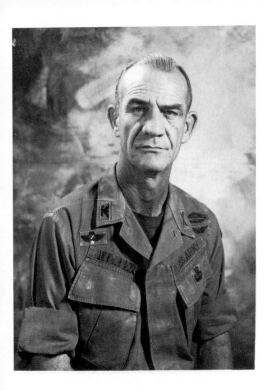

1. ____
Colonel William H. Miller,
Senior Adviser, 5th ARVAN
Division. Author's collection.

2. ____
Colonel Tran Van Nhut,
Province Chief, Binh Long
Province. Author's collection.

3. ___

Lieutenant Colonel Ed Benedit, Colonel Bill Miller, and Major Allan Borsdorf discuss operations while studying the map in the 5th ARVN Division command post bunker. Courtesy Colonel William Miller.

4. ___

Lieutenant General James F. Hollingsworth, formerly commander, Third Regional Assistance Command (shown here as Commanding General, I Corps Group, Korea in 1973). Author's collection.

5. _____

Column of T-54 tanks that were knocked out as they attacked down the main
street of An Loc. Courtesy U.S. Army.

6. _____

Cessna O-2A flown by the forward air controllers of 21st Tactical Air Support
Squadron. Courtesy Bill Carruthers.

7. _____

Aerial view of An Loc looking south, taken by forward air controller orbiting over the city, April 1972. Courtesy Bill Carruthers.

8. _____

AC-130 Spectre gunship. On the aircraft's left side can be seen the 20mm, 40mm, and 105mm guns that made this aircraft so deadly. Courtesy Bill Carruthers.

9.

C-130 aircraft making
an AWADS drop. U.S.
Air Force photo.

10.

A-35 Dragonfly fighter-bombers from the 8th Special Operations Squadron.
Courtesy Bill Carruthers.

11. ____

The city marketplace in An Loc showing the result of several weeks of constant fighting and enemy shelling. Photo courtesy Bill Carruthers.

12. ____

T-54 tank killed by 8th ARVN Regiment in the center of the city.
Photo courtesy U.S. Army.

13. ____

AH-1G Cobra attack helicopter armed with 2.75-inch rocket
launchers. Photo courtesy U.S. Army.

14.

T-54 tank destroyed by 7th ARVN Regiment on the western perimeter of An Loc.
Photo courtesy U.S. Army.

15. ___

B-52 bomber conducting an ARC LIGHT mission.
Douglas Pike Photo Collection, The Vietnam
Archive, Texas Tech University.

16. ___

T-54 tank destroyed along Highway 13 south of
An Loc. Photo by Watermark.

17.
Huey assault helicopters from 229th Aviation Battalion arrive at Lai Khe to pick up reinforcements for An Loc. Photo courtesy Chad Richmond.

18.

View of An Loc downtown. Photo courtesy U.S. Army.

19.
___
Helicopters from the 229th Aviation Battalion land fresh troops from the 18th ARVN Division south of An Loc in June 1972. Photo courtesy Chad Richmond.

20.
___
ARVN soldier who along with his compatriots withstood repeated North Vietnamese assaults in April and May 1972. The M72 LAWs that were used so effectively against the NVA tanks can be seen to his right. ARVN photo.

21. ____

Madonna statue that was one of the few things left undamaged in the north end of An Loc. Author's collection.

22. ____

Lieutenant General Nguyen Van Minh (second from left), Brigadier General Le Van Hung, and President Nguyen Van Thieu in An Loc, 7 July 1972. ARVN photo.

The second aircraft, flown by Captain Caldwell, approached the drop zone but just 30 seconds away from the release point, the aircraft ran into a hail of antiaircraft fire from the NVA gunners. Shells struck both the cockpit and the cargo hold. Rounds smashed the control panel in the cockpit, killed the flight engineer, Tech Sergeant Jon Sanders, and wounded the copilot, Lieutenant John Hering, and the navigator, Lieutenant Richard Lenz. Hot air ducts in the cargo department ruptured, spilling 700-degree (Celsius) air into the cargo department. Incendiary rounds set some of the pallets of 105mm howitzer and 81mm mortar ammunition in the cargo hold on fire; one of the loadmasters, Staff Sergeant Charles Shaub, although having burned hands, extinguished the fire and cut loose the burning pallets. Two of the pallets exploded in midair only seconds after they left the plane. The crippled C-130, flying on only two engines, limped back to Tan Son Nhut Air Base north of Saigon. En route, Shaub put out another fire in the left wheel well, and he and the other loadmaster, Sergeant David McAleece, manually extended the landing gear. As the plane entered the approach pattern, it lost the third engine, but Caldwell safely landed the crippled aircraft. He and Shaub were both awarded the Air Force Cross for their heroic actions on this mission. The third aircraft was unable to drop because of problems with its ramp and door. None of the 26 tons dropped by the two C-130s was recovered.

Colonel Iosue, realizing that the situation called for a change in tactics, instructed two of his senior pilots, Majors Ed Brya and Robert Highley, to work out a new plan. Iosue took advantage of his previous experience as commander of all air force forward air controllers in Vietnam to arrange for his crews to talk to the FACs who were controlling the airspace over An Loc.[28] Brya and Highley realized that if they approached the city using normal air drop procedures at the customary drop speed of 130 knots, the aircraft would be sitting ducks. Together with the FACs, they came up with new tactics that called for the aircraft to approach the drop zone at treetop level from one of six different directions at 250 knots; the FACs would assess the enemy air defense situation and advise the C-130 crews on what appeared to be the safest inbound and outbound headings. The pilots would fly the recommended track into the DZ, then pop up to the 600-foot release altitude (necessary for the parachutes to open) two minutes out, slowing down long enough to drop their loads. After the cargo was dropped, the aircraft would drop back down to treetop level to leave the target area as rapidly as possible.

On 16 April, two C-130s, one piloted by Colonel Iosue and the other by Major Brya, headed for An Loc. They abandoned the CARP system because it required too much attention from the flight crew, who were too busy dodging antiaircraft fire. Instead they dropped the loads manually. Though the aircrews thought they had identified the drop zone, which was a clearing south of the city to the east of Highway 13, it turned out that they had been given the wrong coordinates and the loads were not recovered.[29]

On 18 April, another attempt was made. As soon as the aircraft, flown by Captain Don "Doc" Jensen and Major Leigh Pratt, slowed to drop speed, it began taking intense NVA antiaircraft fire. With the right wing burning, one engine out, and another on fire, the crew ditched the cargo and managed to crash-land in a marshy area near Lai Khe, where army helicopters from 229th Aviation picked up the crew, while Cobras from F/9th Cavalry provided covering fire.[30]

By this time, three fixed-wing aircraft, including the two VNAF C-123s, had been lost to ground fire over An Loc. One pilot, talking to a reporter, said: "That place [An Loc] is like the Alamo. . . . The NVA let one or two birds come in, then open up with .51-caliber machine guns and blow the daylight out of the third."[31] The ground fire was so intense that the 374th Wing instituted a new item to their preflight checklist; the pilot and copilot made sure that their shoulder harnesses were locked to prevent them from falling on the control yoke if they were hit.[32]

The 374th tried another approach, this time turning to the ground radar directed air delivery system (GRADS) method. The GRADS system employed high-altitude, low-opening (HALO) parachute devices; using a timing mechanism, the parachutes opened about 500 to 800 feet above the ground. This technique resulted in less exposure to the aircraft from ground fire because the aircraft were able to fly at an altitude between 6,000 and 9,000 feet, placing them out of range of most enemy antiaircraft guns. However, there was a problem with the packing of the parachute bundles; they opened too early because of parachute rigging malfunctions and the lack of a reliable delayed-action parachute release. Most of the parachutes drifted outside the drop zone and into enemy hands. Other pallets broke apart during descent. On still other drops, the chutes failed to open at all and the pallets smashed into the ground.[33] On one such occasion, the pallet "streamered" in, hitting the command bunker of the province chief in the southern part of the city and wounding several soldiers. Other pallets were hit by antiaircraft fire as they dangled from their parachutes.

The 374th Wing continued the GRADS drops for four more days, both at night and during daylight hours. During these missions, not a single C-130 was hit by antiaircraft fire, but the percentage of successful load recovery remained dismal.[34]

The supply situation in the city became so desperate that often fire-fights broke out between ARVN units competing for the few cargo bundles that were recoverable. Whenever a pallet hit the ground, soldiers would come out of their bunkers and make a mad dash for it. One adviser observed that the few supplies that made it into the city went to the "strongest, swiftest, and the closest to the pallet drop."[35] In some cases, there were ugly confrontations between friendly units over who would get the supplies. Soldiers of the 5th ARVN fired on ARVN rangers on several occasions, and an American officer carrying C-rations was even challenged by ARVN troops at gunpoint. Colonel Miller was openly critical of the ARVN's ability to organize the supply recovery efforts. He later reported seeing hospital patients in the streets, some of whom were amputees, struggling with the soldiers to recover food for themselves.[36] The North Vietnamese, realizing that the resupply situation inside the city was becoming critical, began to fire at the area where the pallets landed, killing and wounding many South Vietnamese who were trying to recover the supplies.

On 24 April, Colonel Iosue turned to night container-delivery system drops with a flight of seven blacked-out C-130s. They enjoyed the element of surprise, but it was more difficult to identify the drop zone in the dark. Nevertheless, with covering fire provided by the AC-130s, they managed to get their loads close enough to the drop zone for the South Vietnamese to recover most of them. Several attempts were made to illuminate the drop zone with searchlights on the AC-130 Spectres, but this approach was discontinued because of the exposure of the illuminating aircraft to ground fire. On 25 April, 11 C-130s tried another night attempt, but the aircraft were met with heavy antiaircraft fire. One C-130, flown by Major Harry A. Amesbury Jr., took several hits, quickly lost altitude, and crashed two miles south of the city, killing all six crew members on board.[37] Several more nighttime attempts were made, but each time the aircraft suffered heavy damage from ground fire. On the night of 3 May, a third C-130 was shot down, with all six crewmen aboard lost. Colonel Miller requested that these missions be scrapped, since he believed that the NVA was benefiting more by the drops that went astray than was the ARVN.

Miller was correct. One captured NVA officer demoralized his ARVN interrogators, who were existing on brackish water and an ever-decreasing supply of canned fish and rice, when he asked for a can of C-ration fruit cocktail. He said he had grown very fond of it when his unit had retrieved cases of the stuff dropped by the American airplanes.[38] On 1 May, General Hollingsworth estimated that during the period 15–30 April, less than 30 percent of the USAF C-130 tonnage had been recovered by ARVN forces; most of the rest fell into North Vietnamese hands.[39] The 5th ARVN Division reported that resupply efforts during this period were "extremely hazardous, woefully ineffective, utterly frustrating, and counterproductive."[40]

The situation on the ground had become desperate, with food and ammunition stocks critically low and medical and sanitation conditions rapidly deteriorating. Something had to be done. The air force had tried desperately to resupply the city, but had paid a high price; 3 C-130s had been shot down and 38 had been hit by enemy fire over An Loc. Thirteen aircrew men were killed in this heroic but unsuccessful effort.

On 29 April, the NVA had fired the first SA-7 Strela shoulder-fired surface-to-air missile at U.S. aircraft in Quang Tri Province near the DMZ. At An Loc, the night drops had proved only marginally successful, and with the possible introduction of SA-7s to the situation, the return to low-level resupply operations was unthinkable. Accordingly, the 374th returned to the high-altitude GRADS method. Still they were plagued by parachute and rigging malfunctions. Part of the problem lay with the ARVN riggers, who had little experience in the methods of rigging for HALO drops.[41] In an attempt to remedy the situation, the army brought in 76 riggers from the 549th Quartermaster Company (Aerial Resupply), located in Okinawa. Still there were problems, so the air force brought in its airdrop experts from Taiwan to assist in solving the rigging and parachute problems. The Vietnamese and American riggers worked 20-hour shifts, side by side, in exposed conditions on the eastern side of the main airstrip at Tan Son Nhut.

The answer was finally found when the decision was made to use high-velocity drogue parachutes. Instead of using a standard parachute to allow a load to descend slowly to the earth, the high-velocity method used a slotted drogue chute that was designed to stabilize, but not retard, the speed of the load during descent. Though the cargo would hit the ground at about four times the speed of a normal drop, special packing allowed safe and accurate deliveries.[42]

The first high-velocity drop was made on 8 May. Of 140 bundles dropped on 11 missions during the period 8–10 May, 139 landed within the drop zone. Aside from the improved accuracy, the delivery system allowed the aircraft to operate at about 10,000 feet—out of range of the SA-7 Strelas. There were still some technical problems; 24 loads disintegrated while in descent, partly attributable to parachute malfunction. There were six occasions when mortar ammunition exploded on impact, resulting in sympathetic detonations lasting for periods up to four or five hours.[43] Some of the chutes struck bunkers, injuring the occupants; a lieutenant from 36th Ranger Battalion was crushed when one of the pallets landed on him. Despite these difficulties, the high-velocity approach proved to be the solution to the aerial resupply problem. The recovery rate would rise to over 90 percent through May and June.

Meanwhile on the ground, Colonel Le Quang Luong, commander of the 1st Airborne Brigade, had been put in charge of the DZs and recovery; the improved accuracy of the drops and more efficient distribution of the supplies rapidly improved the logistic situation for all units. Major Kenneth Ingram, one of the 5th ARVN Division advisers, later said that the successful airdrops "had almost an undefinable impact in raising their [the ARVN defenders'] morale, giving them hope and raising them from a total situation of frustration to one of confidence."[44] Colonel Miller later described the resupply situation: "We had 21 days of lean times—we were down to eating a slim rice ration—when it got worked out and the drops began coming in nicely. Believe me, that antiaircraft fire was worse than anything you could imagine even from World War II."[45] The antiaircraft fire took its toll, and the resupply effort proved costly. From mid-April to mid-May, the 374th Tactical Airlift Wing made 57 low-level and 90 mid- or high-level drops at An Loc. During that time, five C-130s were shot down, the first C-130s to be lost in combat since 1969. Additionally, 56 aircraft were hit, 17 crew members were killed or missing in action, and another 10 were wounded.[46]

By the end of the first week in May, the situation inside the city had improved greatly. The resumption of near normal aerial resupply and the limited success of medical evacuation improved ARVN morale considerably. Also, the fact that the South Vietnamese still held the town despite two major assaults and the seemingly never-ending shelling contributed greatly to the spirits of the South Vietnamese soldiers. The NVA had failed to take the city, and their strangulation and starvation tactics had not worked.

Despite the growing success of the air drops, the North Vietnamese antiaircraft umbrella was still deadly. On 2 May, an AC-119K Stinger gunship flown by Captain Terrance Courtney and Lieutenant Jim Barkalow was attempting a daylight mission to destroy some ammunition that a C-130 cargo aircraft had dropped too close to the enemy. While orbiting the city looking for the target, the Stinger was struck by three or four rounds of 37mm antiaircraft fire in the right wing, blowing off the right jet engine and disabling the right reciprocating engine. The wing caught fire and most of the 10 crew members bailed out before the aircraft crashed, but 3 crewmen, including Captain Courtney, were killed. The on-scene FAC followed the aircraft until it crashed and then directed two USAF HH-53 rescue helicopters scrambled from Tan Son Nhut Air Base to pick up six of the surviving crew members. A U.S. Army helicopter from 229th Aviation picked up the other survivor. Because of the vulnerability of the AC-119s to antiaircraft fire, the Stingers' daylight missions over An Loc were terminated.

CHAPTER SEVEN

NVA HIGH TIDE

North Vietnamese Prepare for Renewed Attack

IN TURNING BACK the enemy attacks of 19–22 April, the South Vietnamese had caused the NVA to miss their deadline for establishing the Provisional Revolutionary Government (PRG) in An Loc on 20 April. The sense of fatalism that earlier had all but overwhelmed the defenders gradually began to loosen its grip, but the troops were worn out from the seesaw battle and the never-ending artillery barrage. The lull following the failure of the second battle for An Loc gave the defenders a much-needed respite and permitted them to consolidate their positions and strengthen the weak spots in the perimeter.

Despite the slight upswing in morale, the tactical situation in the city remained largely unchanged. By consistently probing on the west side of the perimeter, the enemy managed to secure a small portion of the city block near where Highway 246 intersected with the perimeter road. Aside from this small incursion, the ARVN held the southern third of the city and the NVA held the northern third. The area between the two forces remained contested ground. The northern portion of the city had been pulverized by repeated air strikes; one FAC, Major Robert L. Murphy, reported that from the air it looked like "acres of grey ash."[1] The rest of the city fared little better from the constant bombardment of the area; virtually every building and other structure had been damaged or destroyed. Burned-out tanks littered the city streets. The jeeps and trucks of the South Vietnamese had all lost their tires to shrapnel, but the ARVN continued to run them on the rims when they could get outside to use the vehicles. The shells continued to fall, but the NVA appeared to be having logistical difficulties, because they had turned to using more mortars than artillery. On several instances in my area in the southern part of the perimeter, 105mm shells landed with shipping plugs in the fuze wells. Perhaps this indicated that they had run out of fuzes for the captured guns.

Colonel Miller had once again become frustrated with General Hung. After the jubilation of blunting the attack on 19–20 April had faded, Miller urged Hung to put his troops on the offensive to retake the northern part of the city. However, no amount of pleading was able to force Hung to give such an order. Miller reported that the general sat in his bunker, with only limited contact with his regimental commanders, and waited for U.S. airpower to save the day. Miller wrote in his journal on 22 April: "I cannot get ARVN to push out for patrols, or any form of security. . . . ARVN still lacking a sense of urgency in any quarter and time does not seem to bother them."[2]

Miller believed that the NVA units surrounding An Loc were repositioning themselves for yet another assault. He was correct. While elements of the 7th NVA Division in the south continued to block the relief attempt by the 21st ARVN Division, the North Vietnamese began to marshal forces for the next attack on the city.

The NVA plan to take An Loc by 20 April had been thwarted by the determined South Vietnamese stand and the massive volume of American airpower. The stubborn defense by the South Vietnamese troops and the continuous air support had taken a toll on the attackers. A postwar PAVN report stated that the attacks of 13–23 April had resulted in heavy attrition of the enemy armored forces and that the morale of a number of cadre and enlisted men had "somewhat deteriorated."[3]

Colonel Nguyen Thoi Bung, the commander of the 9th VC Division, was reprimanded by B-2 Front for his failure to capture the city by the announced deadline.[4] The 5th VC Division, which had won the victory at Loc Ninh, was given the responsibility for conducting the new attack, and its commander, Colonel Bui Thanh Van, boasted that his division would "show the 9th how it should be done" and would take the city in two days.[5]

By now, the North Vietnamese controlled all the high ground around the city. The plan for the new attack was to "concentrate superior infantry, artillery, and tank forces to attack from four directions straight toward the center of the enemy's defenses, drive the enemy back, divide enemy forces in order to annihilate them one by one, and in this way eventually completely destroy the entire enemy force defending the city."[6] In order to minimize the effect of the massive U.S. air support that had stymied the previous operations, antiaircraft weapons would move along with the assaulting echelons to strengthen the necessary air defense umbrella.

Intelligence reports at TRAC seemed to indicate that the NVA were indeed making preparations for yet another assault on An Loc. On 1 May, there were reports that the 5th VC Division headquarters had relocated from north of the city south to Hill 169. Other intelligence indicated that the E-6 and 174th Regiments had also moved south to take up positions near the 275th Regiment in the Hill 169–Windy Hill area, which the NVA had occupied since the 1st Airborne Brigade had withdrawn on 19 April. U.S. airborne radio direction finding (RDF) elements also located a number of other NVA units moving toward An Loc. One of these was the 21st Tank Battalion, which had just arrived to reinforce the B-2 Front.[7] The 141st and 165th Regiments of the 7th NVA Division had moved north from their earlier blocking positions in the Tau O area along Highway 13 to positions just three kilometers south of An Loc. The 271st and 272nd Regiments of the 9th VC Division continued to hold their positions in the northeastern part of the city. Thus, the NVA had ringed the city with more than seven regiments, over 10,000 troops, all within a 2,000-3,000-meter circle of the An Loc perimeter.[8]

As the North Vietnamese positioned their force, they did so carefully, and it was not clear to Colonel Miller in An Loc what the enemy planned to do next. On 8 May, he wrote: "Overall, can't figure the enemy at this time. If he is gone, he left a hell of an indirect covering force. If he's utilizing an economy of force role, it is working well for him. I still give him the capability to attack if he so elects."[9] The North Vietnamese had not left.

Colonel Nhut, Binh Long province chief, sent out Montagnard tribesmen assigned to the province reconnaissance element to ascertain what the NVA were doing. Dressed in civilian clothes, they crossed into enemy territory to gather intelligence. On their return to friendly lines, they reported that the enemy indeed appeared to be making preparations for a new attack.[10] Putting all the intelligence together, it soon became apparent to Hollingsworth at TRAC that the NVA were preparing to make a go-for-broke effort with the seven regiments that had converged on An Loc.

Defending against these forces were barely 4,000 ARVN troops, including both regular and territorial forces. General Hung and his advisers reported that at least 1,000 of his troops were wounded, but those who were able continued to man their defensive positions. Colonel Nhut reported that the strength of his territorial forces had dwindled to fewer than 700, with many of them wounded, some so badly that they could not man their bunkers.[11]

That the NVA was planning a new attack was confirmed on 5 May when an NVA officer from the 9th VC Division was captured. He told his captors that the 5th VC Division would make the new attack from the southeast supported by elements of the 9th Division from the northeast and coordinated with 7th Division attacks from the southwest. The lieutenant did not know when the attack would occur, but estimated that it would be within a week.[12]

In view of the indicators of a new attack, an attempt was made by III Corps to reinforce the city by air, but the NVA had moved their antiaircraft weapons closer to the city. When a VNAF helicopter carrying troops from 2nd Battalion of the 8th Regiment was shot down on 9 May, the effort was abandoned.

As it became apparent that the NVA was preparing to launch a new attack, morale again plummeted. The city and its defenders had held off two major attacks, but continued to be pounded by enemy artillery. Colonel Miller later reported that the town by this time was smashed "as if hit with [a] solid steel hurricane. One third of the town was in rubble, the rest was no-man's land or in enemy hands."[13] Miller's deputy, Lieutenant Colonel Ed Benedit, later said that it was "hard to recognize that there is a city anymore. To say that it is battered is a gross understatement."[14] The city was littered with rubble, skeletal remains of houses, dangling parachutes from air drops, and charred military and civilian vehicles.

The American advisers on the ground realized that the situation in the city was critical and told General Hollingsworth that they doubted the ARVN could hold against another determined attack.[15] The South Vietnamese troops knew that they would not be evacuated if they were wounded. The continuous artillery bombardment, which was marked by periods of increased intensity, had a demoralizing effect on the ARVN resolve. The advisers were afraid that the ARVN would break if the NVA attacked in force. The Americans stepped up their efforts to bolster their counterparts' morale. Realizing that the situation inside the city was reaching a dangerous stage, General Hollingsworth took to the air once again in a renewed attempt to encourage the division commander, the province chief, and the advisers to hold their positions, but it was clear to all concerned that the outlook was dire at best, and in the minds of many, beyond hope. The troops had held on since early April, but they were worn out, both physically and mentally. Concerned with the deteriorating morale among the South Vietnamese in An Loc, Hollingsworth made it a point to speak by radio with the American advisers daily to get a sense of what was really going on in and around the city on the ground. The advisers confirmed that the situation was dire and was getting worse as they waited for the next fight to unfold. They did not have to wait long.

A worried Hollingsworth reported to Abrams: "My attempts to belittle the capability of the enemy and to strengthen friendly forces' morale seemed almost hopeless. Enemy positions and movements, intensity of antiaircraft fire, and the increase in enemy artillery and rockets against An Loc pointed to an imminent all-out attack."[16]

The Third Attack

At TRAC headquarters, all intelligence seemed to confirm that the enemy was preparing to make another big push to take the city. More frequent reports of enemy movements and a tremendous increase in shelling indicated that the time of the attack was near. Based on patterns established in the previous attacks, Hollingsworth thought the attack would come very soon.

He was correct. The new NVA plan called for the concentration of superior infantry, artillery, and tank forces to attack from four directions straight toward the center of the South Vietnamese defenses in order to divide the forces so that they could be annihilated one by one. The ultimate objective was the total destruction of the South Vietnamese forces in the city.[17]

At 0530 on 9 May, the enemy commenced strong ground probes all around the ARVN perimeter, but particularly in the south and southeast. The ground attacks abated within two hours, but as the NVA troops pulled back, the volume of enemy artillery fire drastically increased. Based on the patterns he had observed in the previous two attacks, General Hollingsworth correctly guessed that the main enemy effort would come on the morning of 11 May.[18] Accordingly, he planned 18 B-52 boxes (target sets for three-ship missions) and almost 200 tactical air strikes to support the besieged defenders. Armed with his air support plan and intelligence reports, Hollingsworth flew to Saigon to speak with General Abrams at MACV headquarters. He convinced Abrams that the enemy main attack

on An Loc was coming and that the ARVN could not hold without maximum air support. General Abrams agreed and promised to send him
everything that he needed for the battle.[19]

On 10 May, the enemy continued the pattern from the previous day,
with heavy shelling and limited ground probes throughout the day. Hollingsworth chose this time to bring Colonel Miller out. He had been
fighting the battle night and day since early April and was near exhaustion.
Since Miller was slated to assume command of a brigade in the 101st Airborne Division at Fort Campbell, Kentucky, Hollingsworth replaced him
with Colonel Walter Ulmer, a West Pointer who had arrived at Lai Khe in
early May. Ulmer had previously served on the MACV staff in 1963–64
and been senior adviser to the 40th ARVN Regiment in the Central Highlands. After an avalanche of briefings from TRAC staff officers at Lai Khe,
he was flown into An Loc just after daylight on the morning of 10 May by
Lieutenant Colonel Jack Dugan, commander of the 12th Aviation Group.
The Huey helicopter, escorted by several Cobra gunships flying cover,
touched down briefly at the "H" panel in the southern end of the city near
the province headquarters; as Ulmer leaped out, Miller jumped in and Dugan lifted off to get out of the area before the inevitable incoming artillery
that accompanied any attempt to land a helicopter in the city.[20]

As Ulmer tried to get his bearings, the North Vietnamese launched
several strong probes against the ARVN perimeter. The strongest of these
came on the east side, where the 52nd Rangers fell back in disarray. The
senior adviser to the 3rd Ranger Group, Lieutenant Colonel Richard J.
McManus, later blamed the 52nd Battalion's commander, Major Dau,
for what was one of the few times that ARVN rangers, who were normally
among the best South Vietnamese troops, did not acquit themselves well
on the battlefield.[21]

With the increase in artillery and ground probes, Hollingsworth became more convinced that the enemy main attack would come the next
day. Accordingly, he readjusted the 18 ARC LIGHT boxes and added 7 more.
That afternoon he once again called Abrams, advising him that the main
attack would start the next morning and requesting that he be allocated
one B-52 strike every 55 minutes for the next 25 hours beginning at 0530
hours, 11 May.[22] The MACV commander agreed, and Hollingsworth's staff
quickly drew up plans for their use and transmitted them through channels
to the 7th Air Force planners at Tan Son Nhut Air Base in Saigon.[23]

Colonel Ulmer did a quick assessment of the situation once he got on
the ground. He had been told at Lai Khe before boarding the helicopter

that the enemy was going to make a big push, and everything he had seen in the short time since his arrival seemed to point to its coming soon. He saw nothing but chaos around him; the briefings at Lai Khe had not prepared him for the devastation that pervaded the city. There were dead and dying lying all about. The fear on the faces of the South Vietnamese troops in the command bunker was clear. Ulmer watched General Hung closely; he knew that Hung and Miller had not gotten along, but he was prepared to give him the benefit of the doubt. Nevertheless, he was worried about the safety of the advisers now in his charge; given the seemingly deteriorating situation, he radioed to General Hollingsworth, "I feel we must begin to prepare and think of possible extraction."[24] TRAC agreed and began to make plans for a helicopter evacuation. However, those plans would never be activated, because the enemy had plans of their own.

At 0035 hours on 11 May, the NVA drastically increased its bombardment of the ARVN perimeter, which by now measured only 1,000 by 1,500 meters. For the next four hours, 7,500 rounds, or one shell every five seconds, fell on the ARVN positions. Major Kenneth Ingram, an adviser with the 5th ARVN, said later that the barrage was so heavy that to leave your bunker was "certain death."[25] Captain Moffett, with the 3rd Ranger Group, said that the noise "kept going up to a crescendo . . . it sounded like somebody was popping popcorn . . . and about 4 or 4:30 it stopped—bam—just like somebody dropped a baton. Everything stopped at once."[26] For the next 30 minutes, there was a deathly silence.

At 0500, the artillery barrage resumed in earnest, and during the next 12 hours the city was struck by 10,000 rounds of enemy indirect fire.[27] Under cover of this barrage, the NVA commenced the ground assault from all sides of the city, with the main attacks focused in the northeast and west. On the northern perimeter, the 274th Regiment attacked the positions held by the 81st Rangers. Several enemy tanks penetrated the South Vietnamese lines, but were destroyed. Still, the airborne rangers were forced back by the tide of the attack.

In preparation for the next all-out effort to take the city, the North Vietnamese introduced a new element in an attempt to drive off the ever-present air support. The SA-7 Strela was a Soviet-made shoulder-fired heat-seeking surface-to-air missile that had been seen earlier in I Corps, but had not been used previously in III Corps. The first SA-7 sighting in the An Loc area was most likely one fired in mid-April at a Cobra helicopter flying low level southwest of town. As the pilot turned to engage an enemy personnel carrier on the ground, he saw a missile streak past him, leaving a slightly spiraling thick smoke trail. He continued his mission and reported the missile to military intelligence upon return to base, but intelligence continued to maintain that no surface-to-air missiles had deployed in III Corps.

On 8 May, another Cobra pilot from F/9th Cavalry reported a missile fired at him when he was flying at 2,000 feet south of the city. Just after midnight on 9 May, a FAC orbiting over An Loc reported a possible SA-7 launch. Still, TRAC intelligence did not acknowledge that there were missiles in the area, listing the sighting as "unconfirmed."

With the renewal of the ground attack on 10 May, any doubts about the presence of Strelas around An Loc were removed. There were plenty of "confirmed" sightings in the sky over An Loc of the telltale plume of white smoke as the missiles spiraled up toward their intended targets. The Strela missiles were used against Cobra gunships, tactical aircraft, and forward air controllers, but the pilots pressed the fight. Risking withering ground fire, as well as the shoulder-fired missiles, they pulled out all the stops to support the ARVN against the coordinated infantry and tank attacks. One Cobra had its hydraulics shot up during an attack run, but made it back to Lai Khe safely.

As the advisers tried to bring airpower to bear, the North Vietnamese intensified their efforts to breach the ARVN defenses; they seemed to realize that this was their last chance to take the city. In the west, the 272nd Regiment supported by tanks attacked the positions of the 7th ARVN Regiment. The South Vietnamese soldiers knocked out two tanks, but the NVA infantry surged forward and captured the province public works office, only 300 meters from the 5th ARVN Division command post bunker. The 3rd Battalion of the 7th ARVN was forced to pull back.

Additional North Vietnamese troops attacked the province forces and elements of TF 52 on the southern perimeter and the 8th Airborne Battalion in the rubber plantation south of the city. Once again, in these attacks the NVA demonstrated their ineffectiveness in coordinating combined arms operations. The tanks preceded the infantry, but fortunately for the defenders, the tank crews once again appeared to be disoriented, stopping frequently and moving slowly through the streets. Attacking without external fuel drums, many of the tanks ran out of gas before they had expended their ammunition. The rest were eventually destroyed by ARVN soldiers, Cobra helicopters, or tactical aircraft. A postwar North Vietnamese report on the armored operations in An Loc stated that during this attack on the city, the "organizational arrangement was not tight, the combat formation was poor, and our forces did not work together from the start. . . . The

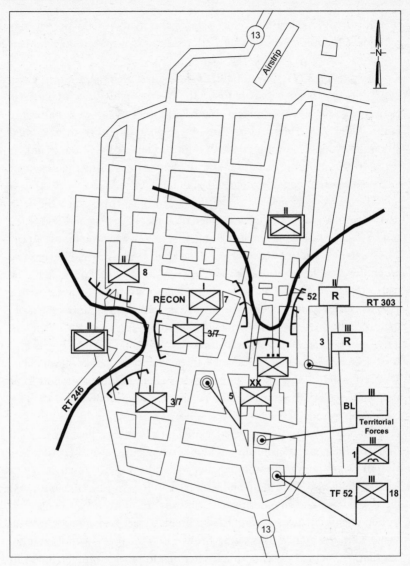

Map 10. NVA High Tide, 11–12 May 1972

spearhead was unable to carry out the tactical plan and . . . did not generate [sufficient] assault power."[28] Map 10 depicts the North Vietnamese attack on 11–12 May 1972.

Despite the NVA's difficulties in coordinating their tanks, which Colonel Ulmer described as "amateurish," the North Vietnamese infantry still managed to forge two salients in the ARVN lines in the west and northeast.[29] They then attempted to widen these penetrations by driving tanks and infantry repeatedly into the ARVN lines. The NVA plan was to link up the two salients in the center of the city, thereby separating the defenders into enclaves that could be defeated in detail.

The NVA had moved in additional 23mm, 37mm, and ZSU-57/2s (twin 57mm antiaircraft guns mounted on tank chassis), in addition to the SA-7 Strela heat-seeking antiaircraft missiles to provide cover for the attack. The focus of this effort was directed at the Cobra gunships and the forward air controllers. The NVA hoped to eliminate the FACs to degrade the effectiveness of the close air support. They also wanted to drive away the Cobras, which were very effective against the attacking infantry and tanks that were trying to negate the tactical aircraft by "hugging" the defenders. The Cobras were able to bring their minigun fire and 2.75-inch rockets in very close to the defenders where the tactical aircraft could not work. The NVA knew that they had to neutralize the effect of the air support to be victorious, so they threw everything possible into the air over An Loc. This was clearly going to be a go-for-broke effort.

The situation in the city was declared an extreme tactical emergency. Air force, navy, and marine aircraft handlers loaded all available ordnance; aircraft made rapid turnarounds after expending their ordnance to get back to their bases to load up and rush back to the An Loc area to support the defenders. The situation was so dire that the forward air controllers turned no aircraft away, regardless of ordnance load. New aircraft units arriving from the United States were thrown into the battle without normal familiarization or safety check flights in order to provide uninterrupted air support to the city in imminent danger of falling. The aircraft arriving in the area were piled up over the city, with the FACs directing strike after strike into the attacking North Vietnamese.

Despite the relentless attack from the air, the desperate North Vietnamese were on the verge of a major victory when the friction of war intervened. Elements of the 271st Regiment, 9th VC Division, had pushed very close to the 5th ARVN Division command bunker, but they made a wrong turn. A North Vietnamese report after the battle noted that "instead of attacking southeastward, the [regimental element] had attacked north-eastward." Instead of focusing its combat power on the nerve center of the 5th ARVN defense, the NVA soldiers seized the provincial public works building, "an objective of no tactical value."[30] The North Vietnamese had missed a golden opportunity.

Meanwhile, General Hung and Colonel Ulmer had realized that the enemy was trying to separate the ARVN defenders. Hung ordered the 5th Airborne Battalion from the southern part of the perimeter to blunt both NVA penetrations in the northeast and west. The paratroopers responded rapidly. Fighting tenaciously, they halted the enemy advances. Once the penetrations were stopped, the air force (both U.S. and VNAF) went to work, reducing the western salient with repeated bomb strikes. The enemy troops in the northeastern salient were too close to the ARVN defenders to use bombs, but the AC-130 Spectre gunships were able to bring accurate and effective 40mm and 105mm cannon fire on the attackers, driving them back.

At one point, Lieutenant Colonel Gordon Weed, commander of the 8th Special Operations Squadron, made two low-level passes in his A-37 through a curtain of intense enemy antiaircraft fire to destroy a North Viet-namese T-54 tank that was firing point blank into the 5th ARVN command post. On the first pass, his 250-pound bomb scored a direct hit on the tank, but the bomb was a dud. The tank stopped firing, but it was not immobi-lized. Weed made another pass through a hail of 37mm and .51-caliber fire, and this time the bomb scored another direct hit; the subsequent explosion destroyed the tank and drove back the supporting infantry troops.

During the course of the battle that day, 297 sorties of tactical air support were flown in the face of some of the most intense antiaircraft fire ever encountered in South Vietnam; 260 sorties were flown each day for the following four days. The airspace over An Loc during the four days of pitched battle was called by one observer a "mass of confusion."[31] At least three FACs were over the city at all times, constantly putting in air strikes as the aircraft arrived on station. In addition, several AC-130 Spectre gunships were also orbiting, striking targets in support of ARVN forces in contact.

Further complicating the mission for the airmen was the presence of the SA-7 Strela heat-seeking missile. Several near misses on AC-130 Spectres and the downing of two Cobra gunships by SA-7 missiles caused all aircraft in the area to take extreme evasive maneuvers when deliver-ing ordnance on target. The FACs played a key role in ensuring that this weapon did not tip the scales in favor of the attacker. They made maximum use of available aircraft on immediate ground targets while minimizing the exposure of the aircraft to the heat-seeking missile and withering ground fire.

While the FACs continued to employ all available tactical air support sorties on targets in direct support of the ARVN forces engaged in near hand-to-hand combat, General Hollingsworth increased efforts to ensure that B-52s were available to strike enemy staging areas. He had "borrowed" an additional five B-52 missions from Second Regional Assistance Command (MR II) to bring the total of B-52 strikes against the forces surrounding An Loc to 30 within a 24-hour period. Wave after wave of ARC LIGHT strikes pounded the area surrounding the city; they were a tremendous morale booster for the defenders, who could readily see the effects.[32] The American advisers requested that the strikes be brought closer to the South Vietnamese perimeter, and several of them were moved to as close as 800 meters from the ARVN positions.[33] Lieutenant Colonel Art Taylor, senior adviser to the 1st Airborne Brigade and an infantryman in the Korean War, later said that neither he nor the Vietnamese had ever seen a more awesome display of firepower.[34]

In one instance, a large enemy force was inflicting heavy casualties on the 81st Ranger Battalion on the eastern perimeter. A B-52 strike diverted to that location virtually annihilated the enemy force, estimated to be a regiment. There were other reports of panicked enemy troops fleeing in disarray from the areas that had been struck by the B-52s. General Hollingsworth reported to General Abrams after the battle that "B-52 strikes and tacair allowed us to punish the enemy severely."[35]

An NVA soldier captured early on the morning of the 11th revealed that his regiment had been ordered into the craters of an earlier air strike as a jumping-off point for an attack. His commander was betting that a second strike would not be called in on the same site. The results of the interrogation were forwarded to Hollingsworth, who called in another strike on the original target. Later, he said: "I'm so proud of that strategic air force. . . . That crew diverted the strike in 20 minutes, put it in . . . and destroyed that whole damn regiment, right in the same holes where they had gone to reorganize when I'd missed them in the morning."[36]

Throughout the battle, Colonel Ulmer urged his advisers to do "everything we could to thump people on the back and tell . . . all of the Vietnamese friends of ours . . . to keep hanging in there."[37] This was one of the major roles of all advisers in An Loc for the duration of the battle. That the advisers were enduring the same hardships as their counterparts went a long way to encouraging them to hang on, even in the darkest moments of the battle.

By midafternoon on the 11th, the repeated B-52 strikes and continuous tactical air support, combined with a tenacious defense by the ARVN forces in the city, had broken the main enemy attack. Nevertheless, fierce fighting continued periodically throughout the rest of the day. The NVA continued to rain massive amounts of indirect fire on the city, while the defenders replied with devastating air strikes. However, stopping the NVA was not without its price; the withering enemy antiaircraft fire downed a VNAF A-1, one A-37, two Cobra gunships, and two FAC O-2 aircraft during the course of the day's action.[38]

Captain Robert J. Williams and Warrant Officer Rodney L. Strobridge, of F/79th Artillery, "Blue Max," were flying in a Cobra gunship in support of the defenders against the NVA attack. Major Larry McKay, the commanding officer of Blue Max, later reported that Williams and Strobridge had just rolled in and destroyed two tanks in the southwest corner of the city when the radio crackled: "MISSILE, MISSILE, MISSILE!" Before they could react, a heat-seeking missile shot toward the Cobra's exhaust. The missile exploded, severing the tail boom from the fuselage; the aircraft went into a flat spin and crashed. Captain Williams's last radio transmission was, "Oh, my God!" No further radio contact was made with Williams and Strobridge. No one saw the helicopter hit the ground, but both men were thought to have died in the crash. They were listed as Killed in Action, Body Not Recovered.[39]

Another Blue Max Cobra was shot down that day while escorting a medevac heading to An Loc to attempt an evacuation. It was hit by a Strela missile and exploded in midair. The medevac pilot later reported that "one minute it was there, and the next it was gone." There were no survivors.

The NVA tanks and infantry made another attack on 12 May and again penetrated the town's defenses. As the tanks moved in, the NVA artillery lifted. This permitted the ARVN defenders to come out of their holes and take on the attackers at short range. In some cases, this degenerated into hand-to-hand combat. VNAF A-1 Skyraiders, armed with 250-pound bombs, and a Spectre gunship with the PAVE AEGIS 105mm system aboard concentrated on the western salient. In the northeast, the NVA salient was so narrow that only the accurate fire of the Spectre could be used.

The 81st Rangers saw several T-54s moving toward An Loc along Route 303, east of the town. At one point the road crossed a stream by way of a narrow concrete bridge. The rangers, accompanied by a U.S. adviser, devised a bold scheme; they would knock out the lead tank exactly on the bridge, thereby creating a major obstacle. The rangers moved to within 30 meters of the bridge and waited on both sides of the road with M72s ready. As the lead tank reached the middle of the bridge, six M72 rounds hit it and stopped it dead in its tracks.[40]

During the course of the day's battle on 12 May, a number of SA-7 Strela missiles had been fired at the FACs and other aircraft. At 1830, one found its mark, striking an AC-130. The aircraft sustained extensive damage, but the crew was able to get it back to base.

During the night of 12 May, the NVA mounted yet another desperate attempt to take the city. Under cover of darkness and extremely bad flying weather, the NVA attacked with PT-76 tanks (suggesting that earlier battles had resulted in the decimation of the enemy's T-54 resources) from the north and east, supported by infantry attacks from the west and south.

Without air cover, the defenders found themselves in deep trouble. Hollingsworth responded to the situation by diverting six ARC LIGHT strikes against the NVA troop concentrations. These strikes, accomplished in close proximity to friendly positions, broke up the enemy attacks; Hollingsworth reported that the B-52 raids "spoiled another apparent enemy effort to seize An Loc."[41]

Shortly after midnight the weather improved slightly, and two AC-130 Spectre gunships arrived on station and responded to the defenders' call for fire. The Spectres continued to be extremely effective against the enemy troop formations and equipment. Hollingsworth later cited the Spectre's "magnificent performance" during marginal flying weather.[42]

The heavy shelling of An Loc would continue unabated for the next three days, but the intensity of the ground attacks decreased in frequency, intensity, and duration. There were only two more significant attempts to breach the ARVN perimeter between the 11th and the 15th, and both efforts were blunted by the ever-present B-52 strikes. The most significant activity was at 0145 hours on 14 May when the South Vietnamese observed troop movement to the west and southwest; at the same time, tank fire was received from the west. The enemy may have been preparing for another go at the ARVN perimeter, but three timely B-52 strikes eliminated this threat.

Still, the fighting on the ground remained intense as the South Vietnamese tried to reduce the enemy penetrations. Although the NVA attacks had ultimately failed, they held stubbornly to the gains they had made, fighting desperately from bunkers and ruined buildings. Sergeant First Class Cao Tan Tai of the 8th ARVN Regiment, in position on the roof of a building, killed two tanks. He hit the first one from a distance of 10 meters with an M72 LAW, which hit the front part of the turret and somehow ignited the ammunition inside the tank. Again with a LAW, he struck the second tank's front road wheel. With the tank immobilized, he then fired two more LAWs into the turret from a range of 20–30 meters. Both tanks started to burn. The surviving crew members tried to escape but were killed by small-arms fire. In another action, an element of the 36th Ranger Battalion captured a ZSU-57/2.

On 14 May, the defenders in An Loc were joined by an unexpected visitor. During a mission over the city, Lieutenant H. "Pep" McPhillips, a forward air controller, was shot down when his O-2 observation plane was hit by an SA-7 Strela missile. He parachuted out of the aircraft and landed in the rubber trees south of the town near the 5th Airborne Battalion. The paratroopers rushed out to rescue him. He could not be evacuated for several days, so he stayed in the command post bunker of the 1st Airborne Brigade. Every day a South Vietnamese sergeant brought him water (he had broken his ankle in the parachute landing). McPhillips described the sergeant, who had been wounded five times, as "a little guy who kept going because he figured that was his job."[43]

McPhillips later observed that conditions during the battle were quite bad. The casualties were so heavy that many of the wounded, those who could walk or hobble, were sent back into action. The lieutenant reported that the noise in the bunkers from mortars and artillery shells was "awful" and that the ARVN soldiers had to keep filling sandbags to repair the damage to the bunkers from the constant shelling.

By nightfall on the 15th, it appeared that the NVA forces had called off their attack plans and withdrawn further into the surrounding rubber plantations. Hollingsworth concluded that the South Vietnamese had weathered what turned out to be the final big battle during the fight for An Loc. He reported to Abrams that "the enemy had lost his capability for further offensive actions in Binh Long Province."[44] That was true, but the shelling of the city had continued with more than 3,000 rounds on 13 May, 2,000 on 14 May, 2,600 on 15 May, and 2,000 on 16 May.

Stabilizing the Situation

By 16 May, the situation in An Loc looked much brighter. Despite the continued shelling, the defenders had beaten back yet another desperate attack by the NVA. The aerial resupply effort had hit its stride. An effort was made to reestablish artillery support in the area. On 11 May, two 155mm howitzers had been airlifted to an existing ranger camp at Tong Le Chon. The range of these weapons permitted coverage for the western portion of the city.

On 17 May, Marine Air Group 12 began to arrive at Bien Hoa Air Base. Marine pilots flew in the right seat of the side-by-side-seat A-37s of the 8th SOS (Special Operations Squadron) aircraft for orientation before conducting missions over An Loc. Soon air force A-37s and marine A-4s conducted joint close-support strikes that increased the aerial firepower available to the city's defenders.[45] From 20 to 23 May, tank and infantry attacks tended to move south of An Loc, but heavy artillery continued to fall on the town itself. On 23 May, the NVA launched a tank attack with six to eight tanks, moving slowly north in column without infantry or artillery support. They were engaged by F-4 fighter aircraft with 500-pound bombs, and several of the tanks were destroyed. ARVN soldiers knocked out the rest with M72s and XM202s.[46] Also on that day, the NVA launched a tank assault on the 8th Airborne Battalion south of the city. Eight tanks were destroyed, three of them within the airborne perimeter, but the rest were forced to withdraw; 45 NVA bodies were found after the fight. In the aftermath, two airborne soldiers mounted what they thought was a dead tank, but the engine started and the tank began to move. The tankers tugged on the tank hatch from the inside, while the airborne tried just as hard to get it open. The latter eventually won and dropped a grenade into the turret that killed the crew.[47]

It was slowly becoming evident that what one adviser termed the almost "ritualistic" pattern of action and reaction had taken a heavy toll on the attackers, as well as the defenders.[48] Although the NVA troops still ringed An Loc, this last attempt had cost the enemy dearly. Almost his entire armor force had been destroyed; over 40 tanks and armored vehicles littered the battlefield in and around the city. The continual aerial bombardment had decimated whole NVA units, and General Hollingsworth reported that he believed that enemy units had "withdrawn from the immediate vicinity of An Loc as a result of the heavy losses inflicted by TACAIR and B-52 strikes."[49] The general was correct; the official NVA history written after the war states: "Three waves of assaults against Binh Long city (on 13 and 15 April and on 11 May) were all unsuccessful. Our units suffered heavy casualties and over half of the tanks we used in battle were destroyed."[50] The attacks on 11–12 May proved to be the North Vietnamese high tide; the bitter fighting had been close, but the beleaguered defenders had held the city against overwhelming odds.

Eventually repeated air strikes by B-52s and close air support aircraft enabled the ARVN forces to counterattack and retake what remained of the enemy salients. On 8 June, 1st Battalion, 48th Regiment, from TF 52 successfully eliminated enemy forces from the northeast salient, taking only minor casualties while claiming 61 enemy killed. That same day, a medevac mission was also successfully accomplished, raising the defenders' morale greatly. On 12 June, the 7th Regiment was successful in driving enemy forces from the western salient, but unfortunately lost several junior officers and NCOs in the process.

However, the battle of An Loc was not over yet; the city was still cut off from the south. With the North Vietnamese failure to capture An Loc for the third time, the Party Committee of COSVN concluded that they had failed to overrun the city not "because the enemy was strong and un-beatable, but mainly because of our own shortcomings." They reported to the Politburo in Hanoi that "our failure to overrun Binh Long has limited our success and affected the development of our campaign." Accordingly, they decided to change their strategy from one of trying to take An Loc to one of "besieging, wearing down, and destroying enemy personnel."[51] In accordance with this decision, they shifted their focus toward the south, where fighting still raged along Highway 13 as the 7th NVA Division continued to block the 21st ARVN Division from moving north and relieving the still besieged city.[52]

CHAPTER EIGHT

THE FIGHT FOR HIGHWAY 13

The 21st ARVN Division

WHILE THE BATTLE raged to the north, the South Vietnamese and NVA were locked in a desperate struggle for control of Highway 13. The 21st ARVN Division, conducting operations in the mangroves of Ca Mau in MR IV, had been alerted for movement on 7 April and was placed under the operational control of III Corps. The division advance party was dispatched the following day. Despite heavy VC attack from the U Minh Forest area in An Xuyen, the division extracted itself rapidly, and the 32nd Regiment closed into Lai Khe by air on 10 April. By 12 April, the entire division, including divisional artillery, had displaced from the southern Mekong Delta to the Lai Khe area. During the period 12–23 April, division dispositions placed the 31st Regiment in the vicinity of Suoi Tre hamlet, the 32nd Regiment south of Chon Thanh, the 33rd Regiment north of Lai Khe, and the 9th Armored Cavalry Regiment in Lai Khe.

The division's initial mission had been to secure Highway 13 from Lai Khe to Chon Thanh, 30 kilometers south of An Loc. They were then to secure the Chon Thanh area as a base for subsequent operations. It was hoped that the division would be able to eventually fight its way up the highway to relieve the besieged troops at An Loc. However, the North Vietnamese had sent an entire division south to block this effort. The 21st ARVN, commanded by Major General Nguyen Vinh Nghi, was accustomed to conducting operations in the swamps and canals of the Delta against lightly armed Viet Cong. The officers and men of the division were not prepared for the intensity of combat that they would soon encounter in the unfamiliar terrain of Binh Long Province. Intense fighting would rage up and down Highway 13 between Lai Khe and An Loc for more than three months.

The 32nd Regiment initially deployed to the Chon Thanh area by vehicle on 11 April without incident. However, NVA tanks and troop-laden Molotova trucks were reported to be six kilometers northeast of Chon Thanh. It appeared that the NVA commanders were attempting to cut Highway 13 into segments. In an effort to block this from happening, General Nghi attempted a high-speed advance up the highway from Lai Khe, led by the 31st Regiment supported by tanks and armored personnel carriers from the 9th Armored Cavalry Regiment. About 15 kilometers north of Lai Khe, this force ran into heavy enemy contact with the 101st NVA Regiment, an independent formation normally under regional command, reinforced with the K-6 Battalion of the 165th Regiment. Three tanks were lost to enemy fire. Some drivers panicked, running over ARVN soldiers accompanying the armored vehicles. The subsequent battle resulted in a six-kilometer retreat by the South Vietnamese, leaving behind dead and wounded ARVN. During the retreat, the commander of the tank and APC element, Lieutenant Colonel Truong Huu Duc, was killed as he flew overhead in a helicopter directing the movement of the tanks and APCs below. A .51-caliber machine-gun round tore through his forehead, killing him instantly. This was only the beginning of the 21st Division's bitter fight to open the highway.

Colonel J. Ross Franklin, senior adviser to the 21st Division, a veteran of Korea with more than three years' service in Vietnam, told one journalist: "You people write that the 21st is not clearing the highway to An Loc. That's not our job. We're here to find and engage the NVA 7th Division, which is the only big enemy outfit not committed to this Hanoi offensive. We're fighting the 7th, engaging it and keeping it at bay. So you guys in Saigon can sleep tonight."[1]

Despite Franklin's protestations to the contrary, the attempts by the troops from the Delta to fight their way up the highway were seen as a relief effort aimed at lifting the siege in An Loc. These efforts and their lack of progress would be the subject of much media attention for the next three months. Those of us in An Loc looked to the south hopefully, but as time passed, we eventually gave up on the 21st and disparaged their efforts; faced with our own version of hell, we could not conceive why the troops from the Delta could not break through and rescue us. In truth, the fighting along the highway rapidly degenerated into a bloody war of attrition that resulted in extremely heavy casualties on both sides.

By 18 April, it became apparent to all observers that the 7th NVA Division had moved into the area in force. On the morning of 22 April, a civilian refugee column moving south along the highway from Chon Thanh came under fire from the NVA near the hamlet of Bau Bang. During this action, a blue bus loaded with civilians was struck by an enemy rocket-propelled grenade (RPG), killing 4 and wounding an estimated 20 civilians. The battle that ensued to break the NVA roadblock, which had effectively cut all road traffic between Chon Thanh and Lai Khe, came to be known as the "Battle of the Blue Bus." On 24 April, the 32nd and 33rd Regiments launched assaults from the north and south, respectively, in an attempt to put the NVA forces manning the roadblock between two pincers. At the same time, the 31st Regiment was air assaulted from Suoi Tre to an LZ north of Chon Thanh to secure the town and the highway north for 10 kilometers. Map 11 depicts the fighting along Highway 13, April–June 1972.

After 10 days of extremely hard fighting, the lead ARVN elements reached a point 15 kilometers north of Lai Khe, where they encountered a heavily entrenched NVA force astride the highway. General Nghi, the 21st Division commander, who had only recently been assigned, attempted to maneuver elements of the division against the NVA forces, but the attacks were conducted in an uncoordinated fashion. What ensued was an almost daily pattern of attempting to attack in the morning hours, followed in the afternoon by attempts to evacuate casualties and prepare for the next day's attack. The division commander was not adept at coordinating the efforts of several regiments against an entrenched enemy. As Colonel Franklin, senior adviser to the 21st Division said, "It doesn't take a lot of guys in bunkers to stop an uncoordinated attack."[2]

On the morning of 24 April, the South Vietnamese engaged in a pitched battle with NVA forces along Highway 13 north of the village of Bau Bang. It would take five days of heavy fighting to reduce the NVA forces in those positions and finally reach Chon Thanh on 29 April. The NVA forces withdrew to the west.

While fighting was concentrated south of Chon Thanh during the last week in April, the 21st ARVN Division was ordered to continue the attack north up Highway 13 from Chon Thanh to effect a linkup with the ARVN airborne forces south of An Loc. On 1 May, the 31st Regiment came under intense fire six kilometers north of Chon Thanh from the other two

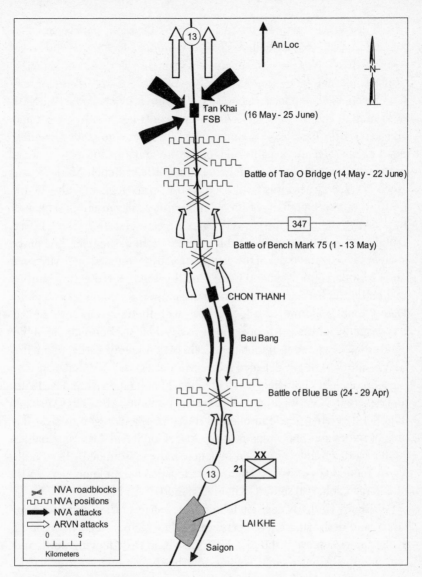

13

An Loc

Tan Khai
FSB   (16 May - 25 June)

Battle of Tao O Bridge (14 May - 22 June)

347

Battle of Bench Mark 75 (1 - 13 May)

CHON THANH

Bau Bang

Battle of Blue Bus (24 - 29 Apr)

13   XX
      21

LAI KHE

Saigon

NVA roadblocks
NVA positions
NVA attacks
ARVN attacks
0   5
Kilometers

Map 11. The Fight for Highway 13

battalions of the 165th Regiment, 7th NVA Division, which were entrenched in yet another belt of fortified positions blocking the highway. The North Vietnamese were dug in, well-camouflaged, and could not be displaced despite being pounded for five days by 8 B-52 strikes, 142 sorties of tactical air support, and over 20,000 rounds of artillery.[3] The NVA used mortars and rockets very effectively against the South Vietnamese attackers; on 4 May, the NVA employed AT-3 Sagger wire-guided missiles, never before seen on the battlefields of South Vietnam. During the course of the battle, which became known as the Battle of Bench Mark 75, the 165th NVA Regiment was reinforced with its sister regiment, the 209th. On 6 May, two battalions of the 32nd Regiment began envelopment of the enemy's main defensive positions to the east, and on 8 May the 3rd Battalion, 31st Regiment, was airlifted to the north of the main line of resistance. The commander of the 31st was seriously wounded on 9 May, and on 11 May part of the 2nd Battalion, 32nd Regiment, was overrun. During that battle the battalion second-in-command was killed, as was Captain Harold John Faldermeyer, a U.S. adviser with the unit. On 12 May, the responsibility for the entire operation was passed to the commander of the 32nd ARVN Regiment. It took two weeks of continuous battle before the ARVN attackers finally defeated the heavily entrenched NVA units, reaching a point eight kilometers north of Chon Thanh on 13 May. The 165th and the 209th NVA Regiments withdrew to positions at the Tau O Bridge. The South Vietnamese consolidated their forces and began to clear the area of mines and make repairs to the road. Combined ARVN casualties in this battle included 76 killed in action and 236 wounded.[4] The South Vietnamese now controlled Highway 13 to a point eight kilometers north of Chon Thanh, still some 17 kilometers short of An Loc.

With the COSVN decision to shift to a strategy of "besieging, wearing down, and destroying enemy personnel," they focused their main effort to the south to prevent the 21st ARVN Division from moving north and relieving the besieged city.[5] Accordingly, they ordered part of the 9th VC Division that had failed to take An Loc to move south and join the fight to block the highway.[6]

As the NVA reinforced their units along Highway 13, the ARVN 32nd Regiment was given the task of clearing the roadblock where the NVA 209th Regiment had dug in a strong defensive network of blocking positions centered on the southern edge of the deep swamps of the Tau O stream, which crossed Highway 13 six to seven kilometers south of Tan

Khai. This action became known as the Battle of the Tau O Bridge and resulted in the bitterest fighting of the battle along Highway 13.

After the Battle of Bench Mark 75, the North Vietnamese had regrouped and occupied prepared positions farther to the north. The 209th NVA regiment had fallen back from its earlier position and established a strong defense astride the highway. Their positions, consisting of bunkers with an average of two feet of overhead cover, connecting trenches, and telephone communications, ran in depth to the north, using high ground and other terrain features to maximum advantage. The North Vietnamese employed a blocking position called *Chot*, which was generally an A-shaped underground shelter arranged in a horseshoe configuration with multiple outlets assigned to different companies. Every three days, the troops that manned the position were rotated so that the NVA continually enjoyed a supply of fresh soldiers. These positions were organized into large triangular patterns called *Kieng* (tripod), which provided mutual protection and support.[7] Together they formed a solid defense in depth across the highway. In order to reduce casualties from air strikes, the NVA forces tried to "grab the belts" of the South Vietnamese, staying within 20 to 50 meters of ARVN lines while pounding the South Vietnamese with mortars and rockets. Faced with these formidable defenses, the ARVN made little progress. What ensued was a meat grinder that took its toll on both sides.

The 209th NVA Regiment was reinforced with a reconnaissance element from the 7th NVA Division, the 94th Sapper Company, and the 41st NVA Anti-Tank Company. Extensive bombardment by B-52s, tactical air strikes, and artillery could not dislodge them. Part of the problem, according to the senior adviser to the 21st ARVN Division, was that the ARVN troops came to rely too heavily on the B-52 strikes, and "subsequent maneuvers were generally not aggressive and units were committed piecemeal."[8]

For 38 days, the ARVN and NVA fought desperately along Highway 13. The South Vietnamese troops were able to advance only haltingly against the entrenched NVA, sometimes advancing only 50 meters a day. Colonel Franklin later said, "Once in a while we would break through and push a mile, but the attack was being fought piecemeal . . . all the good leaders had been killed."[9] On many days, the South Vietnamese troops made no progress at all. However, the NVA had sustained heavy casualties and could conduct only a holding action against the ARVN. On 23 May, they tried to mount a tank and infantry attack on the ARVN from the north, but a Spectre gunship engaged; the tanks were destroyed and the infantry withdrew.

The fight along Highway 13 had evolved into a bloody stalemate that continued without letup for another month. The situation along the road was grim. One reporter described it this way: "Huge trees, their charred limbs poking into the sky, break the monotony of the flat, bushy terrain that flanks the highway. Mounds of charred artillery casings left behind by South Vietnamese troops stand out like pockmarks on the roadside. Brass rifle cartridges sparkle everywhere in the sun."[10]

Both sides were reeling from the constant pounding they were inflicting on each other. By 26 May, half of the total infantry force of the 21st ARVN Division of 12,000 men had become casualties. At the same time, they had inflicted a heavy toll on the North Vietnamese. Two captured NVA officers indicated that their units' casualties were heavy; some companies of the 209th Regiment were down to only 10 men. Constant allied bombardment was causing major breakdowns in enemy morale and fighting spirit to the extent that some troops were "no longer responding to orders from their superiors."[11] Another POW report indicated that the 7th NVA Division had received 360 replacements in May, but had received none during the first 18 days of June. The troops received rice only once a day, and "morale was low due to the fear of B-52 strikes, sickness, and poor leadership."[12]

One NVA unit history written after the war described how conditions had deteriorated for the North Vietnamese: "We were then in the middle of the rainy season. Our combat trenches and shelters were constantly flooded. The positions of the besieging units were well within enemy artillery range and had been relentlessly bombed and shelled since the day we began the attack on the town. The soil was pulverized and then turned muddy by rain water, seriously impeding troop movements, the conveyance of food to the front, and the evacuation of wounded combatants to the rear."[13]

While the fighting continued on the ground, the air over Highway 13 remained extremely dangerous for the army aviators trying to support the South Vietnamese. On 24 May, a Blue Max Cobra flown by Warrant Officers Isaac Yoshiro Hosaka and John R. Henn Jr. in the vicinity of Tan Khai was struck by a Strela missile. The aircraft crashed and exploded with no survivors. On 8 June, a medevac helicopter from the 215th Medical Company was shot down, but the crew and passengers were picked up.

On the morning of 13 June, a UH-1H from A Company, 229th Aviation, was shot down.

As the helicopter pilots braved the intense fire over the highway, the fighting continued without letup on the ground. Despite the hardships on both sides, they continued to flail away, inflicting even more casualties on each other. On 19 June, the South Vietnamese made another concerted effort to break through using 13 tanks. As the column of tanks and infantry moved up the road toward the enemy positions, they became bunched up, making a lucrative target for NVA gunners. The incoming mortar and rocket fire was extremely accurate. One rocket hit the ARVN command group. The U.S. regimental adviser, Lieutenant Colonel Burr M. Willey, accompanied by his dog Moose, ran to render aid. Another rocket hit in the same area, killing Willey instantly. Colonel Willey was on his third tour in Vietnam and, according to journalists Peter Arnett and Horst Fass, "was full of sympathy for the Vietnamese soldiers fighting an endless war."[14]

The North Vietnamese gunners continued to take a heavy toll on the helicopter pilots trying to assist the ARVN in their attempts to break through the North Vietnamese positions. A Cobra flown by Captain Edwin G. Northrup and First Lieutenant Stephen E. Shields was shot down over Tan Khai with no survivors. Another AH-1G, flown by First Lieutenant Louis K. Breuer and Chief Warrant Officer Burdette D. Townsend Jr., exploded in midair; it was suspected that the aircraft had been struck by an SA-7 missile. Two days later, Captain Mike Brown of the Blue Max was hit by an SA-7 at an altitude of 4,000 feet. He had been flying in support of the ARVN forces in the vicinity of Tan Khai on Highway 13, approximately six miles south of An Loc. Captain Brown had just completed a gun run in which he was providing suppressive fire in support of ARVN troops along the highway. As he broke away from the run and began to gain altitude, he was hit by an SA-7 missile. The explosion of the missile blew away his tail boom; the tail was severed in the battery compartment area just behind the engine, the radios were out, and the aircraft virtually fell out of the sky. Brown, through some very skillful flying, still managed to get the aircraft safely to the ground, crashing into the jungle where the trees and bamboo helped cushion the impact of the aircraft. As Brown and his injured copilot, Captain Mark Cordon, got out of the demolished aircraft, they realized that they had landed in the middle of the NVA positions. Luckily, Warrant Officer Ron Tusi and Captain Harry Davis, also from Blue Max, witnessed the crash and saw that the pilots had survived.

They put out a call for help to pick up the downed pilots. Warrant Officer Bill Wright, from B Company, 229th Aviation, was flying south in a Huey along the highway from An Loc, where he had picked up five ARVN KIA in body bags. The crash of the Cobra had not made a large hole in the tree canopy, but Wright forced his Huey into the area, clipping the trees with his rotor tips in the process. Brown and Cordon climbed up the wreckage of the Cobra to reach the hovering Huey.

Meanwhile, Tusi, not sure that the Huey was going to be able to make the pickup, jettisoned his rocket pods and landed close to the crash site. Leaving his copilot to hold the aircraft, he got out of the Cobra and ran through the bush looking for Brown and Cordon. Seeing the Huey lift off with the two downed pilots, he ran back to his aircraft and took off again. With Brown and Cordon on board, Wright flew to Lai Khe. From there, Cordon, with an injured back from the crash, was placed aboard a medevac and flown to 3rd Field Hospital in Saigon. Brown later said that he was just happy to be back on the ground safely and away from the smell of the ARVN dead in the rescue helicopter.[15] This incident illustrates the type of actions performed again and again by the army pilots and crewmen during the fight for Binh Long Province.

The fighting along the highway continued relentlessly. On 21 June, the 32nd Regiment was replaced by the 46th Regiment of the 25th ARVN Division. The soldiers from the Delta were exhausted. During its unsuccessful effort to clear the enemy from the Tau O area, the 32nd Regiment suffered heavy casualties; 84 were killed and 315 were wounded.[16]

The 31st Regiment continued to fight along the highway, but made little progress. On 21 June, Lieutenant Colonel Charles Butler, senior adviser to the 31st, was killed. Less than a week later, the regimental commander was killed and one of the American advisers was wounded in an NVA attack on the regimental command post.

As the preponderance of the 21st ARVN Division dealt with the virtual meat grinder along Highway 13, General Minh, the III Corps Commander, had come to the conclusion that providing fire support to both the defenders of An Loc and the would-be relief force from the 21st ARVN was crucial. With the increase in NVA pressure on An Loc during 10–14 May, it became imperative to deploy artillery north to a position capable of providing fire support to the defenders within An Loc, as well as to the ARVN attempting to effect a linkup from the south. He ordered the 9th Cavalry Regiment and other elements of the 9th ARVN Division, which had been moved from the Mekong Delta to Lai Khe and placed under his operational control, to establish a fire support base at Tan Khai on Highway 13, just 10 kilometers south of An Loc.

On 15 May, while the 32nd ARVN Regiment tried to force the NVA positions at the Tau O Bridge, a task force composed of the 9th Armored Cavalry Regiment, one battalion from the 15th Regiment of the 9th ARVN Division, and three 105mm howitzers from the 93rd Artillery Battalion made a forced march paralleling Highway 13 to the east, bypassing enemy resistance around the Tau O Bridge, to occupy positions at Tan Khai. At the same time, the 2nd Battalion, 15th Regiment, made a helicopter assault into an area 1,500 meters east of Tan Khai and then moved to occupy the hamlet in preparation for the forces arriving from the south. The next day additional troops plus eight 105mm and two 155mm howitzers were helicoptered to the area to establish Fire Base Long Phi (Flying Dragon). On 16 May, VNAF Chinooks and a U.S. Sikorsky Sky Crane helicopter lifted three more 105mm howitzers and an additional battery of 155s into Tan Khai. Resupply of the base was by CH-47 and later by parachute drop.

By 18 May, the 15th Regiment had secured Tan Khai and the immediate surrounding area and began to move north to effect a linkup with the troops in An Loc. The firebase served to alleviate some of the pressure on An Loc, and the word of its establishment helped raise the morale of the defenders inside the city.

The North Vietnamese realized the importance of the firebase at Tan Khai and rushed reinforcements to the area. On the morning of 20 May, the 141st NVA Regiment, reinforced with three tanks, attacked the new ARVN firebase. The attacks continued for two days, but the NVA were eventually driven off, primarily by air strikes. Failing to overrun the South Vietnamese foothold, the North Vietnamese turned to indirect fire to reduce the ARVN defenses. They poured a large volume of mortar, rocket, recoilless rifle, and 105mm fire into the firebase. The defenders took heavy casualties, but held out for three days against repeated attacks. The existence of this firebase brought the defenders in An Loc desperately needed relief from enemy pressure. The defenders would continue to hold this small outpost for the next 45 days; it would be the only ARVN redoubt in enemy-held territory between An Loc and the 21st Division north of Chon Thanh.

CHAPTER NINE

BREAKING THE SIEGE

Breakthrough on Highway 13

BY THE EARLY days of June, the situation at An Loc had improved considerably. There was a lull in the fighting, and even the incoming artillery had decreased significantly. The around-the-clock air strikes had taken a horrendous toll on the NVA forces. ARVN intelligence estimated that the three NVA divisions, the 5th, 7th, and 9th, had already suffered over 10,000 casualties in the fight for the city and along Highway 13.[1] There were reports that the North Vietnamese began using Cambodian fillers, indicating that they were having difficulties in replenishing their personnel losses.

The massive air strikes had destroyed many of the antiaircraft weapons that ringed the city, permitting the first sustained aerial resupply to the defenders since the battle began. Additionally, the reduced air defense threat permitted the delivery of much-needed personnel replacements and the evacuation of the more seriously wounded.

The defenders had held their position against overwhelming odds and, with the increase in resupply and the arrival of fresh soldiers, morale in An Loc soared. Taking advantage of the success of the air strikes and the devastation they had wrought on the enemy, the ARVN commanders shifted to the offensive, with the objective of expanding the city's defensive perimeter.

When the ARVN troops began to push their perimeter outward, they soon saw the death and destruction wrought by the continual massed air strikes. Three kilometers south of An Loc, in a B-52 target area, ARVN soldiers discovered 208 enemy dead from one regiment, all apparently killed by a single B-52 strike. Inside the city, several NVA regimental command post complexes were found to have been completely destroyed by the murderously accurate AC-130 Spectre gunship fire. Unburied NVA bodies littered the terrain in and around the city.

As the situation inside An Loc improved, the South Vietnamese forces to the south, who were still fighting desperately to reach the city, began to make headway. With the establishment of the ARVN firebase at Tan Khai, the South Vietnamese now had a base from which to launch forces to link up with the defenders in An Loc. Once the area was secure, the 3rd Battalion of the 15th Regiment and the regimental light command post arrived. Additionally, elements of the 33rd Regiment had arrived after moving overland from the south. A new task force was formed under the command of the deputy commander, 15th Regiment. The task force began preparations for the launching of operations from the area west of Tan Khai to open the road to An Loc and effect a linkup with the besieged defenders.

As TF 15 commenced operations from Tan Khai, two battalions of the 33rd Regiment advanced toward An Loc along the east side of Highway 13. Now two large ARVN forces advanced on different sides of the highway toward the besieged city.

As these forces attacked north, the firebase at Tan Khai came under three days of heavy attack from the 141st Regiment, 7th NVA Division. The North Vietnamese were trying to eliminate this outpost, which threatened their operations in the entire area. The battle started on 20 May and lasted for three days. With the help of tac air, the South Vietnamese turned back the attackers and continued to provide artillery support of the ARVN at Tau O, the forces moving north, and the defenders in An Loc.

Initially, the two ARVN forces attacking north from Tan Khai advanced against only light enemy resistance, but on 22 May, when TF 15 was about one kilometer from Thanh Binh village, it was hit by heavy artillery, surrounded, and attacked. The situation deteriorated rapidly; casualties were heavy, and the wounded could not be evacuated, nor could the force be resupplied. The next day, the NVA mounted a major counterattack against the task force. A desperate battle ensued, but the South Vietnamese gave as good as they received. The attackers were forced to withdraw, leaving behind 14 bodies. With the enemy departure, the task force was able to evacuate its wounded and was resupplied with food and water.

On the 24th, the 9th Cavalry Squadron, returning to Tan Khai with wounded from the 15th and 33rd Regiments, fought a major battle along the highway with the 141st Regiment of the 7th NVA Division. Twenty-three vehicles were lost to 75mm recoilless rifle fire, rocket-propelled grenades, and mines. The commander of the armored column was killed, and 159 were wounded.[2] The squadron's losses were so severe that it had to be kept at the firebase at Tan Khai for reorganization and reequipping.

On the 25th, TF 15 resumed its advance toward An Loc, but almost immediately it ran into heavy enemy resistance again, bringing the ARVN attack to a halt. For the next several weeks, the task force would fight desperately to evict the NVA, who just as desperately tried to hold every inch of ground. Sometimes the South Vietnamese troops moved only 50 meters a day, mostly on their stomachs through rubber plantations and open fields. They took horrendous casualties. "Because the contact was so [heavy], the bodies would just lie there," recalled Major Craig Mandeville, who served as assistant senior adviser to the regiment. "You couldn't get up and bury them."[3] By this time, there were only about 239 combat-effective soldiers left in the regiment, and many of these were wracked by dysentery from the diet of rice and untreated water.[4]

Meanwhile, the 33rd Regiment of the 21st ARVN Division had continued to move north on the east side of the road and had reached the Xom Ruong road junction, where it, too, met heavy enemy resistance that halted its advance. Another Cobra from Blue Max was shot down while flying in support; both pilots perished in the crash. Now both ARVN columns had been halted by the enemy on both sides of the road.

The turning point on Highway 13 came on 4 June when the reconstituted 6th Airborne Battalion was lifted by helicopter into Fire Base Flying Dragon at Tan Khai to help break the deadlock. With them came 300 replacements for the 15th Regiment. Immediately after landing, the paratroopers began advancing north. Two days later, the paratroopers ran into stiff enemy opposition. Most of the 6th were new recruits, but the battalion cadre were veterans of the earlier battle at An Loc. Led by the battalion commander, Lieutenant Colonel Nguyen Van Dinh, who had vowed to avenge the earlier destruction of his unit, the paratroopers overcame the enemy positions with light casualties. After linking up with TF 15 at a point only three kilometers south of An Loc, Dinh turned over the replacements to the task force commander. The next day, the task force was resupplied and evacuated its wounded. Later that day, the 6th Airborne Battalion and TF 15 advanced in parallel toward An Loc. On 8 June, the paratroopers fought a major engagement east of Thanh Binh village. The fresh troops overwhelmed the NVA, who withdrew, leaving 73 dead on the battlefield. Later that afternoon, the 6th Battalion linked up with the 8th Airborne of the 1st Airborne Brigade in the rubber plantation south of An Loc.[5]

TF 15 had paid a heavy price during the bitter fighting to link up with the ARVN forces in An Loc; they sustained 138 killed, 511 wounded, and 57 missing.[6] Colonel Tran Van Nhut, the Binh Long province chief, personally went out to greet the task force; he gave Lieutenant Colonel Ho Ngoc Can, the task force commander, and Major Mandeville, his counterpart, a bottle of cognac, the "last bottle left in the entire province."[7]

Despite the linkup between ARVN forces, the road was still not open all the way from Chon Thanh to An Loc, as the NVA still held positions that interdicted movement north. On 6 June, the 33rd Regiment was still bogged down along the highway. Lieutenant Colonel Edward J. Stein, senior adviser to the regiment, was with the regimental commander and his 12-man staff when it was ambushed and cut off. Pinned down by heavy mortar and small-arms fire, the group could not establish radio contact with any other unit. Fortunately, Stein was able to make contact with Lieutenant James W. Beaubien, a FAC from 21st TASS, orbiting in the area at 8,000 feet. Beaubien flew to Stein's position and began to mark targets for two A-37s. In the face of heavy antiaircraft fire and dealing with a low cloud ceiling, Beaubien successfully directed the attack, thereby saving Stein and his entire party. The lieutenant was awarded the Distinguished Flying Cross for braving the intense enemy ground fire to support the ARVN during the attack.

The battle for Highway 13 had been a bitter, bloody fight. The 21st ARVN had failed to open the highway by the assigned deadline and was disparaged roundly in the press for its inability to push forward. It must be acknowledged, however, that despite leadership problems, the South Vietnamese soldiers fought hard. For example, the 32nd Regiment sustained over 40 percent casualties. In the final analysis, the 21st Division had indeed failed in effecting the linkup with the forces in An Loc. Nevertheless, their attack tied down and ultimately all but destroyed nearly an entire NVA division, making them unavailable for the fight in An Loc.

Although the road was still not open, the situation in An Loc continued to improve for the South Vietnamese. By 8 June, ARVN units had cleared the center of the city of most enemy resistance and greatly expanded the area controlled by friendly units. On 10 and 11 June, dozens of helicopters came to evacuate 228 wounded, many of them with infections incurred during the long wait for evacuation. They brought 232 replacements, including one helicopter full of those previously wounded during the earlier fighting. One of them, Phan Van Ranh, said, "I'm happy to be back with my brothers."[8]

On 13 June, III Corps ordered the 48th ARVN Regiment, a unit from the 18th ARVN Division, to begin replacing the battered troops of the 5th Division.[9] For two days, helicopters from A and B Companies of 229th Aviation escorted by Blue Max Cobras transported the fresh troops from Lai Khe into landing zones on the highway south of the city. Former Warrant Officer Mike Wheeler reported that the soldiers he saw on the ground in An Loc were "in very rough shape"; their uniforms were in tatters and they appeared malnourished.[10] Another pilot observed, "Some of the South Vietnamese flown out were barefoot, some were dazed and some were too exhausted to do more than shuffle."[11] He was correct; the surviving troops who had been in An Loc since the beginning of the NVA offensive were exhausted from the constant fighting, never-ending artillery, and stress of just trying to hang on in the face of overwhelming odds.

The insertion of the fresh regiment was not without incident. The helicopters took fire going into the LZ, on the ground, and on the way out of the area. On 13 June, farther to the south of An Loc near Tan Khai, several other Hueys from 229th Aviation were inserting more fresh ARVN troops when one of the helicopters, flown by Warrant Officer Josh Dunigan and Captain John Bowers, was struck by ground fire and crashed just south of the LZ. Fortunately, another helicopter from 229th, braving the continuing NVA fire, immediately went in to pick up the downed crew, who had not been seriously injured in the crash.

On 17 June, the 48th retook the hills to the south of the city and from that vantage point began to direct tactical air strikes on the remaining enemy concentrations to the west and north of the city. The 81st Rangers and the 3rd Ranger Group recaptured the northern part of An Loc, while the 7th Regiment recaptured the western portion of the city that had fallen into enemy hands on 11 May. Captain Charles R. Huggins of Titusville, Georgia, an adviser with the 81st Ranger Battalion, said that most of the North Vietnamese had fled, leaving behind their dead, wounded, and weapons. "In the end," he said, "the NVA were scared to death. They were crowded in bunkers, sometimes as many as 15 in a fighting position with only two firing points. They wouldn't fight."[12] On 12 June, General Hollingsworth reported to Abrams: "At 1200 the ARVN reported the entire city of An Loc was under friendly control."[13] By mid-June, the defensive perimeter had been expanded to encompass most of the outlying hamlets and the commanding terrain that surrounded the city.

From that point on, the enemy shelling of An Loc was greatly reduced. For the first time since early April, the ARVN soldiers were able to move around above ground without risking almost certain death. The situation had so improved that the 1st Airborne Brigade, less the 81st Ranger Battalion, was ordered to attack south along Highway 13, clearing the enemy in the zone while moving to a PZ near Tan Khai. They began the move south on 18 June, reducing NVA positions en route. Arriving at the assigned PZ on the 18th, the brigade was extracted by helicopter to Chon Thanh, where they boarded trucks for the trip back to their original home stations in Tan Son Nhut, Bien Hoa, and Vung Tau. On 24 June, the 81st Ranger Battalion was extracted from a PZ just east of An Loc. The departure of the 81st ended the airborne brigade's being under the operational control of III Corps. The airborne troopers had performed magnificently during the battle, but they had paid a high price. The brigade sustained 346 killed, 1,093 wounded, and 66 missing; the 81st Rangers alone had suffered 61 killed and 271 wounded.[14] Nine airborne advisers were wounded during the battle for An Loc.

In mid-June, the city was visited by General Hollingsworth, who was accompanied by Sir Robert Thompson, special adviser to President Nixon. Thompson remarked that the victory at An Loc far exceeded the one that the Viet Minh had won at Dien Bien Phu.[15] On 16 June, Hollingsworth again flew into the city. This time he was accompanied by Lieutenant General Nguyen Van Minh, III Corps commander, who was making his first trip into the city since the fighting had started nearly three months earlier. That day, General Hollingsworth told a reporter, "I would think the enemy is fully aware of their total disaster. Two and two-thirds divisions [of enemy troops] is one helluva rent to pay for twenty-five percent of a small inconsequential province capital for less than thirty days' occupancy."[16]

The Siege Is Lifted

On 18 June, General Minh declared that the siege of An Loc was broken. Despite this proclamation, the battle was not completely over. ARVN and NVA forces continued to exchange fire as the South Vietnamese forces attempted to destroy the remaining enemy. North Vietnamese artillery and rockets continued to fall on the city, but at a greatly reduced rate—only several hundred a day by this point.

Intelligence sources noted that the headquarters of the 5th VC Division had moved to Cambodia, north of Svay Rieng, and that the main elements of the 9th VC Division were heading west toward the Cambodian border. On 26 June, the remaining pockets of NVA notwithstanding, General Hollingsworth reported to General Abrams that "unless we receive our share of replacements designated for COSVN, the campaign is over."[17]

On 7 July, President Thieu made an unannounced visit to An Loc. As Cobra gunships patrolled the skies overhead, a group of helicopters landed. Out stepped the president wearing a khaki safari suit and a black helmet. He was accompanied by General Cao Van Vien, the chief of the Joint General Staff; a retired French general named Paul Vanuxem; General Minh; General Hollingsworth; and a number of foreign and Vietnamese journalists. The party made its way to the 5th Division command post where they were greeted by an emaciated Brigadier General Le Van Hung, whose eyes blinked incessantly in the bright sunshine. Later, the president confided jokingly to an aide, "Hung looked deceitful to me. Why do you think he kept constantly squinting and blinking his eyes?" The aide replied most seriously, "Why, Mr. President, General Hung had not seen sunlight for a long, long time."[18]

President Thieu awarded both General Hung and Colonel Nhut the National Defense Medal, Third Class. Standing amid the rubble in front of the command bunker, President Thieu gave a short speech: "Binh Long is not the symbol of one battle. . . . Binh Long is a national as well as an international symbol. The Binh Long victory is not a victory of South Vietnam over communist North Vietnam only, the Binh Long victory is also a victory of the Free World over the theory of people's war [and the] revolutionary war of world communism."[19]

Following the speech, he decreed that General Hung and all combatants who had taken part in the battle were promoted on the spot to the next higher rank. After the ceremony, Thieu and his party toured the city and visited with the troops, who were shocked to find the president in their midst. Thieu was stunned at the devastation wrought during the siege. He knelt in prayer in front of a large statue of Christ that was one of the few things mostly intact (it was missing the right arm) in the city after nearly three months of constant shelling and bombing. He also knelt in prayer at a cemetery filled with the dead from the 81st Airborne Rangers who had given their lives in the desperate fighting.

As the party completed their rounds of the city, Colonel Nhut took them to the province bunker, where he had laid out refreshments. During his visit there, the president took a pen and wrote in large letters on the operations map, "Heroic Binh Long."[20]

The North Vietnamese campaign may have been over, but the fighting was not. The battle to clear Highway 13 continued. In the city, mortars and rockets continued to fall, albeit at a drastically reduced rate than seen in April and May.

That An Loc was still dangerous was made only too clear on 9 July. Brigadier General Richard J. Tallman, General McGiffert's successor as Hollingsworth's deputy, who had been promoted to his rank only eight days earlier, landed in the city with several of his key staff officers to observe the progress of ARVN operations and coordinate the reinforcement effort. Colonel Ulmer and several other advisers, including Major Joe Hallum (also from the 18th ARVN Division) and myself, went out to meet the helicopter.[21] The general and his party departed the aircraft and as it lifted off, an artillery round landed close by. The general, his party, and the advisers dove for cover. After the round impacted, the group leapt up and began to run toward the province command post bunker. The next round landed right in the middle of the group. Three American officers who had accompanied General Tallman, Lieutenant Colonel Stanley J. Kuick, Major Peter M. Bentson, and First Lieutenant John Todd Jr., were killed instantly. Lieutenant Colonel Kuick was the TRAC chief of staff and was due for promotion to colonel. Major Bentson was assistant chief of staff for operations, and First Lieutenant Todd was aide to General Tallman and the son of Colonel John Todd, deputy commander of the 1st Aviation Brigade at Long Binh, 12 miles north of Saigon. Sergeant First Class Son, the Binh Long senior adviser's interpreter, was also killed instantly. General Tallman, Major Hallum, and I were wounded. My wounds were relatively minor, but Hallum had taken a severe shrapnel wound in the upper chest and right shoulder, and the general had sustained a massive head injury and other wounds. We were immediately evacuated by U.S. helicopter to 3rd Field Hospital in Saigon, where the general, mortally wounded, died on the operating table.[22] Major Hallum was further evacuated to the United States, while I remained in country after a month-long stay in the hospital.

Despite this tragedy, the conditions inside the city had improved greatly. They got even better when General Minh ordered the entire 18th ARVN Division into An Loc to relieve the battered and exhausted 5th ARVN Division. The 18th arrived by a massive helicopter airlift on 11 July. Brigadier General Le Minh Dao directed his troops to commence operations immediately to expand the perimeter and eradicate the remaining enemy resistance in and around the city. They drove the remnants of the 272nd NVA Regiment from Windy Hill, Hill 169, and Ton Loi village east of An Loc, and on 31 July, the 18th attacked to clear the NVA from the Quan Loi area. This greatly reduced the shelling that had plagued the city since early April.

In mid-July, General Minh moved the 25th ARVN Division from Tay Ninh to Chon Thanh to replace the 21st ARVN, which had fought hard but still had not broken the NVA roadblocks astride Highway 13 south of An Loc. The 25th Division was fresh to the battle and was able to complete the job started by the 21st. They encircled the remaining enemy positions along the highway and destroyed them by 20 July.

During the course of the effort to relieve the embattled city, the 21st sustained 662 killed and 3,381 wounded.[23] The fighting had been fierce. About 6 percent of the killed, wounded, and missing were officers; 5 out of the 9 infantry battalion commanders and 21 out of 27 company commanders had been killed or wounded.[24] The U.S. advisers from the 21st ARVN had also suffered, with 4 killed and 18 wounded. Still, the exhausted division had inflicted horrendous casualties on the North Vietnamese forces and tied down the better part of four regiments in the process. The 7th NVA Division had been virtually destroyed in the heavy fighting along Highway 13. Although the 21st was unable to open the road, it tied down an entire division that no doubt would have turned the tide had it been used on An Loc itself. Additionally, after the failed third attack on An Loc, the 5th VC Division was forced to divert its attention from the besieged city to dispersing its forces to meet the threat posed by the 21st Division approaching from the south; the redirecting of enemy ground forces and indirect fire south to engage the 21st ARVN greatly relieved the pressure on An Loc. The 21st paid a heavy price in its attempt to open Highway 13, but its efforts had not been in vain.

ARVN Victory amid the Rubble

The Battle of An Loc was over. The city had withstood a battering given to few other cities during the war. The ceaseless shelling, estimated at over 78,000 rounds during the three-month period, had reduced the city to almost total ruins.[25] No building or structure was left untouched. The province hospital was destroyed, and the government elementary school and the Catholic school near the church were heavily damaged. Rudolph Rauch of *Time* magazine, one of the first American correspondents to reach An Loc after the siege began, visited the city in June and reported: "There are perhaps six buildings left in the town, none with a solid roof. There is no running water or electricity. Every street is shattered by artillery craters and littered with the detritus of a battle that saw every kind of war. Everywhere you walk you hear the crackle of shifting shell fragments when you put your foot down."[26] Phan Nhat Ham, a young reporter with the South Vietnamese Army who was present in the city during the battle, wrote after the war that An Loc "was completely smashed, broken into pieces, reduced to rubble. Nothing remained. . . . Like a giant termite that lives under a layer of dirt, the town was buried in bunkers deep in the earth, the deeper the better."[27]

The statue of the ARVN soldier that stood in the southern part of the town still stood, but was pockmarked by shrapnel. The few vehicles still working moved around on their wheel rims; *Time* correspondent Rauch wrote that it was common to see seven or eight Vietnamese "lurching through the town in a Jeep without tires."[28] The stench of garbage and death permeated the air; dead bodies and animal carcasses lay everywhere. The bodies of North Vietnamese soldiers had been left where they fell. After lying for weeks in sun and rain, they had decomposed to skeletons.

The ARVN defenders in the city had sustained 5,400 casualties, including 2,300 killed or missing.[29] One battalion of the 5th ARVN was down to 26 effectives from an original strength of 300 soldiers. Many of those who had survived the battle were wounded. There were graves along the streets, in schoolyards, and in vacant lots. Sixty dead from the 81st Airborne Ranger Battalion had been buried by their comrades under intense fire in two neat rows near the city market. Major John Howard, one of the airborne advisers, best described the aftermath of the fighting: "The graves, the burned-out vehicles, and the rubble were mute testimony to the intensity of the battle that had been fought there."[30]

The civilians who had remained in the city had suffered horribly during the bitter fighting. As the ARVN forces began to expand the perimeter and retake parts of the city lost to the North Vietnamese earlier in the battle, the plight of the civilians became only too clear. They had been forced underground in basements and makeshift bunkers during the heavy shelling. Going with little food, water, or medical attention for weeks, they were in pitiful condition, suffering from malnutrition and disease. Colonel Ulmer later remembered: "It was indescribable: people of all ages inadequately nourished, wounded, crying. They were all over the city way down in the cellars and the bottoms of houses."[31] A perfect example was two little emaciated and frightened girls, the daughters of a warrant officer at the province headquarters, who had lived in the northern part of the city for the entire period of the heaviest fighting, some 71 days. Their mother and two brothers had been killed early in the battle.[32] Another young woman, Pham Thi Nghia, spent 64 days in her bunker which during the course of the battle received a direct hit from an NVA rocket, killing her mother and her son.

The provincial authorities soon focused on providing aid and assistance. The new province senior adviser, Lieutenant Colonel William B. Nolde, who had replaced Lieutenant Colonel Corley, called for maximum U.S. helicopter support and for a U.S. doctor. In response, a U.S. Army surgeon, Major Risch, arrived in the city and began to work with the Binh Long Province surgeon, Captain Quy, who had been in An Loc since the battle began. Working 16 to 18 hours a day, the two doctors tried to save as many of the wounded as they could. Despite their heroic efforts, the death rate was still very high because of infection caused by the filthy conditions that still prevailed within the city. Another gallant surgeon was Captain Cao Phu Quoc, of Medical Company 183 from the 18th ARVN Division, who had done what he could to alleviate the suffering of both soldiers and civilians. He was killed by artillery earlier in the battle when he went to help a wounded paratrooper near the city soccer field.

Even those civilians who made it out of An Loc did not escape the suffering. Refugees had been trying to escape the fighting since the battle began in April. As the fighting slowed in early June, a long column of thousands of Vietnamese and Montagnards began to stream southward along Highway 13. Many were picked up by Chinook helicopters at Tan Khai, but others were killed or wounded along the highway by enemy snipers, indirect fire, and land mines.[33] One group of civilians was moving down the highway toward government-controlled territory in mid-June when the North Vietnamese opened up on the refugees with point-blank rocket fire, taking a heavy toll. "I don't know why they fired on us," said one old man who survived the attack, "since it was clear we were not soldiers."[34] Others, particularly those with adolescent boys, were stopped at North Vietnamese checkpoints along the highway. Some of these young boys were seized as forced labor.[35]

In another incident, a Chinook helicopter full of civilians crashed south of the city in mid-June. It was not known whether enemy fire or equipment malfunction caused the crash, but the 5-man VNAF crew and all 47 refugees were killed.

Despite the toll on civilians and soldiers, the South Vietnamese defenders and their advisers, with the help of tactical airpower, had decisively defeated three of the finest divisions in the North Vietnamese Army and held the city against overwhelming odds. It is estimated that the North Vietnamese suffered 10,000 soldiers killed and 15,000 wounded during the battle.[36] The area in and around the city was littered with over 80 burned-out NVA tanks and other vehicles.[37]

The South Vietnamese victory prevented a direct threat to the national capital in Saigon. In addition to inflicting a military defeat on the enemy, the ARVN defenders won a decisive psychological victory as well. They had stood up against the very best of the North Vietnamese Army, defeated them, and prevented them from establishing their "liberation government" in the South. A Saigon government pamphlet commemorating the victory said: "Dien Bien Phu fell once the Communists had broken through the defenses [but] An Loc held—and held. Where Dien Bien Phu lasted 56 days before collapse, An Loc held on for 70 days before driving the Communists out, leaving the town strewn with the wreckage of field guns and derelict Soviet T-54s."[38]

Nguyen Van Thieu and his government emerged from the crisis stronger than ever, at least on the surface. He and his army had been victorious. The brutality of the North Vietnamese invaders had not won them many converts in the South. The victory seemed a turning point for South Vietnam.

CHAPTER TEN

EVALUATING THE BATTLE OF AN LOC

The Failure of the Nguyen Hue Campaign

AFTER NEARLY SIX months of bitter and desperate fighting, the South Vietnamese had defeated the NVA invasion. An Loc had held, and the ARVN had repelled the NVA assault on Kontum in the Central Highlands. Although the Communists retained control of some territory in the South, their overall campaign goals remained unrealized. In the process, they had also nearly exhausted themselves militarily. The South Vietnamese had lost more than 8,000 killed in action during the NVA offensive, and wounded were about three times that number. However, the North Vietnamese suffered losses that included over 100,000 casualties and at least one-half of their artillery and tanks.[1] With the exception of Quang Tri, the North Vietnamese had failed to capture any provincial capital, and Quang Tri was retaken by the South Vietnamese on 16 September.

In planning for the 1972 campaign, the North Vietnamese had made several near fatal errors in judgment at the strategic level. First, they launched the offensive too early. Had they waited until later in 1972 or early 1973, it is likely that U.S. combat power in theater would have been negligible given the schedule of American troop withdrawals. Suffering from hubris, the North Vietnamese launched the attack in early 1972 to ensure that they could hand the South Vietnamese a decisive defeat while the United States still had forces in country and could share in the humiliation.

In launching the offensive while the United States still had substantial air assets in theater, the North Vietnamese leaders grossly underestimated the amount of additional airpower that Nixon could bring to bear in support of the South Vietnamese. In addition, the North Vietnamese put too much store in the lessons of LAM SON 719 and greatly underestimated the staying power of the South Vietnamese forces when they were supported by U.S. advisers and American airpower. These strategic errors were compounded by poor campaign planning and mistakes at the operational and tactical levels of war.

Ultimately, the entire operational campaign was flawed. Once launched, the offensive consisted of three virtually independent attacks on three fronts separated by great distances. There did not appear to be a main effort. Operating on classical exterior lines, the North Vietnamese did not have the capability to reinforce success and mass forces against South Vietnamese weak points when they were identified. At various times on all three of the major battlefields of Quang Tri, Kontum, and An Loc, had the NVA been able to bring more forces to bear, they most likely would have overwhelmed the ARVN defenders. This was certainly true in III Corps. If the North Vietnamese had had additional troops to throw against An Loc in mid-April or early May, they probably would have prevailed. As the campaign was designed and executed, the three divisions that began the campaign in Binh Long were never reinforced. The same was true with the North Vietnamese forces committed during the battles for Quang Tri and Kontum. Taking on three major attacks simultaneously, the North Vietnamese spread their forces too thinly and were unable to reinforce success.

The failure to maintain the initial momentum of the attack in Binh Long Province also played a key role in the inability of the North Vietnamese to take An Loc. After taking Loc Ninh in 48 hours, they had hoped to attack An Loc no later than 9 April. An uncommonly candid postwar review of the battle by the Military History Institute in Hanoi concluded: "Because we [the North Vietnamese] were not able to seize the initial opportunity which presented itself to us, the enemy had been able to bring in reinforcements, establish an active defense, and increase his use of B-52s. The situation had become more complicated and difficult."[2] Had the North Vietnamese struck An Loc right after Loc Ninh fell, the city would have been virtually defenseless and no doubt would have fallen very quickly.

Logistics also played an important role in the inability of the North Vietnamese to maintain the momentum of the attack. This was true in

MR I and II, but particularly so in the battle in Binh Long Province, which was at the far end of the Ho Chi Minh Trail from North Vietnam. Given the intensity of the combat, the North Vietnamese used vast quantities of ammunition and fuel. Supplying their three divisions in Binh Long was a monumental task that often dictated the operational tempo of the attackers. The result was an attack–lull–attack cycle that repeated itself several times during the three-month-long battle. The NVA would make desperate attacks that in almost every case nearly succeeded in overwhelming the defenders, but when they were repelled by massive U.S. air support, the North Vietnamese would have to pull back and gird themselves for the next round of fighting. Thus, the NVA found it difficult to maintain the pressure, which allowed the defenders to "take a breath" between major attacks and prepare themselves for the next onslaught.

Another operational blunder was that the North Vietnamese became mesmerized by terrain objectives. This was true in all three major attacks, but particularly so in the battle for An Loc. The NVA continued to dash themselves against the An Loc defenses despite the devastation wrought by the attack helicopters, fighter bombers, gunships, and B-52s. This was true long after the town ceased to have any military significance. By the end of April, all that the shelling and repeated ground attacks did was "move the rubble around." In the previously mentioned postwar review of the campaign, Senior General Hoang Van Thai, one of the senior military commanders in the region, is quoted as acknowledging that the "second attack on Binh Long [probably meaning the 11 May attack] was a mistake."[3]

The general was correct, but his observation also applies to the attack on 19 April. The campaign in Binh Long might have ended differently had the NVA left a force to tie down the South Vietnamese troops in An Loc immediately after taking Loc Ninh, and massed the remainder of its forces against the 21st Division farther south on Highway 13. In that case, it likely would have been able to mount a direct threat against Saigon. As it was, NVA forces concentrated themselves around An Loc and its approaches, providing lucrative targets for tactical air strikes, attack helicopters, AC-130s, and B-52s.

The Communists' operational errors were further compounded by mistakes at the tactical level. The North Vietnamese employed their tanks poorly. Rather than use the inherent speed, mobility, and shock action of their armored forces to strike deep into the South Vietnamese lines, they repeatedly used them piecemeal and more as infantry support vehicles.

NVA commanders had difficulty coordinating the combined effects of tanks, infantry, and artillery. In a report to the Soviet Politburo in Moscow in late June 1972, Lieutenant General Tran Van Quang, deputy chief of the North Vietnamese General Staff, acknowledged that some of their problems resulted from having "not sufficiently established a clear system of command and control of our forces." He also cited "a lack of high quality tactical training and combat experience."[4] In another report, the North Vietnamese Armor Command made the following assessment of the failure of the armored forces at An Loc:

> The primary reason for our failure to achieve victory . . . was that the combined arms force commanders and their staff assistants for armor did not [know] how to use their forces correctly, leading to the use of our armor in small, isolated increments, never achieving a powerful armored punch from the beginning. These commanders not only lost the element of surprise and the assault capability that surprise provides, they did not correctly apply the principle of conducting massed armored attacks against the primary targets in key battles launched at the most decisive moment in order to achieve victory.[5]

In addition to the mistakes made with their armored forces, a related tactical error had to do with the way the North Vietnamese conducted their attacks. They repeatedly squandered their numerical advantage at the point of decision by using suicidal frontal assaults. Since these infantry attacks often were not properly coordinated with the armored forces for the reasons enumerated above, the North Vietnamese infantry took horrendous losses, usually for little or no gain. As the battle progressed and the NVA took more casualties as they threw their forces against the An Loc defenses, this had a tremendously negative impact on troop morale, eventually to the point that desertion became a serious problem in frontline units.[6] The NVA kept making the same mistakes over and over again, wasting its forces in the process.

Ultimately the Easter Offensive failed strategically because the campaign plan was based on fundamentally flawed assumptions. These flaws were further compounded by fatal errors at the operational and tactical levels, ultimately resulting in the overall defeat of the offensive.

Assessing South Vietnamese Performance

The North Vietnamese clearly underestimated the ability of the South Vietnamese soldiers to stand against their all-out onslaught. They had observed the debacle in Laos in 1971 and believed that the South Vietnamese would fold if pressed hard enough. Yet, when the smoke cleared, the ARVN were still standing.

The Nixon administration used the South Vietnamese victory at An Loc to declare the president's Vietnamization policy a success.[7] Citing the "fierce determination" of An Loc's defenders, administration officials proclaimed the victory as clear proof that the policy of turning the war over to the South Vietnamese was working.[8] The ARVN had indeed won a decisive victory against overwhelming odds in the desperate battle for An Loc, and in many cases, the courage, skill, and endurance of South Vietnamese officers and soldiers were exemplary. Published MACV reports at the time lauded the bravery and performance of the South Vietnamese defenders; however, the reports failed to reveal just how close the outcome of the battle had been.[9]

Despite the fact that the North Vietnamese had been defeated, the performance of the South Vietnamese during the demanding battle for An Loc had been uneven at best. Some units had fought with almost superhuman valor and skill. Lieutenant Colonel Laddie Logan remarked after the battle that "the 81st [Ranger Battalion] never gave up an inch of ground, and they never left a single one of their dead unburied, even under the heaviest artillery fire."[10] Many of the ARVN took everything the NVA threw at them and stood fast, despite taking horrendous casualties. The 3rd Ranger Group, commanded by Colonel Nguyen Van Biet, had over a thousand soldiers when the NVA launched their first attack; after three months of fighting, all but 346 were dead or wounded. There was little medical support, but the soldiers, for the most part, continued to fight, doing the best they could under the harrowing circumstances.

The performance of the Territorial Forces under Colonel Tran Van Nhut was generally outstanding throughout the siege of An Loc. The Binh Long RF/PFs were well equipped and well trained. Many had lost one or more of their family members and seen their homes destroyed during the battle. They had a cause to fight for, and they acquitted themselves very well against the North Vietnamese regulars. Their morale remained high despite heavy casualties; they started the battle with a strength of slightly more than 2,000, but lost 350 killed, 250 missing, and 900 wounded.[11]

In April and May after the NVA had tightened the ring around An Loc, reconnaissance operations by the 5th ARVN Division ceased almost completely. However, members of the province reconnaissance and intelligence platoon, often dressed as civilians, repeatedly infiltrated the enemy lines to gather intelligence.

The townspeople had nothing but praise for the Regional and Popular Forces, the airborne brigade, and the ranger battalions. The rangers had a particularly good relationship with the locals. They shared their food with the civilians, who in turn cooked for the rangers and did their laundry. If one of the civilians was wounded, the ranger medics attended to him or her.

However, not all the South Vietnamese soldiers covered themselves with glory. Many of the townspeople of An Loc had nothing but scorn for many of the soldiers of the 5th ARVN Division. Soldiers of the division engaged in considerable looting and in some cases even fired into houses to force the occupants out before plundering it.[12]

Although the officers of the division did not encourage looting, they apparently lacked sufficient control and discipline to prevent it. Part of the problem lay with the lack of field grade officer presence about the town. Leadership was the key ingredient; where the leaders were aggressive and physically shared the same hardships as their soldiers, the soldiers' performance was exemplary. Colonel Ulmer later related one such case. During the last major attack on An Loc, the NVA had surrounded part of an ARVN battalion in the city jail on the night of 10–11 May. The South Vietnamese soldiers had run low on ammunition and were virtually defenseless. The NVA sent a message to the ARVN commander, telling him that he had fought well, but that he was surrounded. He could surrender with honor and be protected, but if he did not surrender, he and his soldiers would be killed. The battalion commander replied that he was not about to surrender on those terms. In a few hours, the NVA overran his position. The commander and his soldiers fought to the last man. Their bodies were found on 12 June when the 7th ARVN Regiment cleared the area in house-to-house fighting.[13] The commander and his men had made the supreme sacrifice.

In another case, the regimental commander of the 7th Regiment, then Lieutenant Colonel Quan (soon after promoted on the spot by President Thieu to colonel), was himself wounded three times during the battle. For the critical period in mid-May, he commanded while being propped up in his cot.[14]

Unfortunately, courage and bravery under fire were not uniform among the defenders of Binh Long. Some 5th ARVN troops were observed selling the air-dropped food and medical supplies. On several occasions, 5th ARVN soldiers fired on airborne and ranger troops who were attempting to retrieve air-dropped supplies.

More damaging than the selfishness demonstrated by some of the 5th ARVN soldiers was the cowardice demonstrated by some officers. The commander of 1-5 Cavalry Squadron surrendered himself and most of his unit to the North Vietnamese at Fire Base Alpha north of Loc Ninh. The commander of the 9th Regiment at Loc Ninh wilted under the NVA assault, and it is likely that he surrendered rather than go down fighting. The Loc Ninh district chief abandoned Captain Wanat as they tried to escape to the south. Such cowardly behavior infected the common soldiers as well. This was seen, for example, when the "olympic wounded" abandoned their wounded compatriots in order to clamber aboard medevac helicopters in the panic to get out of the city.

The U.S. Role

General McGiffert said that the battle of An Loc was "an American show in its essence."[15] Indeed, as Major John Howard, an adviser with the airborne brigade, said, it was "the war we came to fight."[16] The United States had always been less than comfortable in fighting a counterinsurgency war in South Vietnam. American forces were not principally equipped and organized for such operations; they were designed to bring superior technology and firepower to bear on a foe who fought in the open under "normal" rules.

The American way of war called for U.S. forces to close with and destroy the enemy by firepower and maneuver. There is some debate about whether the emphasis was on firepower rather than maneuver. Nevertheless, the North Vietnamese and Viet Cong normally refused to provide the appropriate targets for this type of attrition-based warfare that relied heavily on technology and firepower. Although North Vietnamese and Viet Cong forces were confident in their own tactical skills, they knew that they could not match the Americans' ability to mass indirect and aerial fires for extended periods. Consequently, the Communist forces fought their own style of war designed to negate the American advantages. They generally refused to fight the type of battles that would allow the Americans to prevail, opting for hit-and-run tactics, refusing to get involved in set-piece battles of long duration.[17]

In 1972, General Giap and his fellow North Vietnamese generals made a serious mistake when they decided to abandon their previously successful strategy and initiate conventional attacks against the South Vietnamese. An Loc was a battle the Americans were trained and equipped to fight. When ARVN leadership and resolve wavered, General Hollingsworth and his advisers provided the technical expertise and fighting spirit to stabilize a desperate tactical emergency.[18] American firepower and American advisers fighting in the American way of war enabled the ARVN defenders to win a great victory.

U.S. Airpower

Although U.S. airpower provided the margin of victory on all three major battlefields of the Easter Offensive, the role played by air support at An Loc is particularly illustrative. During the three-month siege of An Loc, U.S. airpower provided the South Vietnamese garrison and its handful of U.S. advisers with their major means of fire support and interdiction of enemy forces at the tactical level, as well as their primary source of resupply. This triad of support not only broke the NVA's stranglehold on the town, but also destroyed the better part of three divisions that would have been poised to move on Saigon had An Loc fallen.

As previously discussed, this air support took many forms, but key to the defenders' ability to hold the city against repeated attacks was the performance of the forward air controllers. During the height of the battle, the FAC on station over An Loc had to keep track of as many as 10 sets of aircraft above him, all with different ordnance, capabilities, and times on target. Adding to the complexity was the intense antiaircraft fire that pervaded the skies over An Loc. As the FACs dodged intense fire from the ground, they worked tirelessly to ensure the most efficient use of all aircraft to support the ARVN and their advisers on the ground. Colonel Ulmer later said that the FACs "had accomplished virtually the impossible" and were "contenders for the 'Most Valuable Player' award."[19] You will get no argument on that statement from any of the advisers who survived the bitter fighting at An Loc. Figure 9 reflects the number of fixed-wing sorties flown in support of the South Vietnamese and their American advisers in 1972.

Figure 9. Fixed-wing Sorties in South Vietnam, 1972

A. Fixed-Wing Strike Sorties in South Vietnam

	March	April	May	June
USAF tac air	247	3,032	7,516	5,310
USAF gunships	24	407	491	325
U.S. Navy	128	4,683	3,247	2,040
U.S. Marine Corps	—	537	1,381	1,937
VNAF tac air	3,118	4,612	5,276	3,950
VNAF gunships	31	292	310	182
USAF B-52s	689	1,608	2,223	2,207
Totals	4,237	15,171	20,444	15,951

B. Strike Sorties in South Vietnam, April 1972, by Region

Service	MR I	MR II	MR III	MR IV	Total	Percent
USN	2,022	1,118	1,378	314	4,832	27.6
USAF	2,510	1,397	2,825	377	7,109	40.6
USMC	43	497	3	0	593	3.1
VNAF	1,292	1.153	1,533	1,012	4,990	28.6
Total	5,867	4,165	5,739	1,703	17,524	

C. Distribution of B-52 Sorties in South Vietnam, April–June 1972

	MR I	MR II	MR III	MR IV	Total
April	554	691	363	0	1,608
May	842	991	363	44	2,240
June	1,503	503	161	40	2,207
Total	2,899	2,185	887	84	6,055

Source: Major A. J. C. Lavalle, ed., Airpower and the 1972 Spring Offensive, United States Air Force Southeast Asia Monograph Series (Washington, D.C.: U.S. Government Printing Office, 1976), p. 106.

The tools at the disposal of the FACs were many. The fixed-wing gunships played a key role, day and night. The AC-119 Stingers were initially very effective in the early fighting in Binh Long. When the Stinger worked at its normal operational altitude of 3,500 feet over Loc Ninh and An Loc, its 7.62mm miniguns and 20mm cannon were very accurate. However, the Stinger required a relatively permissive air environment, and as the antiaircraft fire over the city intensified, the Stingers were forced up and away from the city. Still, they were able to perform area reconnaissance and engage targets of opportunity. In these roles, they proved most effective in impeding the flow of supplies to the NVA forces around the provincial capital.

The more advanced AC-130 Spectres saved the advisers and their counterparts on too many occasions to count. They were extremely effective because of both their firepower and accuracy. They were capable of taking very specific directions from the advisers on the ground and bringing fire to within 10–20 meters of friendly troops. This was particularly useful when the fighting was house to house early in the battle. Major Ken Ingram, an adviser with the 5th ARVN Division who spent 31 days in An Loc, later lauded the AC-130 gunships, saying, "There is nothing the NVA could do when the Spectre was overhead except crawl into a hole and hope that it didn't hit them."[20] The accuracy of the Spectres' onboard weapons systems was greatly enhanced when the air force was able to drop lightweight X-band beacons to the advisers. Using these beacons, which pinpointed friendly positions, the Spectres could bring fire in extremely close to the defenders. On one night in June, I was with a battalion in the rubber south of the city. We had a beacon and were communicating with the Spectre on station. He alerted us to movement near our position and asked if we had anyone moving. We replied that we did not. He informed us that "personnel were attempting to drive large animals" into our defensive barbwire very close to our command post. We told him to engage, and the Spectre pilot warned us to "keep our heads down." He engaged with 40mm cannon, and there was no more movement that night. The next day, we found NVA bodies and water buffalo carcasses just outside our position. The steady drone as the Spectres orbited the area at night was very comforting to the advisers and the South Vietnamese soldiers.

Close air support by air force, navy, and marine fighter-bombers was also critically important throughout the battle. All aircraft performed well, but two are worthy of note. The F-4 was prized because of its capacity for armament. The slower but more accurate A-37 was one of the most

effective fixed-wing platforms for close-in fighting. The advisers appreci-
ated all the tactical aircraft, but the A-37 won a special place in their hearts.
General McGiffert later summed it up very well when he said that the "A-37
proved to be the very best compromise" for close air support at An Loc.
General Vogt, 7th Air Force commander, stated that the work of the 8th
Special Operations Squadron and its A-37s was "absolutely spectacular."[21]

The B-52s also won a special place in the saga of the battle. Over 700
ARC LIGHT sorties were flow in April and May in support of the defense
of An Loc. These strikes inflicted horrendous damage on the NVA, but
maybe just as importantly they pumped up the morale of the beleaguered
defenders, who were heartened time and again by the devastation the giant bombers inflicted on the NVA. Often, the big bombers were the only
margin between hanging on and being overrun.

Air force airlifters also played a key role. Although beset by difficulties
in providing aerial resupply in the dangerous skies over An Loc, the C-130
pilots and crews braved intense fire to press on with their mission. Their
steadfastness in the face of this deadly fire greatly impressed the South
Vietnamese and their advisers. Once they overcame the initial problems,
the air crews provided timely resupply that enabled the defenders to fight
on as the North Vietnamese tightened the cordon around the city.

Playing an integral role in the American air support were the various
components of army aviation, especially the pilots and crews from 229th
Assault Helicopter Battalion. Not enough can be said about the Cobras,
who selflessly flew into the maelstrom to take out the tanks bearing down
on the defenders. They flew tirelessly to support the troops on the ground.
For example, F/79th Aerial Rocket Artillery, the Blue Max, flew 1,623
combat hours in the month of April alone. This is very likely the greatest
number of combat hours ever logged by any U.S. Army aviation unit of
comparable size in the 10-year history of the war.[22]

The assault helicopters, including both Hueys and Chinooks, also
played an important role, providing medevac, resupply, and troop lift. Like
the Cobra crews, the pilots, crew chiefs, and door gunners of these aircraft
braved the intense antiaircraft umbrella over the city and along Highway
13, spending many very long days in the cockpit to make sure that the
North Vietnamese would be defeated. One adviser observed that the tireless aviators "took fire going in and out" of the city and the surrounding
area, often two or three times a day.[23] To a man, the advisers greatly re-
spected all of the U.S. helicopter pilots for their bravery and skill. We knew
that we could count on them in a crisis, no matter how bad things got.

In planning for the campaign, the North Vietnamese knew that American air support would be a critical factor, and allowed for it by providing a robust antiaircraft capability to support their assault. However, they underestimated the sheer volume of air support that would be brought to bear. For their inability to sufficiently impede aircraft of all types, North Vietnamese ground troops paid a horrendous price. In his after-action report, Colonel Ulmer summed up the situation very well when he wrote that air support was "the predominant factor in swaying the balance of power over a numerically superior, well equipped enemy force" at An Loc.[24]

The Role of the U.S. Advisers

It is impossible to assess South Vietnamese combat performance and the ultimate outcome of the battle at An Loc without considering the role of the U.S. advisers on the ground in the city. They served in several key roles.

First, they provided encouragement to their counterparts. This encouragement was particularly important in the darkest hours of the repeated North Vietnamese attacks. The mere presence of the advisers was the embodiment of the U.S. commitment to stand by the South Vietnamese in time of dire peril. The Americans were right there in the bunkers with their counterparts, sharing the hardships and facing the same dangers. A post-battle review of the action conducted by MACV revealed the importance of the advisers' presence in the city to the ability of the soldiers and civilians to withstand the North Vietnamese onslaught. It stated, "The people of An Loc knew that the US advisers were still in the city, and they felt confident of continuing critical air support as long as the adviser stayed. The sight of aircraft regularly boosted the morale of both soldiers and civilians."[25] After the offensive was defeated, Lieutenant General Ngo Quang Truong, who led the counterattack to retake Quang Tri, wrote: "The American response during the enemy offensive was timely, forceful and decisive. This staunch resolve of the U.S. to stand by its ally stunned the enemy. Additionally, it brought about a strong feeling of self-assurance among the armed forces and population of South Vietnam."[26] This was clearly the case in the successful defense of An Loc.

Obviously, one of the most critical roles served by the American advisers relates to the importance of U.S. tactical air support. The advisers provided the link between the ARVN defenders and the American tactical aircraft and helicopters supporting the battle. Without the advisers and their radios, the defenders on the ground in the city and surrounding area would have been unable to communicate with the aircraft. The advisers were tireless in coordinating the around-the-clock air strikes that prevented the North Vietnamese forces from overrunning the city. General McGiffert said of the advisers, "their primary duty and their primary reason for existence was coordination of U.S. tac air [tactical air support] and without them it [the defense of An Loc] would have just been damn near impossible."[27]

The advisers also provided General Hollingsworth and the other senior Americans who controlled the air assets their only feeling for "ground truth." Determining exactly what was going on in the city was particularly difficult in the beginning stages of the battle when confusion and near panic reigned. The advisers in An Loc talked daily by radio with Hollingsworth and his operations personnel. This allowed the general to coordinate the B-52 airstrikes that proved so crucial in the battle for the city. General McGiffert described this role of the advisers in the following manner: "It was the only way we could get any kind of objective analysis of what was really going on in there; it was talking to them [the advisers] every day."[28]

The last and maybe most crucial role performed by the American advisers in An Loc is less tangible. Many of the ARVN fought bravely and maintained their fighting edge under the most trying conditions. Unfortunately, others allowed panic and fear to rule and fought less than valiantly. On several occasions, the defense of An Loc was only a breath away from crumbling. General McGiffert said that the advisers "were the glue that kept them [the ARVN] together."[29]

The fact that the advisers remained with their counterparts in and around An Loc and were in constant contact with General Hollingsworth and the support he controlled greatly encouraged the South Vietnamese defenders and provided excellent leadership by example. Leadership in the South Vietnamese armed forces had long been a problem and was still a problem in 1972. The crucible of An Loc only served to exacerbate this shortcoming. In looking at leadership at An Loc, one must actually consider it in two separate categories: one assessment for the regular forces and one for the RF/PFs.

Most advisers who took part in the battle and many outside observers acknowledge that the leadership of Colonel Tran Van Nhut, the province chief, was outstanding. He was calm and cool under pressure and very aggressive. He did not wait for air support to take care of the enemy and was very offensive-minded. He and his deputy, Lieutenant Colonel Nguyen Thong Thanh, who was also well regarded by the advisers, "led from the front" and were very visible to their troops, particularly during the darkest hours.[30] The superior leadership provided by Nhut and Thanh had a great influence on their junior leaders and individual soldiers, who, in most cases, remained steadfast in the face of the repeated NVA assaults, taking horrendous casualties in the process. Because of their leaders, the performance of the RF/PFs, as previously noted, far outshone that of most of the regular forces.

In the regular forces, leadership and morale were generally high in the elite airborne and ranger units, but were often less than satisfactory in the non-elite units; this was particularly true at the higher echelons of command. General McGiffert stated later that the 5th ARVN Division commander "choked" under the pressure and "just didn't do a damn thing for a long time."[31] He also felt that the regimental commanders, with some exceptions, were no better than mediocre. According to McGiffert: "There was no control. There was no supervision; there was no command emphasis to get out into the crew positions."[32]

This situation was so bad at several points during the siege that some advisers felt that the city would probably have fallen if the NVA had left the road open to the south so the ARVN troops could have escaped.[33] In many cases, troops who did not wish to be there had no choice but to fight in order to survive. Given this situation, the advisers in An Loc often did a lot more than advise their counterparts; in many cases, the Americans stepped into the void and assumed virtual command of the ARVN units they were with, providing the leadership so badly needed.[34] A Senate Foreign Relations Committee looking into the 1972 offensive later reported: "No one with whom we talked, American or Vietnamese, thought that the South Vietnamese could have held had there not been American advisers."[35]

Another part of the problem with the South Vietnamese leadership had to do with the tactical competence of the South Vietnamese leaders. U.S. advisers had been working with ARVN commanders for years, and much emphasis had been placed on the conduct of tactical operations and planning. However, the focus of this training had been mostly on conducting counterinsurgency operations. The situation in An Loc was far removed from the type of circumstances that even the best of ARVN commanders had previously experienced. Facing tanks was a far cry from chasing guerrillas. As one adviser later described the situation that existed in An Loc: "Regimental and higher level leadership was not tactically or psychologically prepared for a battle of the duration and intensity of the Binh Long campaign; battalion level leaders lacked preparation for the close coordination necessary between fire and maneuver elements."[36] In many cases, the American advisers provided the expertise in handling battles of such magnitude.

The Bottom Line

All of the above said, it must be remembered that when the battle was over in An Loc, the South Vietnamese troops had held on despite some serious systemic problems. As General Hollingsworth said "the real credit goes to the little ARVN soldier. He is just tremendous, just magnificent. He stood in there, took all that fire and gave it back."[37] Perhaps the best analysis was given by *Time* magazine correspondent Rudolph Rauch, who quoted one of the American advisers in An Loc: "The only way to approach the battle of An Loc is to remember that the ARVN are there and the North Vietnamese aren't. To view it any other way is to do an injustice to the Vietnamese people."[38]

Even with all its shortcomings, the ARVN had withstood everything the NVA could muster. The South Vietnamese soldiers had endured almost unbelievable hardship and still triumphed in the end. Although there had been some glaring errors, the South Vietnamese established that with sufficient continuing air support from the United States they had at least a chance of surviving anything the North could throw against them.

Perhaps the greatest tribute to these soldiers who endured so much was the one inscribed on a monument erected by the grateful people of An Loc in honor of the 81st Rangers. This monument stood amid a cemetery especially built for the members of that unit who gave their lives in defense of the city. It read:

An Loc Xa Vang Danh Chien Dia
Biet Cach Du Vi Quoc Vong Than

This translates: "Here, on the famous battlefield of An Loc Town, the Airborne Rangers have sacrificed their lives for the nation." Such sacrifice was not limited to the airborne rangers. An Loc remained free because South Vietnamese soldiers stood and fought when they had no other choice.

CHAPTER ELEVEN

AFTERMATH

Vietnamization Declared a Success

UNFORTUNATELY, THIS GREAT victory led to a fatal set of perceptions both for the Americans and the South Vietnamese. Many ARVN soldiers fought valiantly under conditions never seen before in the history of the Southeast Asian war. Yet, the battle had been close, and many South Vietnamese units had not done well. Nevertheless, the Nixon administration promoted the South Vietnamese victory as a vindication of the Vietnamization program. The president made statements declaring that the South Vietnamese had demonstrated that they were ready to prosecute "their war" without American help. Many in the American press agreed; Joseph Alsop wrote after the battle of An Loc, "ARVN has a damn good record in this fighting; ARVN has proven itself."[1]

Lieutenant General Phillip Davidson, former MACV J-2 Intelligence, maintains that President Nixon put the best face on the South Vietnamese performance in 1972 to validate the Vietnamization policy and provide the justification for completing the American withdrawal from Vietnam.[2] Davidson further maintains that even as early as 1968, "any cold-blooded analysis of the capacity of the South Vietnamese to carry out their part of Vietnamization would have argued against its adoption."[3] This evaluation was supported by examining battles prior to 1972, such as the LAM SON 719 debacle in 1971, which clearly demonstrated that the South Vietnamese were not ready to take over the war. All of that is true, but the Easter Offensive did prove that the South Vietnamese at least had a chance to succeed as long as U.S. support continued.

Even though South Vietnamese forces had learned some valuable lessons and made strides in improving their combat capability during the Vietnamization period prior to 1972, ARVN forces were not prepared for what happened at An Loc. They were plagued by the same kinds of problems that had bothered them for the entire Vietnam War: politicized commanders, inept leadership, and tactical incompetence at the higher levels of command. The ARVN were victorious at An Loc because the American advisers and U.S. airpower had negated the debilitating effects of these long-standing maladies. The same was true on the other battlefields of 1972, clearly demonstrating that the South Vietnamese still relied heavily on U.S. support for survival.

The fact that U.S. tactical leadership and firepower were the key ingredients in the battle for An Loc and elsewhere during the Easter Offensive was either lost in the mutual euphoria of victory or ignored by Nixon administration officials who wanted to get the United States out of Vietnam in the most expeditious manner. The victory at An Loc and elsewhere during the Easter Offensive would eventually be used to rationalize the complete withdrawal of U.S. forces from the war.

The Peace Talks and the Christmas Bombing

Given the ARVN success on the battlefield, the North Vietnamese negotiators became more amenable to meaningful negotiations in Paris. Anxious to achieve a settlement before the 1972 presidential election, the chief American negotiator, Henry Kissinger, worked out a deal with North Vietnamese representative Le Duc Tho by October. Under this proposed agreement, all U.S. troops would be withdrawn from Vietnam, while the North Vietnamese troops would remain in South Vietnam but could not increase their number. South Vietnamese president Nguyen Van Thieu would remain in power but acknowledge the legitimacy of the Communist National Liberation Front and explore the prospect of a coalition government. Not surprisingly, Thieu objected to this deal. He prepared a set of counterproposals, and Kissinger presented them to the North Vietnamese in Paris. Shortly thereafter, the talks collapsed, and the North Vietnamese walked out of the negotiations.

Five days later, President Nixon launched Operation LINEBACKER II, a massive bombing campaign against North Vietnam. Wave after wave of B-52s and other aircraft pounded bridges, power plants, railroad lines, and industrial installations. The "Christmas bombing," as it became known, ignited a storm of protest not just in the United States but also around the world. Nevertheless, the North Vietnamese agreed to come back to the negotiating table in Paris.

Kissinger and Tho reached an agreement on 9 January that was not appreciably different than the one Thieu had scuttled earlier, and the South Vietnamese president had to be pressured into accepting it. He went along only after being promised military and economic aid and receiving assurances from Nixon that the United States would respond with full force if North Vietnam violated the cease-fire agreement. On 27 January, Secretary of State William Rogers and Le Duc Tho signed the peace settlement in Paris.

The Paris Peace Accords

Under the provisions of the "Agreement on Ending the War and Restoring the Peace in Viet Nam," a cease-fire would go into effect at 8:00 A.M. Saigon time, 28 January 1973. All military forces of the United States and its allies such as South Korea and Australia would leave South Vietnam, and the United States was to dismantle its military bases in South Vietnam, removing or destroying military equipment so as to make the bases unusable for military purposes.[4] The agreement said nothing about a pullout of the North Vietnamese forces in South Vietnam, but it forbade the introduction of additional military personnel into the south. All prisoners of war were to be released within 60 days. The United States promised to contribute to healing the wounds of war and to postwar reconstruction of North Vietnam.

The cease-fire went into effect as scheduled. The prisoners of war, including those captured in Loc Ninh in April 1972, were returned. By the end of March, all American troops had left Vietnam.[5]

1973–1974, the Cease-Fire War

Unfortunately, the signing of the treaty did not mean the end of the war. The cease-fire proved to be only a momentary respite from the fighting, which resumed after a brief pause. The South Vietnamese were struggling to remain an independent nation; the North Vietnamese wanted unification of both Vietnams on their terms. Since the remainder of the Communist military units that had come south and survived the desperate battles of 1972 were still in place, open combat soon broke out with the South Vietnamese as the Communists tried to consolidate control of the areas they occupied. During the first three months of "peace," the South Vietnamese lost 6,000 soldiers in fighting with the North Vietnamese.[6]

Although the North Vietnamese forces occupied areas in the South, they had been hurt badly during the 1972 combat. Needing time to regroup and refit, they instituted a program of quiet infiltration to bring in supplies and fresh replacements from the North. Large volumes of tanks, other armored vehicles, rockets, long-range artillery, and antiaircraft weapons were moved south. Replacements came down the Ho Chi Minh Trail, and North Vietnamese units in the South were reorganized and refitted. This effort even included the building of a pipeline from Quang Tri in northern MR I to Loc Ninh in MR III. The North Vietnamese were able to do all this because the U.S. Congress had mandated the cessation of bombing along the Ho Chi Minh Trail. Unimpeded, the North Vietnamese rapidly rebuilt their forces in the South.

Most of the million-man South Vietnamese Army was tied down in the defense of static positions. When the North Vietnamese units were stronger, they began to try to expand their influence. This resulted in relatively low-level but constant combat between the ARVN and the NVA as each side jockeyed for position and territory. In 1973, the South Vietnamese forces fared fairly well against the North Vietnamese in what President Thieu called the "Third Indochina War." However, by the end of the year, the ARVN began to experience severe shortages in ammunition, fuel, medical supplies, and other matériel. As the South Vietnamese got weaker, the North Vietnamese were growing stronger. In 1973, the South Vietnamese suffered 25,473 battle deaths, exceeding that of any previous years with the exception of 1968, the year of the Tet Offensive, and 1972.[7]

The Initial Attack on Phuoc Long

The fighting continued into 1974. Late that year, the North Vietnamese decided to test the waters with a limited attack; they wanted to see how the South Vietnamese would deal with a major new offensive. They also wanted to see how the United States would react. In December, they attacked Phuoc Long Province with both regional and mainforce NVA units.

This time, unlike the action in An Loc, the infantry and armor forces were well coordinated and they routed the South Vietnamese forces, killing or capturing 3,000 soldiers, taking control of vast quantities of war matériel, and "liberating" the entire province.

The United States did nothing. President Nixon had left office in disgrace in August, and most Americans wanted nothing further to do with Vietnam. Nixon's successor, Gerald R. Ford, faced an increasingly hostile Congress that slashed military aid to South Vietnam. General Van Tien Dung, commander of NVA forces, realized that President Thieu, without American help, was now relegated to fighting a "poor man's war."[8] The post-treaty balance of power had clearly shifted in favor of the North Vietnamese.

On the heels of the victory at Phuoc Long, the Communist war planners developed a two-year strategy that called for large-scale offensives in 1975 to create conditions for a "general offensive, general uprising" in 1976.[9] The strategy hinged on the assumption that the United States, having pulled out, would not return to Vietnam. The thrust of the strategy was to determine which battles would have the greatest impact on the Thieu government. Having determined the high-value targets, the North Vietnamese planners massed armor and infantry to overwhelm the ARVN defenders at those points. NVA plans called for "blooming lotus" attacks, in which the critical point was captured and NVA control spread out in every direction.[10]

Campaign 275

On 10 March 1975, the North Vietnamese launched the general offensive with an attack on Ban Me Thuot in the Central Highlands. The ARVN were spread very thinly throughout the country, and the Central Highlands was no exception. The NVA overran the city in two days, and the ARVN fell back in panic.

The NVA then turned on Pleiku and Kontum to finish securing the Highlands before the advent of the monsoon season. The success of the NVA onslaught panicked President Thieu, and he ordered ARVN forces to withdraw from the Highlands. The NVA cut the roads to the south, blocking the retreating forces. To compound the problem, the civilian populace also tried to escape to the south, intermingling with the ARVN force as they tried to withdraw. The resulting mass confusion turned the retreat into a rout that led to the virtual destruction of the ARVN forces in the Central Highlands. South Vietnam had been cut in half; six provinces had been lost, and two ARVN divisions ceased to exist as a fighting force. The confidence of both the army and the South Vietnamese people was shaken to the core.

Dung and the other North Vietnamese generals were surprised by the rapid success of these initial attacks in the Central Highlands. They quickly developed contingency plans to exploit the situation against the reeling South Vietnamese forces. NVA forces struck both Hue and Da Nang; the ARVN response was no better than in the Highlands, and the South Vietnamese fell back in disarray. Within 10 days, both critical cities fell to the Communists.

The Thieu government and the remnants of its army were in dire straits. Thieu had lost contact with the northern half of the country, and at least 50 percent of his army had given up after putting up only token resistance. Thieu ordered the evacuation of Nha Trang and Cam Ranh Bay.

Still the United States did nothing, even though it was obvious that the South Vietnamese forces were in danger of collapsing. Congress refused to authorize emergency military assistance for South Vietnam, and the mood of the country would not permit President Ford to recommit American forces. General Dung stepped up the timetable for the "Ho Chi Minh Campaign" and ordered his troops to execute a "deep advance" on Saigon.[11] The drive from Da Nang to Saigon took less than a month. By mid-April, the North Vietnamese completed the destruction of the few pockets of South Vietnamese resistance, and the remaining provinces along the coastline "fell like a row of porcelain vases sliding off a shelf."[12] The only real resistance was put up by the 18th ARVN Division at Xuan Loc, but these forces were overwhelmed in several days. Map 12 depicts the final North Vietnamese offensive in March–April 1975.

The Fall of Saigon

The North Vietnamese continued the attack toward Saigon, and on 30 April NVA tanks crashed through the gates to the presidential palace. The South Vietnamese, who had come to rely so heavily on American support, had folded in less than 55 days when that support was not forthcoming. The ARVN, with few exceptions, became ineffective as a fighting force almost immediately when the North Vietnamese attacked. The same army that

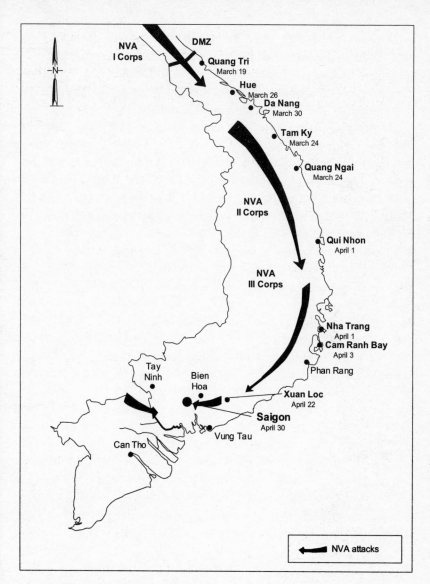

Map 12. The Fall of South Vietnam, 1975

had been victorious with American help in 1972 was virtually helpless by itself. Without American tactical airpower and the advisers that had provided the "backbone" of resolve in 1972, the ARVN fell apart. As retired U.S. Army Brigadier General Douglas Kinnard later put it, Vietnamization was revealed as "the fraud and deception that it was."[13]

Kinnard's characterization of Vietnamization may be a bit harsh, but evidence is irrefutable that the South Vietnamese would not have performed as well as they did in the spring of 1972 if the American advisers and U.S. tactical air support had not been there. The North Vietnamese proved this in 1975 after the advisers and U.S. air support were no longer available. Although some South Vietnamese soldiers fought valiantly, the ARVN force as a whole, without the "steel reinforcing rods" provided by the American advisers and air support, crumbled like a house of cards.[14]

The North Vietnamese had suffered a strategic defeat in 1972, but took the long-term approach to reap a greater victory in 1975 after the United States had departed and left the South Vietnamese to their own devices. Perhaps if U.S. support had been there as it had been in 1972, the outcome might have been different. Tragically, the promised support was not provided. The ultimate result was that South Vietnam ceased to exist as a nation, and the United States lost the first war in its history.

EPILOGUE

MORE THAN 30 years after what General Ngo Quang Truong called "the longest and bloodiest siege of the war," it is appropriate to look at what happened to some of the key participants in the Battle of An Loc.[1]

Vo Nguyen Giap, the architect of the 1972 Easter Offensive, fell into disfavor when the campaign failed. The Politburo allowed him to retain his post of minister of defense, but stripped him of command of the People's Army of Vietnam and gave it to his chief of staff, General Van Tien Dung. Dung would lead the Ho Chi Minh Offensive in 1975 that culminated in the fall of Saigon. Thereafter, Giap's life consisted of a round of visits to mostly Communist countries. He resigned as defense minister in 1980 and was dropped from the Politburo in 1982, but remained deputy prime minister until 1991. Today, he lives quietly in Hanoi.

Tran Van Tra, commander of the Communist forces at An Loc in 1972, returned to Hanoi in October 1974 to help plan the final campaign in the South. After completing the plan, he returned to the battlefront to oversee the final phase that included the surrender of Saigon. Initially, he served as head of the Military Occupation Force in Saigon. In 1982, Tra published his controversial five-volume work, *History of the Bulwark B2 Theater*, in which he, a southerner, criticized the wartime policies of the Democratic Republic of Vietnam. For that he was ousted from the Politburo, and the book was banned in Vietnam. Despite falling from favor in Hanoi, Tra retained his influence among former army officials, with whom in 1987 he organized a war veterans association. The group was vocal in opposition to government policies and was banned in 1990. Tra died on 20 April 1996.

Major General Le Van Hung, former commanding general of the 5th ARVN Division at An Loc, became assistant commander of III Corps after the battle. Later, he assumed command of the 21st ARVN Division, which had returned to the Mekong Delta. In 1975, he was the deputy commander of MR IV at Can Tho under General Nguyen Khoa Nam. At 8:45 P.M. on 30 April 1975, distraught at the fall of Saigon, General Hung took his life with his own pistol. His wife and children escaped to the United States.

After the battle was won at An Loc, Tran Van Nhut was promoted to brigadier general and given command of the 2nd Infantry Division at Quang Ngai. He led his division throughout the cease-fire war. In April 1975, his outnumbered division was overwhelmed by the advancing North Vietnamese troops; he and the survivors of his division were evacuated by sea to Binh Tuy. On 19 April, Binh Tuy fell and the 2nd Division ceased to exist as a fighting force. General Nhut went to Vung Tau, where he hoped to help organize the defenses against the advancing North Vietnamese, but the situation had degenerated too far by that time and defeat was just hours away. Reluctantly, he and his family made their way to one of the waiting U.S. Navy ships, which brought them to the United States where they settled in California. In the ensuing years, he has been very active in the Vietnamese-American community in Santa Ana. In 1998, he received a belated Legion of Merit medal from Secretary of Defense William E. Cohen. The award was given

> for exceptionally meritorious service from 1 April 1972 to 15 August 1972, while serving as Province Chief and Commander of Regional Forces in Binh Long Province, Republic of Vietnam. Colonel Van Nhut demonstrated extraordinary professionalism in cooperation with his American allies during a period of intense combat. His resourcefulness, remarkable administrative skills and heroic leadership were instrumental in securing the combined United States–Vietnamese success in a major military operation.[2]

After leaving Vietnam in May 1972, Colonel Bill Miller returned to Fort Campbell, Kentucky, where he assumed command of the 2nd Brigade, 101st Airborne Division (Airmobile). In the late 1970s, he served as adviser to the Iranian Army before the fall of the Shah. In 1981, he retired from the service after 41 years of dedicated and selfless service in peace and war. Colonel Miller lived in Florida until he passed away in March 2004. He was buried with full military honors at Arlington National Cemetery.

The funeral was attended by several participants in the battle of An Loc, including the author. The Miller name and military tradition live on today in the U.S. Army; his son, Thomas G. Miller, is a major general serving in Iraq at the time of this writing.

Colonel Walter Ulmer went on to a distinguished military career, ultimately reaching the rank of lieutenant general. He served as commander of the 194th Armor Brigade, then deputy commander of the U.S. Armor Center, Fort Knox. In 1975, Brigadier General Ulmer returned to West Point as the 56th Commandant of Cadets. He went on to command the 3rd Armored Division in Germany and ultimately III Corps at Fort Hood, Texas. In 1985, General Ulmer retired from the army after 33 years of distinguished service. From 1985 to 1995, he served as president and chief executive officer of the Center for Creative Leadership, which became internationally recognized as a leader in executive development. Since retiring from that position, General Ulmer has served as a member of the Board of Trustees of the Association of Graduates, U.S. Military Academy, and contributes his time to a number of West Point Society activities.

Lieutenant Colonel Robert Corley, Binh Long Province senior advisor, departed an Loc in June 1972. He retired from the army in 1979 after successive engineer assignments that included service as V Corps Engineer in Frankfurt, Germany, and Facility Engineer, Fort Benning, Georgia. Upon retiring from the service, he became the assistant superintendent of a school district in Spartanburg, South Carolina. After fourteen years as an educator, he left that job to form his own consulting business, which he ran for eight years before retiring again. He and his wife reside in South Carolina.

Lieutenant Colonel William B. Nolde, who replaced Lieutenant Corley as province senior adviser to Binh Long Province, was killed by artillery in An Loc just 11 hours before the beginning of the cease-fire. He was buried with full military honors in Arlington National Cemetery. Colonel Nolde's name is on panel 01W, line 112 of the Vietnam Veterans Memorial wall in Washington, D.C.

Major General Hollingsworth was promoted to lieutenant general in July 1973. He commanded I Corps (ROK/U.S.) Group Korea, the largest field army in the world—185,000 ROK and U.S. soldiers in 13 divisions deployed along the 100-mile demilitarized zone. On 24 August 1976, he retired from active duty after more than 30 years of dedicated service. After retirement, General Hollingsworth went on to become president of the Washington, D.C.–based Hollingsworth Consultants, Inc. He also served on the boards of various aerospace and technology firms. In 1999, he was honored with the unveiling of a seven-foot statue of his image in the Corps of Cadets area on the grounds of his alma mater, Texas A&M University. Entitled "Danger 79er," the statue depicts the general in full battle gear complete with sidearm. In attendance at the dedication were Major General (Ret.) John R. McGiffert, deputy commander of Third Regional Assistance Command; Major General (Ret.) Nyles Fulwyler, formerly G3 operations officer of TRAC; Mr. Frank Muller, formerly General McGiffert's aide-de-camp at TRAC; and the author. We were all proud to participate in the dedication of a fitting tribute to a great warrior.

After the battle of An Loc, the helicopter pilots who braved the deadly skies over Binh Long went about their lives. Some stayed in the service; some got out and went back to civilian life. In May 1974, the 229th Aviation Battalion was honored with a Presidential Unit Citation that recognized their service and bravery during operations around Loc Ninh and An Loc during the Easter Offensive. This was the second such award for the unit, making it the only army aviation unit to receive two Presidential Unit Citations for Vietnam. The debt owed to these aviators by the defenders in An Loc can never be repaid, and the honor bestowed is only a small token of what they are due for their service during the desperate battle in Binh Long Province. A copy of the citation is in appendix 2.

On 11 February 1999, the members of Advisory Team 70, 5th ARVN Division, who had shared the dangers and hardships of the bitter fighting on the ground at An Loc with their South Vietnamese counterparts, were officially recognized for their courageous service. Twenty-seven years after the fact, the advisers were awarded a Presidential Unit Citation. A copy of that citation is in appendix 3.

In April 2003, nearly three decades after the fall of Saigon, a memorial to the U.S.–South Vietnamese partnership during the war was dedicated at Civic Center Park in Westminister, California, the largest Vietnamese community outside Vietnam. The focal point of the memorial is a 12-foot bronze statue depicting two soldiers—an American and a South Vietnamese—in honor of those who died in battle and commemorating the friendship and alliance between Vietnamese and Americans during the Vietnam War. In attendance were large numbers of former Vietnamese servicemen, many in the uniform of their former country.

After those fateful days in An Loc in 1972, I served in the military for 20 more years, retiring in 1992. Since that time, I have taught as a civilian professor on the faculty at the U.S. Army Command and General Staff

College, Fort Leavenworth, Kansas. Although it has been more than 30 years since we stopped the NVA at An Loc, the events of those days are never very far from my mind.

Today there is little in Binh Long Province to indicate that an epic battle was fought there in the spring and summer of 1972. Loc Ninh is an unremarkable, dusty little town near the Cambodian border, An Loc remains the center of a vast rubber plantation, and Chon Than is just another village along the highway running from Cambodia to Ho Chi Minh City. There are few signs of the bloody struggle that left an indelible imprint on the lives of the soldiers on both sides who fought in Binh Long.

Despite the long time that has passed, the memories remain fresh for many of the soldiers who fought there and also for the families of those who fell there. Recently, there was closure for the family of one soldier who died in 1972. On 7 April 2004, exactly 32 years to the day after he died in a bunker in Loc Ninh, the remains of Lieutenant Colonel Richard S. Schott were buried in Shepherdstown, West Virginia. Schott's body had not been recovered because Loc Ninh fell to the Communists, but in 2002 a search team from Joint Task Force Full Accounting, the U.S. command charged with searching for American remains in Southeast Asia, went back to Loc Ninh to look for Schott's remains. After an extensive search, they found several bones and some personal items, including his dog tags, in the area of Colonel Schott's bunker, which is now a cashew plantation. It took two years to positively identify the remains as Colonel Schott's. He was buried with full military honors. For his family, it was a day of celebration; his daughter, Susan Schott of Kearneysville, West Virginia, said, "It's just so wonderful to have my father coming home."[3] May Colonel Schott and all who fell on both sides during the desperate fighting in Binh Long Province forever rest in peace.

ORDER OF BATTLE

Battle of Loc Ninh, 4–8 April 1972

Enemy	Friendly
5th VC Div	9th Regiment (2 battalions)
E6 Regiment	1st Armored Cavalry Squadron*
174th Regiment	74th Border Ranger Battalion*
275th Regiment	1 battalion Regional-Popular Forces
429th Sapper Group (–)	1 105mm battery
69th Artillery Division	Task Force 52*
42nd Artillery Regiment	1st Battalion, 52nd Regiment
208th Rocket Regiment	1st Battalion, 48th Regiment
271st Anti-Aircraft Regiment	1 105mm battery
203rd Tank Regiment	
Elements of 202nd Special Weapons Tank Regiment	*Never made it to Loc Ninh itself

Note: The (–) notation means that an organic, assigned subordinate unit is not located with the parent headquarters. Thus, "429th Sapper Group (–)" indicates that part of that unit is absent.

Battle of An Loc, 9–15 April 1972

9th VC Division	5th Division
271st Regiment	7th Regiment (minus 1 battalion)
272nd Regiment	8th Regiment
95C Regiment	Task Force 52
	1st Battalion, 52nd Regiment
69th Artillery Division	1st Battalion, 48th Regiment
42nd Artillery Regiment	3rd Ranger Group
208th Rocket Regiment	
271st Anti-Aircraft Regiment	1st Airborne Brigade (–)*
	5th Battalion
203rd Tank Regiment (2 battalions)	6th Battalion
	8th Battalion
Elements of 202nd Special Weapons	81st Ranger Battalion
Tank Regiment	
	2 battalions Binh Long RF/PF
429th Sapper Group (–)	
	*Arrived 15 April

Battle of An Loc, 19–22 April 1972

9th VC Division	5th Division
271st Regiment	7th Regiment (minus 1 battalion)
272nd Regiment	8th Regiment
95C Regiment	Task Force 52
	1st Battalion, 52nd Regiment
203rd Tank Regiment (2 battalions)	1st Battalion, 48th Regiment
	3rd Ranger Group
Elements of 202nd Special Weapons	
Tank Regiment	1st Airborne Brigade (–)
	5th Battalion
141st Regiment (7th NVA Division)	6th Battalion
	8th Battalion
275th Regiment (5th VC Division)	81st Ranger Battalion
69th Artillery Division	2 battalions Binh Long RF/PF
42nd Artillery Regiment	
208th Rocket Regiment	
271st Anti-Aircraft Regiment	
429th Sapper Group (–)	

Battle of An Loc, 9 May–30 June 1972

9th VC Division	5th Division
271st Regiment	7th Regiment (minus 1 battalion)
272nd Regiment	8th Regiment
95C Regiment	Task Force 52
	1st Battalion, 52nd Regiment
5th VC Division	1st Battalion, 48th Regiment
174th Regiment	3rd Ranger Group
275th Regiment	
E6 Regiment	1st Airborne Brigade (–)*
141st Regiment (7th NVA Division)	5th Battalion
165th Regiment (7th NVA Division)	6th Battalion
	8th Battalion
203rd Tank Regiment (2 battalions)	81st Ranger Battalion
Elements of 202nd Special Weapons	2 battalions Binh Long RF/PF
Tank Regiment	
141st Regiment (7th NVA Division)	
275th Regiment (5th VC Division)	
69th Artillery Division	
42nd Artillery Regiment	
208th Rocket Regiment	
271st Anti-Aircraft Regiment	
429th Sapper Group (–)	*Withdrawn 18 June

Battle for Highway 13, 10 April–20 July 1972

7th NVA Division	21st Division
141st Regiment (departed for An Loc, 16 April)	31st Regiment
	32nd Regiment
165th Regiment (departed for An Loc, 7 May)	33rd Regiment
	9th Armored Cavalry Regiment
209th Regiment	15th Regiment (OPCON)*
101st Regiment (Independent)	46th Regiment (OPCON)*
Elements of the 69th Artillery Division	3rd Airborne Brigade (30 days only)
42nd Artillery Regiment (–)	
208th Rocket Regiment (–)	
271st Anti-Aircraft Regiment (–)	*The 15th and 46th were placed under the operational control (OPCON) of the 21st ARVN Division during the battle.

Source: Major General James F. Hollingsworth, "Communist Invasion in Military Region III," unpublished narrative, 1972. (Microfiche reel 44, University Publications of America: Records of Military Assistance Command, Vietnam.)

PRESIDENTIAL UNIT CITATION, 229TH AVIATION BATTALION

By virtue of the authority vested in me as President of the United States and as Commander in Chief of the Armed Forces of the United States, I have today awarded

THE PRESIDENTIAL UNIT CITATION (ARMY)
FOR EXTRAORDINARY HEROISM
TO THE
229TH ASSAULT HELICOPTER BATTALION
1ST CAVALRY DIVISION, UNITED STATES ARMY
AND ITS FOLLOWING ASSIGNED AND ATTACHED UNITS:
HEADQUARTERS AND HEADQUARTERS COMPANY, 229TH
ASSAULT HELICOPTER BATTALION
(5 April to 7 July 1972)
DETACHMENT 1, HEADQUARTERS AND HEADQUARTERS
COMPANY,
229TH ASSAULT HELICOPTER BATTALION
(5 April to 15 June 1972)
COMPANIES A, B, AND D, 229TH ASSAULT HELICOPTER
BATTALION
(5 April to 7 July 1972)
TROOP F, 9TH CAVALRY (5 April to 7 July 1972)
BATTERY F, 79TH AERIAL FIELD ARTILLERY (5 April to 7 July 1972)
AND THE
362ND AVIATION COMPANY (5 April to 7 July 1972)

The 229th Assault Helicopter Battalion distinguished itself by extraordinary heroism in action against a hostile force during the period 5 April
1972 through 7 July 1972 while serving in support of the Government of
Vietnam defenders of the provincial capital of An Loc, Binh Long Province during the North Vietnamese Army "NGUYEN HUE" Offensive.
Through their courage, determination, and ingenuity the troopers of the
229th Assault Helicopter Battalion and assigned and attached units, overcame the difficulties engendered by the introduction of new weaponry by
the enemy and the most intensive volume of anti-aircraft artillery fire yet
experienced, while supporting and sustaining the beleaguered defenders against the enemy onslaught. The successful defeat of the enemy by
the forces of the Government of Vietnam would have been vastly more
prolonged and costly were it not for the invaluable support rendered by
the 229th Assault Helicopter Battalion. The outstanding devotion to duty,
perseverance, and extraordinary heroism of the members of the 229th Assault Helicopter Battalion and its assigned and attached units under the
most hazardous conditions are in keeping with the finest traditions of the
United States Army and reflect great credit upon themselves, the Army,
and the United States of America.

                                                            Richard M. Nixon
                                                            15 May 1974

PRESIDENTIAL UNIT CITATION, ADVISORY TEAM 70

DEPARTMENT OF THE ARMY

THIS IS TO CERTIFY THAT
THE PRESIDENT OF THE UNITED STATES OF AMERICA
HAS AWARDED THE

PRESIDENTIAL UNIT CITATION

TO THE

UNITED STATES ARMY COMBAT ASSISTANCE TEAM 70

FOR
EXTRAORDINARY HEROISM IN MILITARY
OPERATIONS AGAINST AN ARMED ENEMY.

APRIL–JULY 1972

GIVEN UNDER MY HAND IN THE CITY OF WASHINGTON
THIS 11THE DAY OF FEBRUARY 1999

SECRETARY OF THE ARMY
By direction of the President of the United States the Presidential Unit
Citation is awarded to:

UNITED STATES ARMY COMBAT ASSISTANCE TEAM 70

for outstanding heroism against an armed enemy:

During the period April 1972 to July 1972, the Combat Assistance Team 70 distinguished themselves in the critical Battle and Siege of An Loc in the Republic of Vietnam. In support of the Army Republic of Vietnam 5th Division, the United States officer-advisers rallied the beleaguered defenders to overcome seemingly insurmountable odds. Though outnumbered by more that 5:1 (36,000 enemy troops to 5,800 defenders), supplied only by air-drops and occasional daring C-130 deliveries and pounded night and day by the war's heaviest and most sustained artillery and tank assaults, An Loc managed to prevail. By coolly coordinating the United States air support and re-supply, pinpointing B52 strikes to break up enemy attacks, helping to direct perimeter defenses, assuring life-saving food, water, and medicine to the Army Republic of Vietnam defenders as well as to some 5000 desperate civilian refugees, and above all by bolstering morale through their example of unflagging determination and *Esprit De Corps*, the United States Army's An Loc advisers performed a pivotal role turning back the enemy's massive surprise offensive of 1972. In so doing, they helped to save Saigon for another three years, assured the safe withdrawal of our remaining combat forces, and assisted in making possible the January 1973 peace agreement for release of American Prisoners of War. The United States Army's Combat Assistance Team 70 served nobly in the highest and most honored tradition of the Army and the United States of America.

NOTES

KEY TO NOTE ABBREVIATIONS

CARL   Combined Arms Research Library, Fort Leavenworth, Kansas
CMH   Histories Division, U.S. Army Center of Military History, Washington, D.C.
MHI   U.S. Military History Institute, Carlisle Barracks, Pennsylvania
Texas Tech   Indochina Collection, Texas Tech University Archive of the Vietnam Conflict, Lubbock, Texas

INTRODUCTION

1. Douglas Pike, *PAVN: People's Army of Vietnam* (Novato, Calif.: Presidio Press, 1986), p. 229.

2. Philip C. Clarke, "The Battle That Saved Saigon," *Reader's Digest*, March 1973, p. 151.

1. PRELUDE TO BATTLE

1. George C. Herring, *America's Longest War: The United States and Vietnam, 1950–1975* (New York: Knopf, 1979), p. 198.

2. James Lawton Collins Jr., *The Development and Training of the South Vietnamese Army, 1950–1972* (Washington, D.C.: U.S. Government Printing Office, 1975), pp. 90–91.

3. Herring, *America's Longest War*, p. 232; Major General Nguyen Duy Hinh, *Vietnamization and the Cease-Fire*, Indochina Monographs (Washington, D.C.: U.S. Army Center of Military History, 1980), p. 47.

4. State of Vietnam, Ministry of National Defense. Memorandum: Principles Authorizing TRIM Advisers with Units and Formations of the Vietnamese National Armed Forces, Saigon, 10 April 1955, CARL.

5. David Fulghum and Terrence Maitland, *South Vietnam on Trial, Mid-1970 to 1972* (Boston: Boston Publishing Company, 1984), p. 56.

6. Prior to 1971, the military regions were known as corps tactical zones.

7. General Cao Van Vien, Lieutenant General Ngo Quang Truong, Lieutenant General Dong Van Khuyen, Major General Nguyen Duy Hinh, Brigadier General Tran Dinh Tho, Colonel Hoang Ngoc Lung, and Lieutenant Colonel Chu Xuan Vien, *The U.S. Adviser*, Indochina Monographs (Washington, D.C.: U.S. Army Center of Military History, 1980), p. 16.

8. The NVA were more formally known as Quan Doi Nhan Dan Viet Nam, or People's Army of Vietnam. This study will use the more common "NVA."

9. Dale Andradé, *America's Last Vietnam Battle* (Lawrence: University Press of Kansas, 2001), p. 340.

10. Jeffrey C. Clarke, *Advice and Support: The Final Years—The U.S. Army in Vietnam* (Washington, D.C.: U.S. Army Center of Military History, 1987), p. 452.

11. A cluster bomb unit consists of a compact group of small fragmentation bomblets enclosed in a cannister. When the cannister is released from the aircraft, the bomblets are scattered over a small area and explode on impact.

12. Quoted in "The War That Won't Go Away," *Newsweek*, 17 April 1972, p. 17.

13. Lewis Sorley, *A Better War: The Unexamined Victories and Final Tragedy of America's Last Years in Vietnam* (New York: Harcourt Brace, 1999), pp. 307–309.

14. Headquarters, Pacific Command, Directorate of Operations Analysis, *Contemporary Historical Examination of Current Operations (CHECO) Report: The Battle for An Loc, 5 April–26 June 1972*, Honolulu, 1973, p. xiii. Hereafter cited as *CHECO Report: Battle for An Loc*.

2. THE NGUYEN HUE CAMPAIGN

1. Andradé, *America's Last Vietnam Battle*, p. 22.

2. This summary of North Vietnamese strategic thinking is drawn from David W. P. Elliott, *NLF-DRV Strategy and the 1972 Spring Offensive* (Ithaca, N.Y.: Cornell University, International Relations of East Asia, IREA Project, January 1974) and Lieutenant General Ngo Quang Truong, *The Easter Offensive of 1972*, Indochina Monographs (Washington, D.C.: U.S. Army Center of Military History, 1980), pp. 157–158. Phillip B. Davidson, in *Vietnam at War: The History 1946–1975* (Novato, Calif.: Presidio Press, 1988), pp. 606–607, suggests that one of the reasons that the senior members of the Politburo voted for launching the offensive in 1972 rather than waiting until 1973 when virtually all U.S. combat power would be gone from the region was that these senior leaders, averaging 60 years of age, wanted to end the war with a resounding military victory, not some negotiated "half loaf" settlement.

3. Military History Institute of Vietnam, *Victory in Vietnam: The Official History of the People's Army of Vietnam, 1954–1975*, trans. Merle L. Pribbenow (Lawrence: University Press of Kansas, 2002), pp. 283–284.

4. Military History Institute of Vietnam, *Report to General Vo Nguyen Giap: A Consolidated Report on the Fight against the United States for the Salvation of Vietnam by Our People*, trans. Duong Bui (Defense Language Institute Foreign Language Center, Presidio of Monterey, California, 1996), p. 30; originally published in Hanoi, 1987.

5. Ilya V. Gaiduk, *The Soviet Union and the Vietnam War* (Chicago: I. R. Dee, 1996), pp. 231–232.

6. Qiang Zhai, *China and the Vietnam Wars, 1950–1975* (Chapel Hill: University of North Carolina Press, 2000), pp. 195–196. The author maintains that Beijing had already begun to increase weapons shipments to North Vietnam earlier in 1971 to convince the Politburo in Hanoi that China's opening to America would not undermine their war effort.

China's aid to North Vietnam would reach record levels in 1972–1973. See Chen Jian, *Mao's China and the Cold War* (Chapel Hill: University of North Carolina Press, 2001), p. 228, for table showing China's military aid to Vietnam, 1964–1975.

7. Ngo Quang Truong, *Easter Offensive of 1972*, pp. 8–9. Louis A. Fanning, *Betrayal in Vietnam* (New Rochelle, N.Y.: Arlington House, 1976), p. 105, asserts that the Soviets provided more than just equipment. Citing Hanoi International News Service in English, 29 March 1972, he writes that the Soviets also provided high-ranking advisers for the invasion. According to Fanning, the Soviet delegation included Marshal Pavel F. Batitsky, a member of the Central Committee of the Communist Party of the Soviet Union; Lieutenant General A. N. Sevchenko, representing the General Political Department of the Soviet Air and Naval Forces; and Lieutenant General of Artillery F. M. Bolarenko, Soviet Antiaircraft Missile Forces. According to the cited article, the visitors spent their time visiting "various air force missile, navy and infantry units."

8. Dave Richard Palmer, *Summons of the Trumpet: U.S.-Vietnam in Perspective* (San Rafael, Calif.: Presidio Press, 1978), on p. 248, wrote that 350 Soviet ships brought weapons and equipment to North Vietnamese ports in 1971. David Fulghum and Terrence Maitland, *South Vietnam on Trial*, p. 120, estimated that Red China and the Soviets sent $1.5 billion in military aid during 1970–1972.

9. Military History Institute of Vietnam, *Victory in Vietnam*, p. 283.

10. U.S. Military Assistance Command, Vietnam, Special Intelligence Report (Declassified): "The Nguyen Hue Offensive—Historical Study of Lessons Learned," Saigon, January 1973, p. C-1, CARL. Hereafter cited as MACV, "Nguyen Hue Offensive."

11. Major General James F. Hollingsworth, "Communist Invasion in Military Region III," unpublished narrative, 1972, in Robert Lester, ed., *Records of the Military Assistance Command, Vietnam, Part 1: The War in Vietnam, 1954–1973* (Bethesda, Md.: University Publications of America, 1988), MACV Historical Office Documentary Collection, microfilm reel 44, p. 21. Hereafter cited as Hollingsworth, "Communist Invasion."

12. Ngo Quang Truong, *Easter Offensive of 1972*, p. 158.

13. Quoted in Fulghum and Maitland, *South Vietnam on Trial*, p. 122.

14. General Cao Van Vien and Lieutenant General Dong Van Khuyen, *Reflections on the Vietnam War*, Indochina Monographs (Washington, D.C.: U.S. Army Center of Military History, 1980), p. 104.

15. "War That Won't Go Away," p. 16.

16. "The Air War Grows," *Newsweek*, 24 April 1972, p. 32.

17. Major A. J. C. Lavalle, ed., *Airpower and the 1972 Spring Offensive*, United States Air Force Southeast Asia Monograph Series (Washington, D.C.: U.S. Government Printing Office, 1976), p. 25.

18. Walter J. Boyne, "The Easter Halt," *Air Force*, September 1998, p. 63.

19. "Vietnamization: A Policy under the Gun," *Time*, 17 April 1972, p. 38.

20. Quoted in Lewis Sorley, "Courage and Blood: South Vietnam's Repulse of the 1972 Easter Invasion," *Parameters*, Summer 1999, p. 40.

3. THE AREA OF OPERATIONS

1. Shelby L. Stanton, *Vietnam Order of Battle* (New York: Galahad Books, 1986), pp. 375, 380.

2. For an account of Hollingsworth's World War II exploits, see Cornelius Ryan, *The Last Battle* (New York: Simon and Schuster, 1966).

3. Andradé, *America's Last Vietnam Battle*, p. 340.

4. Ibid., p. 340. Andradé reports that Hollingsworth made it a point to learn the first name of every officer in his command and was known to write personal letters to the children of his advisers, telling them how sorry he was that their fathers could not be home with them but that they were doing extremely important work in Vietnam.

5. The designation "route" indicates a provincial road, often unpaved, while "highway" denotes a major paved national artery.

6. The border ranger battalions had previously been part of the Civilian Irregular Defense Group (CIDG) program run by the CIA and U.S. Special Forces. CIDG forces conducted a number of missions along the borders of South Vietnam with Cambodia and Laos, such as surveillance and interdiction of Communist infiltration. The conversion from CIDG camps to border ranger battalions began in 1970, and the last two camps were converted in January 1971.

7. The discussion of the relationship between Miller and Hung is based on interviews and communication with Colonel Miller. It was impossible to get General Hung's side of things because he committed suicide shortly after the fall of Saigon in 1975.

8. Military History Institute of Vietnam, *Victory in Vietnam*, p. 295; Military History Institute of Vietnam, *The Nguyen Hue Offensive Campaign in Eastern Cochin China*, trans. Merle L. Pribbenow (unpublished trans., n.d.), p. 15; originally published as *Chien Dich Tien Cong Nguyen Hue Mien Dong Bo—Nam 1972–Luu Hanh Noi Bo* (Hanoi: Military History Institute of the Ministry of Defense, 1988). The campaign political commissar was Major General Tran Do.

9. Military History Institute of Vietnam, *Nguyen Hue Offensive Campaign*, pp. 34–38.

10. The T-54 was the most advanced tank that the USSR had given to any of its allies or satellites to that time. It was powered by a water-cooled diesel engine that delivered ample power for its weight. However, its construction from magnesium alloy made it highly flammable. It had a 100mm gun and carried a basic main gun load of 34 rounds of armor-piercing high-explosive shells. The Soviet PT-76, also used at An Loc, was much lighter than the T-54. However, it was an excellent reconnaissance vehicle with an amphibious capability; it had a waterjet propulsion system that permitted it to traverse fairly wide, swift-flowing waterways.

4. THE BATTLE OF LOC NINH

1. Headquarters, 5th Division Combat Assistance Team, Advisory Team 70, "After-Action Report, Binh Long Campaign, 1972," TRAC, 20 July 1972, pp. 1–2, CMH. Hereafter cited as 5th ARVN Division AAR.

2. U.S. Military Assistance Command, Vietnam, Periodic Intelligence Report (PER-INTREP), no. 4–72, 14 February 1972, p. 12, CMH.

3. 5th ARVN Division AAR, p. 2.

4. U.S. Military Assistance Command, Vietnam, Military History Branch, *Command History, 1972–1973*, vol. II (Saigon, 1973), p. J-1, CARL. Hereafter cited as MACV, *Command History, 1972–1973*.

5. Ngo Quang Truong, *Easter Offensive of 1972*, p. 110.

6. Tong Le Chon Base remained under ARVN control against all odds until April 1974. Although attacked repeatedly, the rangers fought courageously, never giving ground. After the cease-fire in January 1973, the base was besieged and repeatedly attacked by elements of the 7th NVA and 9th VC Divisions, in clear violation of the provisions of the cease-fire agreement.

7. MACV, *Command History, 1972–1973*, vol. II, p. J-1.

8. Ibid., p. J-3.

9. 5th ARVN Division AAR, pp. 3–30.

10. MACV, *Command History, 1972–1973*, vol. II, p. J-2; Military History Institute of Vietnam, *Nguyen Hue Offensive Campaign*, pp. 34–38.

11. Andradé, *America's Last Vietnam Battle*, p. 357; Ngo Quang Truong, *Easter Offensive of 1972*, p. 115.

12. Later, one of the advisers on the ground in Loc Ninh, Captain Mark Smith, maintained that there were also elements of the 9th VC Division participating in the battle. Bo Tu Lenh Thiet Giap [Armor Command], *Mot So Tran Danh Cua Bo Doi Thiet Gap, Tap IV* (A number of battles fought by our armor troops, vol. IV) (Hanoi: General Staff Printing Plant, 1983), p. 54, identifies the tanks at Loc Ninh as being from the 10th Company of the 20th Tank Battalion reinforced with two ZSU-57/2 self-propelled antiaircraft guns.

13. For purposes of clarity, time will be expressed using the military 24-hour clock; thus 6:00 A.M. will be expressed as 0600.

14. Captain Ron Timberlake, F Troop, 9th Cavalry, and Captain Michael Sloniker, A Company, 229th Aviation, 3rd Brigade, 1st Cavalry Division, unpublished narrative, 1999, p. 1, Texas Tech.

15. Most of the description of this battle comes from Captain Mark A. Smith, "Battle of Loc Ninh, RVN, 5–7 April 1972," unpublished narrative (Fort Bragg, North Carolina, 21 October 1976); copy in author's possession.

16. *CHECO Report: Battle for An Loc*, p. 7.

17. Timberlake and Sloniker, unpublished narrative, p. 2.

18. Major General James F. Hollingsworth, back-channel message to General Creighton C. Abrams, "Daily Commander's Evaluation," 6 April 1972, in Lester, ed., *Records*, microfilm reel 44. Further citations of Hollingsworth back-channel messages refer to this source.

19. Colonel Walter F. Ulmer Jr., "Anti-Aircraft Employment on a Battlefield in South Vietnam," *Armor*, May–June 1974, p. 24.

20. Hollingsworth, back-channel message, 7 April 1972.

21. *CHECO Report: Battle for An Loc*, p. 10.

22. Miller later said that he did not know who had requested this strike, but he believed the request came from III Corps headquarters.

23. Quoted in Andradé, *America's Last Vietnam Battle*, p. 372.

24. Smith and the army are at odds about what happened that day in the bunker. There were no other surviving witnesses, and Smith steadfastly maintains that the incident happened just as he reported it. For a full description of the controversy, see Andradé, *America's Last Vietnam Battle*, p. 525 n. 8.

25. Timberlake and Sloniker, unpublished narrative, p. 4.

26. "Major Ran for His Life 4 Days—and Won," *Pacific Stars and Stripes*, 29 April 1972.

27. In 1998, there was an unsuccessful effort by several general officers to have Captain Smith awarded the Medal of Honor. Major Davidson and Captain Wanat were also awarded the Distinguished Service Cross.

28. 5th ARVN Division AAR, p. 7.

29. Quoted in Andradé, *America's Last Vietnam Battle*, p. 374, and imparted to the author by Colonel Miller on numerous occasions during discussions about the battle. It is clear that Miller still feels responsibility to this day for what happened at Loc Ninh.

30. Hollingsworth, back-channel message, 7 April 1972.

31. Captain Marvin C. Zumwalt, Adviser, 52nd Infantry, interview by Major John

Cash, Military Assistance Command, Vietnam, SJS-History, 3rd Field Hospital, Saigon, 18–19 April 1972, pp. 1–2, Texas Tech. Hereafter cited as Zumwalt interview.

32. Dale Andradé, "Three Days on the Run," *Vietnam*, August 1990, p. 40.

33. For some unknown reason (at least to the advisers on the ground), the medevac helicopters had all been painted white, with large red crosses on them, supposedly so the enemy could differentiate the evacuation helicopters from those performing combat missions. Most medevac pilots agreed that all this did was make them better targets for the North Vietnamese gunners.

34. MACV, *Command History, 1972–1973*, vol. II, p. J-8.

35. Zumwalt interview, p. 2.

36. MACV, *Command History, 1972–1973*, vol. II, p. J-8.

37. Lieutenant Colonel Walter D. Ginger, Headquarters, Advisory Team 87, "After-Action Report, Task Force 52," Xuan Loc, South Vietnam, May 1972, p. 5, Texas Tech; Miller, unpublished manuscript, section III, "Hung Tam Task Force 52," p. 5, copy in author's possession.

38. Ginger, "After-Action Report, Task Force 52," p. 6; Miller, unpublished manuscript, section III, "Hung Tam Task Force 52," p. 5.

39. Quoted in Andradé, "Three Days on the Run," p. 42.

40. Ibid., p. 43.

41. The mission was flown in M24 protective masks, because a preceding B-52 strike had mixed CS riot control agent with high explosive (HE) and the gas was still floating over the PZ.

42. Timberlake and Sloniker, unpublished narrative, p. 14.

43. An unsuccessful attempt was made in 1998 to have John Whitehead's award upgraded to the Medal of Honor. The deputy brigade commander remarked on the day that it happened that if Whitehead had landed within sight of journalists, he would have been assured the Medal of Honor.

44. "After Attack on An Loc," *Los Angeles Times*, 17 April 1972.

45. Quoted in MACV, *Command History, 1972–1973*, vol. II, p. J-7.

46. Message, CG TRAC to all U.S. Elms MR3, Subject: Tactical Alert, 7 April 1972, CMH.

5. THE OPENING BATTLE FOR AN LOC

1. Brigadier General John R. McGiffert, interview by Major Walter S. Dillard, Military Assistance Command, Vietnam, SJS-History, Saigon, 10 October 1972, p. 7, MHI. Hereafter cited as McGiffert interview.

2. Ngo Quang Truong, *Easter Offensive of 1972*, p. 115.

3. Major John Howard, "The War We Came to Fight: A Study of the Battle of An Loc, April–June 1972" (U.S. Army Command and General Staff College, Fort Leavenworth, Kans., June 1974, unpublished student paper), p. 29, CARL.

4. Quoted in *CHECO Report: Battle for An Loc*, p. 16.

5. Ian Ward, "North Vietnam's Blitzkrieg—Why Giap Did It: Report from Saigon," *Conflict Studies*, October 1972, p. 5.

6. McGiffert interview, p. 17.

7. "In Furious Battle," *Newsweek*, 24 April 1972, p. 32; Fulghum and Maitland, *South Vietnam on Trial*, p. 152.

8. Nguyen Quoc Khue, "LD3/BDQ Voi Tran Chien An Loc/Binh Long" (3rd Ranger Group and the Battle of An Loc/Binh Long), *Tap San Biet Dong Quan* [Ranger Magazine], issue 7, 2003, p. 81 (trans. Merle Pribbenow).

9. "Reds Cut Viet Road Links," *Pacific Stars and Stripes*, 10 April 1972.

10. Ngo Quang Truong, *Easter Offensive of 1972*, p. 118.

11. This exchange and the rest of the description of the contentious relationship between the South Vietnamese general and his American counterpart come from Colonel Miller's unpublished manuscript, section IV, "Gathering of Forces."

12. Quoted from the minutes of the COSVN Military Headquarters meeting held on the night of 6 April, found in a review of the campaign by the Military History Institute of Vietnam, *Nguyen Hue Offensive Campaign*, p. 39.

13. Bo Tu Lenh Thiet Giap [Armor Command], *Mot So Tran Danh Cua Bo Doi Thiet Gap, Tap IV* (A number of battles fought by our armor troops, volume IV), p. 40.

14. MACV, "Nguyen Hue Offensive," p. C-1.

15. Quoted in *CHECO Report: Battle for An Loc*, p. 16.

16. From author's e-mail and telephone discussion with Mike Wheeler, WO1, an assault helicopter pilot with A Company, 229th Aviation, 11 September 2003.

17. When the battle for An Loc began, there were eight artillery pieces in the center of the city. However, these guns were destroyed by NVA artillery on the first day of fighting. Thus, the defenders had no friendly artillery support for most of the battle.

18. *CHECO Report: Battle for An Loc*, p. 16.

19. The (–) notation means that an organic, assigned subordinate unit is not located with the parent headquarters. Thus, 8th Regiment (–) indicates that one of its battalions is not present.

20. Headquarters, U.S. Military Assistance Command, Vietnam, Pacification Studies Group, Office of the Director, CORDS, "Debriefing: An Loc Siege Experiences," Saigon, 27 June 1972, p. 5, CARL. Hereafter cited as "An Loc Siege Experiences."

21. MACV, *Command History, 1972–1973*, vol. II, p. J-12.

22. Ward, "North Vietnam's Blitzkrieg," p. 6.

23. In August after I got out of the hospital, I visited Combined Intelligence Center, Vietnam. While there, one of the civilian analysts showed me a file drawer full of tank photos taken in Cambodia by persons unnamed. When I asked why word of these sightings was not passed down the chain to those of us in the field, the analysts replied, "Well, Captain, you didn't have a need to know." Obviously, this was not the answer that I was looking for.

24. *Attack Helicopters—The Cobra*, 58 min., Discovery Wings Channel, 1999, videocassette.

25. "An Adviser's 2-Month Nightmare Ends," *Pacific Stars and Stripes*, 4 June 1972.

26. Fulghum and Maitland, *South Vietnam on Trial*, p. 120.

27. K. N. Stacey, "North Vietnamese Armor Operations: The Lessons of 1972 and 1975," *Armor*, July–August 1981, p. 50.

28. Bo Tu Lenh Thiet Giap [Armor Command], *Mot So Tran Danh Cua Bo Doi Thiet Gap, Tap IV* (A number of battles fought by our armor troops, volume IV), p. 41.

29. Ngo Quang Truong, *Easter Offensive of 1972*, p. 121.

30. The VC and NVA had used the agents-in-place method very effectively during the 1968 Tet Offensive when their troops overran Hue, the old imperial capital.

31. "Lai Khe: The Cav at Work," *Armed Forces Journal*, June 1972, p. 18.

32. Timberlake and Sloniker, unpublished narrative, pp. 19–20.

33. Memorandum, DCAT 70 for Brigadier General James F. Hamlet, Subject: Battle of An Loc, An Loc, 5 April 1972 to 10 May 1972, dated 13 May 1972, 2, Texas Tech.

34. Timberlake and Sloniker, unpublished narrative, p. 20. Captains Timberlake and Sloniker returned the thought, writing that "Colonel Miller was an instrument of the attack helicopter's salvation."

35. Tran Van Nhut, "The Unfinished War" (Santa Ana: unpublished manuscript, n.d.), p. 162.

36. Bo Tu Lenh Thiet Giap [Armor Command], *Mot So Tran Danh Cua Bo Doi Thiet Gap, Tap IV* (A number of battles fought by our armor troops, volume IV), p. 6.

37. *Attack Helicopters—The Cobra.*

38. Charles Black, "Mistakes Help An Loc Allied Force," *Columbus Enquirer* (Georgia), 20 May 1972.

39. Clarke, "Battle That Saved Saigon," p. 153.

40. "An Adviser's 2-Month Nightmare Ends"; K. G. Mortensen, *The Battle of An Loc, 1972* (Parkville, Victoria, Australia: Gerald Griffin Press, 1996), p. 69.

41. By 1975, Vy was a brigadier general in command of the 5th ARVN Division. When the North Vietnamese overran the presidential palace in April 1975, Vy committed suicide.

42. Truong Nhu Tang, *Vietcong Memoir: An Inside Account of the Vietnam War and Its Aftermath* (New York: Harcourt Brace Jovanovich, 1983), pp. 167–168.

43. John Morrocco, *Rain of Fire: Air War, 1969–1973* (Boston: Boston Publishing Company, 1985), p. 105.

44. MACV, *Command History, 1972–1973*, vol. II, p. J-13.

45. Lavalle, ed., *Airpower and the 1972 Spring Offensive*, p. 85.

46. Hollingsworth, back-channel message, 14 April 1972.

47. Mortensen, *Battle of An Loc, 1972*, p. 28.

48. Bo Tu Lenh Thiet Giap [Armor Command], *Mot So Tran Danh Cua Bo Doi Thiet Gap, Tap IV* (A number of battles fought by our armor troops, volume IV), p. 46, states that this was the first time that the 8th Tank Company had seen combat.

49. "An Loc Siege Experiences," p. 7. I heard of this incident during the battle, but did not personally witness the events that the province officials described.

50. Tran Van Nhut, "Unfinished War," p. 186.

51. Major John D. Howard, "An Infantryman Remembers An Loc and the Air Force" (U.S. Army Command and General Staff College, Fort Leavenworth, Kans., unpublished student paper, March 1974), p. 1.

52. Leon Daniel, "An Loc Rapidly Becoming a Pile of Rubble," *Pacific Stars and Stripes*, 23 April 1972.

53. *CHECO Report: Battle for An Loc*, p. 19.

54. At various times during peaks in the fighting, there were four FACs orbiting over the city.

55. Hollingsworth, back-channel message, 15 April 1972.

56. Ngo Quang Truong, *Easter Offensive of 1972*, p. 122.

57. Timberlake and Sloniker, unpublished narrative, p. 22.

58. Ngo Quang Truong, *Easter Offensive of 1972*, p. 122.

59. Hollingsworth, "Communist Invasion," p. 9.

60. "Lai Khe: The Cav at Work," p. 18.

61. Hollingsworth, back-channel message, 16 April 1972.

62. MACV, *Command History, 1972–1973*, vol. II, p. J-14.

63. Quoted in 5th ARVN Division AAR, p. D-12.

64. Ibid.

65. Message, Miller to Hollingsworth, 17 April 1972, subj: For Information, CMH.

66. MACV, "Nguyen Hue Offensive," p. C-2.

67. MACV, *Command History, 1972–1973*, vol. II, p. J-15; Hollingsworth, "Communist Invasion," p. 10.

68. Ngo Quang Truong, *Easter Offensive of 1972*, p. 123; Nguyen Duy Hinh, *Vietnamization and the Cease-Fire*, p. 103.

69. "Tells How Reds Died: Chained Inside of Tanks," *Pacific Stars and Stripes*, 18 April 1972. There were other reports that NVA soldiers were tied to their antiaircraft guns and mortars, but I never personally saw this, and such reports are doubtful at best.

70. POWs later said that the chaining was done ceremonially, and individuals had been prompted to volunteer for the chaining ceremony as a mark of distinction. Many of the tankers had their arms tattooed with slogans such as "Drive Fiercely" and "Attack Deeply." "An Loc Siege Experiences," p. 2.

6. SECOND ATTACK ON AN LOC

1. Quoted in Andradé, *America's Last Vietnam Battle*, p. 402.

2. Headquarters, 1st Airborne Brigade, "Combat After-Action Report, 1st Airborne Brigade," Saigon, 22 July 1972, p. 3, CARL. Hereafter cited as 1st Airborne, CAAR.

3. 5th ARVN Division AAR, p. 29. By this time, only one 105mm howitzer remained operational in the city.

4. 5th ARVN Division Daily Journal, 20–21 April 1972, CMH.

5. 5th ARVN Division AAR, p. 32.

6. Clarke, "Battle That Saved Saigon," p. 154.

7. "An Adviser's 2-Month Nightmare Ends."

8. Pham Nhat Nam, "An Loc: The Unquiet East," trans. John C. Shafer (Center for Southeast Asian Studies, Northern Illinois University, DeKalb, Ill., unpublished monograph, n.d.), pp. 10–11.

9. Nguyen Quoc Khue, "LD3/BDQ Voi Tran Chien An Loc/Binh Long" (3rd Ranger Group and the battle of An Loc/Binh Long), *Tap San Biet Dong Quan* [Ranger Magazine], p. 88.

10. "An Loc: A Battlefield in Hell," *Pacific Stars and Stripes*, 1 May 1972. The devastation in An Loc, after a week of almost constant shelling and repeated ground attacks, was like nothing I, or any of the other advisers, had ever seen.

11. "An Loc Siege Experiences," p. 9. The refugees estimated that as many as 500 people were executed in Loc Ninh by the North Vietnamese.

12. Andradé, *America's Last Vietnam Battle*, p. 379; Mortensen, *Battle of An Loc, 1972*, p. 87.

13. Headquarters, Third Regional Assistance Command, Command Center Duty Log, 23 April 1972.

14. Quoted in "The Relief of An Loc," *Newsweek*, 26 June 1972, p. 34.

15. Pham Nhat Nam, "An Loc: The Unquiet East," p. 11.

16. Personal observations of author; Major Raymond Haney, adviser, Task Force 52, interview by Major John Cash, Military Assistance Command, Vietnam, SJS-History, 19 April 1972, 3d Field Hospital, Saigon, p. 2, MHI. The bodies still lay strewn along the highway when we carried Major Haney to an area south of the city where he was picked up by a medevac helicopter.

17. Nguyen Quoc Khue, "LD3/BDQ Voi Tran Chien An Loc/Binh Long" (3rd Ranger Group and the battle of An Loc/Binh Long), *Tap San Biet Dong Quan* [Ranger Magazine], p. 90.

18. Ward, "North Vietnam's Blitzkreig," p. 6.

19. Headquarters, Third Regional Assistance Command, Command Center Duty Log, 16 April 1972, in Lester, ed., *Records*, microfilm reel 44.

20. Nick Thimmesch, "A Grisly Story," *Pacific Stars and Stripes*, 13 May 1972, and personal observation of author.

21. Tran Van Nhut, "Unfinished War," p. 182.

22. Howard, "War We Came to Fight," p. 18.

23. "On Highway 13: The Long Road to An Loc," *Time*, 24 April 1972, p. 27.

24. 5th ARVN Division AAR, p. 12.

25. Ibid.

26. Ray L. Bowers, *Tactical Airlift. The United States Air Force in Southeast Asia* (Washington, D.C.: Office of Air Force History, 1983), p 539.

27. Sam McGowan, "Easter Airlift," *Vietnam*, April 1994, p. 48.

28. In 1973, Major Brya would fly to Hanoi to pick up the first group of American prisoners of war released after the Paris Peace Accords were signed.

29. Bowers, *Tactical Airlift*, p. 543.

30. Headquarters, Pacific Command, Directorate of Operations Analysis, *Contemporary Historical Examination of Current Operations (CHECO) Report: Airlift to Besieged Areas, 7 April–31 August 1972*, Honolulu, 1973, p. 8.

31. "In Furious Battle," p. 33.

32. Transcript of speech by Brigadier General Edward Brya, given at U.S. Air Force Tanker Convention, Seattle, 1995; copy in author's possession. Hereafter cited as Brya speech.

33. In one such instance, the author observed a group of ARVN soldiers crouched around the wreckage of a pallet of peaches as they picked through the crushed cans, eating the remains on the spot as if they were shucking oysters at the beach.

34. Bowers, *Tactical Airlift*, p. 545.

35. Fulghum and Maitland, *South Vietnam on Trial*, p. 153.

36. Bowers, *Tactical Airlift*, p. 547.

37. Major Amesbury's remains were not recovered for 29 years; he was buried with full military honors in May 2001.

38. Morrocco, *Rain of Fire*, p. 118, and personal experience of the author.

39. Hollingsworth, "Communist Invasion," p. 13; *CHECO Report: Battle for An Loc*, p. 30.

40. 5th ARVN Division AAR, p. 38.

41. Bowers, *Tactical Airlift*, p. 545.

42. McGowan, "Easter Airlift," p. 51.

43. 5th ARVN Division AAR, p. 42.

44. *CHECO Report: Battle for An Loc*, p. 38.

45. Charles Black, "Hanoi's Troops—Good Soldiers," *Columbus Enquirer* (Georgia), 19 May 1972.

46. Brya speech.

7. NVA HIGH TIDE

1. Quoted in Andradé, *America's Last Vietnam Battle*, p. 422.

2. 5th ARVN Division Daily Journal, 2225H, 25 April 1972, CMH.

3. Bo Tu Lenh Thiet Giap [Armor Command], *Mot So Tran Danh Cua Bo Doi Thiet Gap, Tap IV* (A number of battles fought by our armor troops, volume IV), p. 52.

4. *CHECO Report: Battle for An Loc*, p. 40.

5. Major John D. Howard, "An Loc: A Study in U.S. Power," *Army*, September 1975, p. 22.

6. *Bo Tu Lenh Thiet Giap* [Armor Command], *Mot So Tran Danh Cua Bo Doi Thiet Gap, Tap IV* (A number of battles fought by our armor troops, volume IV), p. 53.

7. Ibid. The report stated that the unit, which was made up of local force troops from Ha Nam Ninh Province who had just been transferred to the armor branch, had come down the Ho Chi Minh Trail from the North. After a short period of training, they were sent directly to the front.

8. Hollingsworth, "Communist Invasion," p. 16.

9. 5th ARVN Division Daily Journal, 8 May 1972, CMH.

10. Tran Van Nhut, "Unfinished War," p. 216.

11. Hollingsworth, back-channel message, 23 April 1972.

12. Ngo Quang Truong, *Easter Offensive of 1972*, pp. 128–29.

13. Charles Black, "An Loc Is Key to Saigon," *Columbus Enquirer* (Georgia), 17 May 1972.

14. "Adviser: Reds at An Loc Didn't Get it Together," *Pacific Stars and Stripes*, 23 May 1972.

15. Hollingsworth, "Communist Invasion," p. 17; MACV, *1972–1973 Command History*, vol. II, p. J-22.

16. Hollingsworth, back-channel message, 23 April 1972; Hollingsworth, "Communist Invasion," p. 17.

17. Bo Tu Lenh Thiet Giap [Armor Command], *Mot So Tran Danh Cua Bo Doi Thiet Gap, Tap IV* (A number of battles fought by our armor troops, volume IV), p. 53.

18. Hollingsworth, "Communist Invasion," pp. 17–18.

19. MACV, *Command History, 1972–1973*, vol. II, p. J-22.

20. The author also came out on this helicopter. After a brief respite, I would go back in later with a fresh regiment.

21. Lt. Col. Richard J. McManus, Report to Brig. Gen. McGiffert, 1 June 1972, subj: Activities Report, 3rd Ranger Group, 8 April–20 May 1972, p. 1, CARL.

22. McGiffert interview, pp. 32–33.

23. The B-52s in Guam and Thailand were actually Strategic Air Command assets. SAC had an advance element, known as SAC ADVON, at Ton Son Nhut AB that worked closely with 7th Air Force planners in planning ARC LIGHT missions.

24. 5th ARVN Division Daily Journal, 0230H-0600H, 11 May 1972, CMH.

25. *CHECO Report: Battle for An Loc*, p. 42.

26. Ibid.

27. Nguyen Duy Hinh, *Vietnamization and the Cease-Fire*, p. 104.

28. Bo Tu Lenh Thiet Giap [Armor Command], *Mot So Tran Danh Cua Bo Doi Thiet Gap, Tap IV* (A number of battles fought by our armor troops), p. 58.

29. 5th ARVN Division AAR, p. 16.

30. *9th Division*, trans. Foreign Broadcast Information Service (October 1995), pp. 159–60; originally published as *Su Doan 9* (Hanoi: People's Army Publishing House, 1990).

31. Morrocco, *Rain of Fire*, p. 119.

32. "Biggest B-52 Raids of War Pound Reds Besieging An Loc," *Los Angeles Times*, 12 May 1972.

33. 5th ARVN Division AAR, p. 25.

34. Major John D. Howard, "They Were Good Ol' Boys!" *Air University Review*, January–February 1975, p. 36.

35. Hollingsworth, back-channel messages, 12 May 1972.

36. Quoted in Fulghum and Maitland, *South Vietnam on Trial*, p. 154.

37. Ibid.

38. The A-37 was flown by First Lieutenant Michael J. Blassie; his aircraft was hit by ground fire. Lieutenant Blassie's wingman saw him crash into the ground and witnessed an explosion and fire. He did not see any signs of survival. Lieutenant Blassie was listed as Killed in Action/Body Not Recovered. Because of the continued fighting in the area, it was six months before South Vietnamese forces could reach the crash site. Near the site, searchers found a man's remains along with Blassie's identification card, dog tags, and wallet. While the findings were being shipped home, the remains became separated from Blassie's belongings. The Army's Central Identification Laboratory in Hawaii analyzed the remains and labeled them as "believed to be" those of Blassie, but in 1979 the designation was removed when it was decided that the evidence was inconclusive, and the remains were declared as unidentifiable. Those remains were buried in the Tomb of the Unknowns in Arlington National Cemetery on Memorial Day in 1984. In 1998, based on eyewitness accounts and DNA comparison, the remains in the Tomb of the Unknowns were identified as Michael Blassie, and he was subsequently disinterred and buried in the Jefferson Barracks National Cemetery in St. Louis.

39. Later some remains were recovered, but because of legal considerations during the identification process, Rodney Strobridge was briefly listed as possibly being in the Tomb of the Unknown Soldier.

40. Colonel Walter F. Ulmer Jr., "Notes on Enemy Armor at An Loc," *Armor*, January–February 1973, p. 17.

41. Hollingsworth, back-channel message, 13 May 1972.

42. Ibid.

43. S. H. Schanberg, "U.S. Pilot Tells of 6 Days at An Loc in a Bunker beneath the Storm," *New York Times*, 29 May 1972. Later, in a fitting ceremony, McPhillips was awarded the Vietnamese parachutist badge novice level.

44. Hollingsworth, back-channel message, 16 May 1972.

45. Benjamin F. Schemmer, "Bien Hoa Air Base: Short on Toilet Paper, but Long on Teamwork," *Armed Forces Journal*, June 1972, pp. 15–17.

46. XM202 was an experimental flame weapon that included a shoulder launcher and four rockets. These weapons were air-dropped into An Loc as part of the resupply effort.

47. Ulmer, "Notes on Enemy Armor at An Loc," pp. 17, 19.

48. Howard, "War We Came to Fight," p. 24.

49. Hollingsworth, back-channel message, 19 May 1972.

50. Military History Institute of Vietnam, *Victory in Vietnam*, p. 296.

51. *9th Division*, p. 161; also Military History Institute of Vietnam, *Nguyen Hue Offensive Campaign*, pp. 52, 54.

52. Military History Institute of Vietnam, *Nguyen Hue Offensive Campaign*, p. 46.

8. THE FIGHT FOR HIGHWAY 13

1. "An Loc Holds on Despite Relentless Attacks," *Los Angeles Times*, 21 April 1972.

2. Quoted in Fulghum and Maitland, *South Vietnam on Trial*, p. 153.

3. Headquarters, 21st Infantry Division (ARVN), "After-Action Report, Binh Long Campaign, 1972," Can Tho, 1972, p. 4, CMH. Hereafter cited as 21st ARVN Division AAR.

4. Ibid.

5. *9th Division*, p. 161.

6. Ibid., p. 157.

7. Ngo Quang Truong, *Easter Offensive of 1972*, p. 132.

8. 21st ARVN Division AAR, p. K-3.

9. Quoted in Fulghum and Maitland, *South Vietnam on Trial*, p. 162.

10. "A Very Long Road, Where Death Is the Only Easy Rider," *Pacific Stars and Stripes*, 14 April 1972.

11. Quoted in *CHECO Report: Battle for An Loc*, p. 52.

12. Ibid.

13. *9th Division*, p. 160.

14. Peter Arnett and Horst Fass, "U.S. Officer, Pet Die Together on Front Line," *Washington Post*, 21 June 1972; "Colonel Willey's Last Battle," *San Francisco Chronicle*, 21 June 1972.

15. Timberlake and Sloniker, unpublished narrative, pp. 34–35.

16. 21st ARVN Division AAR, p. 5.

9. BREAKING THE SIEGE

1. Ngo Quang Truong, *Easter Offensive of 1972*, p. 134.

2. C. R. Whitney, "Focus on An Loc Shifts to Relief Column," *New York Times*, 27 May 1972.

3. Quoted in Fulghum and Maitland, *South Vietnam on Trial*, p. 153.

4. 21st ARVN Division AAR, p. 7.

5. Howard, "They Were Good Ol' Boys!" pp. 37–38.

6. 21st ARVN Division AAR, 1972, p. 8.

7. Tran Van Nhut, "Unfinished War," p. 230.

8. K. G. Mortensen, *Battle of An Loc*, 1972, p. 53.

9. At the time of the insertion into the city, the 48th Regiment included only two of its three battalions; the 1st Battalion, 48th, was already in An Loc as part of TF 52.

10. From author's e-mail and telephone discussion with former warrant officer Mike Wheeler, A Company, 229th Aviation, 11 September 2003.

11. S. H. Schanberg, "Saigon's Pilots Shun Dangers of An Loc," *New York Times*, 24 June 1972.

12. "Battle for An Loc Ends in Crucial Red Setback," *Pacific Stars and Stripes*, 18 June 1972.

13. Hollingsworth, back-channel message, 12 June 1972.

14. 1st Airborne, CAAR, p. 6.

15. Tran Van Nhut, "Unfinished War," p. 232. Dien Bien Phu was the site of the decisive battle that effectively ended the First Indochina War between the Viet Minh and the French. The French forces were besieged for nearly two months before surrendering on 7 May 1954.

16. "Media Fail to Convey Good News from An Loc," *Baltimore Sun*, 16 June 1972.

17. Hollingsworth, back-channel message, 251000H–261000H, June 1972.

18. Quoted in Ngo Quang Truong, *Easter Offensive of 1972*, p. 135.

19. Speech quoted in *Valiant Binh Long: The 1972 Failure of Communist North Vietnam* (Saigon: Nguyen Ba Tong Printing Co., n.d.), p. 35.

20. Tran Van Nhut, "Unfinished War," p. 235.

21. I had come out of An Loc in mid-May and was replaced by Major Hallum. In early June, I returned when the 43rd Regiment of the 18th ARVN Division was brought in south of the city by helicopter to help bolster the exhausted 5th ARVN.

22. "U.S. General Dies in An Loc Shelling," *New York Times*, 10 July 1972.

23. 21st ARVN Division AAR, p. C-1.

24. Mortensen, *Battle of An Loc, 1972*, p. 43.

25. Clarke, "Battle That Saved An Loc," p. 153. Province officials estimated that 95 percent of the structures in the city were damaged or destroyed.

26. Rudolph Rauch, "A Record of Sheer Endurance," *Time*, 26 June 1972, p. 25.

27. Pham Nhat Nam, "An Loc: The Unquiet East," p. 10.

28. Ibid.

29. Howard, "War We Came to Fight," p. 29.

30. Ibid., abstract.

31. Quoted in Fulghum and Maitland, *South Vietnam on Trial*, p. 165.

32. "The Toll in Battered An Loc—Unknown, But in Hundreds," *Pacific Stars and Stripes*, 17 June 1972, p. 1.

33. "Their Sin—to Leave An Loc," *Pacific Stars and Stripes*, 15 June 1972.

34. Quoted in "Relief of An Loc," p. 34.

35. P. Osnos, "South Vietnamese Refugees Tired, Resigned, Homesick," *Washington Post*, 7 May 1972; Mortensen, *Battle of An Loc, 1972*, p. 17.

36. Ngo Quang Truong, *Easter Offensive of 1972*, p. 134.

37. Ulmer, "Notes on Enemy Armor at An Loc," p. 15.

38. *The Heroic Battle of An-Loc* (Saigon: Government of Vietnam, n.d.), p. 56.

10. EVALUATING THE BATTLE OF AN LOC

1. Ngo Quang Truong, *Easter Offensive of 1972*, p. 158.

2. Military History Institute of Vietnam, *Nguyen Hue Offensive Campaign*, p. 40. The report acknowledges the missed opportunity on p. 100, stating that the opportunity "appeared very quickly and disappeared just as quickly."

3. Ibid.

4. "On the Results of Offensive Actions in South Vietnam and Challenge of Future Armed Struggle," report by the Deputy Chief of the PAVN General, General-Lieutenant Tran Van Quang to a session of the Soviet Politburo, 26 June 1972, translated by U.S. Central Intelligence Agency, 2 July 1993, p. 13, Texas Tech. The report also acknowledged that the North Vietnamese had lost 140,000 personnel during the offensive; Tran said that the NVA had lost over 800 vehicles, including 93 tanks in Binh Long and Tay Ninh (p. 11).

5. Bo Tu Lenh Thiet Giap [Armor Command], *Mot So Tran Danh Cua Bo Doi Thiet Gap, Tap IV* (A number of battles fought by our armor troops, volume IV), p. 61.

6. Ngo Quang Truong, *Easter Offensive of 1972*, p. 160.

7. "Vietnam: The Specter of Defeat," *Newsweek*, 15 May 1972, p. 25.

8. Rauch, "Record of Sheer Endurance," p. 26.

9. Clarke, *Advice and Support*, p. 483.

10. "A Tale of Two Broken Cities," *Time*, 15 January 1973, p. 26.

11. Mortensen, *Battle of An Loc, 1972*, p. 57.

12. MACV, *Command History, 1972–1973*, vol. II, p. J-21.

13. Mortensen, *Battle of An Loc, 1972*, p. 51.

14. Tragically, this courageous officer was killed in May 1973 when his helicopter was shot down not far from Lai Khe.

15. McGiffert interview.

16. Howard, "War We Came to Fight," p. 1.

17. There were any number of exceptions to this approach, most notably in the battle of the Ia Drang Valley, 1965, and Hamburger Hill, 1969.

18. Walter Scott Dillard and John Francis Shortal, "Easter Invasion Repulsed," *Vietnam*, Winter 1988, p. 55.

19. 5th ARVN Division AAR, p. 23.

20. "Report Few Left in An Loc," *Pacific Stars and Stripes*, 2 June 1972.

21. McGiffert interview.

22. According to Headquarters, Division Artillery, 1st Cavalry Division, "History of F Battery, 79th Artillery, 1 February 1972–31 July 1972," n.d., p. 24, Texas Tech.

23. "Copters Rescue An Loc Wounded," *Los Angeles Times*, 11 June 1972.

24. 5th ARVN Division AAR, p. 51.

25. "An Loc Siege Experiences," p. 5.

26. Ngo Quang Truong, *Easter Offensive of 1972*, p. 179.

27. McGiffert interview, p. 26.

28. Ibid.

29. Ibid., p. 27.

30. Mortensen, *Battle of An Loc, 1972*, p. 57.

31. McGiffert interview, p. 22.

32. Ibid., p. 23.

33. Conversations between the author and other advisers in An Loc, April 1972.

34. Clarke, "Battle That Saved Saigon," p. 153.

35. U.S. Congress, Senate Committee on Armed Services, *Staff Report, Vietnam 1972*, 92nd Cong., 2nd sess. (Washington, D.C.: U.S. Government Printing Office, 1972), p. 11.

36. Headquarters, 21st Division Combat Assistance Team, Advisory Team 51, "Senior Officer Debriefing Report, COL Jack Conn," Can Tho, 28 February 1973, pp. K-1-3, MHI.

37. "Viets on Way to Victory at An Loc—Top Adviser," *Pacific Stars and Stripes*, 23 April 1972.

38. Rauch, "Record of Sheer Endurance," p. 26.

11. AFTERMATH

1. Joseph Alsop, "Fighting of the ARVN at An Loc," *Los Angeles Times*, 9 May 1972.

2. Davidson, *Vietnam at War*, pp. 542, 544.

3. Ibid., p. 476.

4. George Katsiaficas, ed., *Vietnam Documents: American and Vietnamese Views of the War* (Armonk, N.Y.: M. E. Sharpe, 1992), pp. 171–76.

5. About 60 U.S. military and civilian personnel remained behind as part of the Defense Attaché Office in the American embassy.

6. Herring, *America's Longest War*, p. 258.

7. Lieutenant General Dong Van Khuyen, *The RVNAF*, Indochina Monographs (Washington, D.C.: U.S. Army Center of Military History, 1979), p. 118.

8. Van Tien Dung, *Our Great Spring Victory: An Account of the Liberation of South Vietnam* (New York: Monthly Review Press, 1977), p. 17.

9. Ibid., pp. 19–20.

10. Ibid., pp. 31–32.

11. Ibid.

12. Arnold R. Isaacs, *Without Honor: Defeat in Vietnam and Cambodia* (Baltimore, Md.: Johns Hopkins University Press, 1983), p. 380.

13. Douglas Kinnard, *The War Managers* (Wayne, N.J.: Avery, 1985), p. 156.

14. Palmer, *Summons of the Trumpet*, p. 255.

EPILOGUE

1. Ngo Quang Truong, *Easter Offensive of 1972*, p. 176.

2. Citation included as appendix in Tran Van Nhut, "Unfinished War."

3. "Community to Mark Fallen Vet's Sacrifice," *Providence Journal* (Rhode Island), 7 April 2004.

BIBLIOGRAPHY

KEY TO BIBLIOGRAPHY ABBREVIATIONS

CARL	Combined Arms Research Library, Fort Leavenworth, Kansas
CMH	Histories Division, U.S. Army Center of Military History, Washington, D.C.
MHI	U.S. Military History Institute, Carlisle Barracks, Pennsylvania
Texas Tech	Indochina Collection, Texas Tech University Archive of the Vietnam Conflict, Lubbock, Texas

INTERVIEWS AND CORRESPONDENCE
(RANKS AND UNITS AS OF MARCH 1972)

Bowers, John. Captain, U.S. Army, Platoon Leader, A Company, 229th Aviation, 3rd Brigade, 1st Cavalry Division.

Brander, Fred. First Sergeant, U.S. Army, Adviser, ARVN Airborne Division (Advisory Team 162).

Brown, Michael. Captain, U.S. Army, Platoon Leader, F/79th Aerial Rocket Artillery, 229th Aviation, 3rd Brigade, 1st Cavalry Division.

Brya, Edward N. Major, U.S. Air Force, Wing Standardization Officer, 374th Tactical Airlift Wing.

Carruthers, William. First Lieutenant, U.S. Air Force, Forward Air Controller, 21st Tactical Air Support Squadron.

Corley, Robert E. Lieutenant Colonel, U.S. Army, Senior Adviser, Binh Long Province Advisory Team.

Dumond, Yves. Freelance photographer, France.

Dunn, Carle E. Major, U.S. Army, Commander, 362nd Aviation Company, 229th Aviation.

Gajkowski, Thaddeus T. (Ted). First Lieutenant, U.S. Army, Section Leader, A Company, 229th Aviation, 3rd Brigade, 1st Cavalry Division.

Hollingsworth, James F. Major General, U.S. Army, Commander, Third Regional Assistance Command.

Ingram, Kenneth. Major, U.S. Army, Artillery Adviser, 5th ARVN Division (Advisory Team 70).

McKay, Larry. Major, U.S. Army, Commander, F/79th Aerial Rocket Artillery, 229th Aviation, 3rd Brigade, 1st Cavalry Division.

Miller, William. Colonel, U.S. Army, Senior Adviser, 5th ARVN Division (Advisory Team 70).

Mortensen, Brother K. G. Missionary.

Murphy, Dan. First Lieutenant, U.S. Army, Section Leader, A Company, 229th Aviation, 3rd Brigade, 1st Cavalry Division.

Murphy, Robert. Major, U.S. Air Force, Forward Air Controller/Air Liaison Officer, 21st Tactical Air Support Squadron.

Orahood, James. Captain, U.S. Army, Platoon Leader, A Company, 229th Aviation, 3rd Brigade, 1st Cavalry Division.

Plummer, Frank S. Colonel, U.S. Army, Senior Adviser, 18th ARVN Division (Advisory Team 87).

Richmond, Charles D. "Chad." Captain, U.S. Army, Platoon Leader, A Company, 229th Aviation, 3rd Brigade, 1st Cavalry Division.

Sloniker, Michael. Captain, U.S. Army, Operations Officer, A Company, 229th Aviation, 3rd Brigade, 1st Cavalry Division.

Tiberi, Paul. Captain, U.S. Army, Adviser, 15th Regiment, 9th ARVN Division (Advisory Team 60).

Tran Van Nhut. Colonel, Republic of Vietnam, Binh Long Province Chief.

Ulevich, Neal. Photographer, Associated Press.

Ulmer, Walter F. Colonel, U.S. Army, Senior Adviser, 5th ARVN Divisions (Advisory Team 70).

Wheeler, Michael J. Warrant Officer, U.S. Army, Rotary Wing Aviator, A Company, 229th Aviation, 3rd Brigade, 1st Cavalry Division.

Williams, Ron. Warrant Officer, U.S. Army, Rotary Wing Aviator, A Company, 229th Aviation, 3rd Brigade, 1st Cavalry Division.

PAPERS AND DOCUMENT COLLECTIONS

Abrams, Creighton W., General, U.S. Army. Papers. U.S. Army Center of Military History, Washington, D.C.

The History of the Vietnam War (microfiche collection). Ann Arbor, Michigan: University Microfilms International, 1991.

Lester, Robert, ed. *Records of the Military Assistance Command Vietnam. Part 1, The War in Vietnam, 1954–1973.* MACV Historical Office Documentary Collection (microfilm edition). Bethesda, Md.: University Publications of America, 1988.

———. *U.S. Army Build-up and Activities in South Vietnam, 1965–1972.* Microfilm edition of Vietnam War Research Collections. Bethesda, Md.: University Publications of America, 1989.

Miller, William H., Colonel, U.S. Army, Retired. Unpublished manuscript, n.d. Copy in author's possession.

Nixon, Richard M. *Public Papers of the President of the United States: Richard M. Nixon.* 6 vols. Washington, D.C.: Government Printing Office, 1971–1975.

Pike, Douglas, ed. *The Bunker Papers: Reports to the President from Vietnam, 1967–1973.* Vols. 1–3. Berkeley: Institute of East Asian Studies, University of California, 1990.

———. Indochina Collection. Texas Tech University Archive of the Vietnam Conflict, Lubbock, Texas.

Southeast Asia Branch Files. U.S. Army Center of Military History, Washington, D.C.

UNPUBLISHED PRIMARY SOURCE MATERIAL

Brya, Brigadier General Edward N. Transcript of speech presented at U.S. Air Force Tanker Convention, Seattle, Wash., 1995. Copy in author's possession.

5th ARVN Division Daily Journal, April–June 1972. CMH.

Ginger, Lieutenant Colonel Walter D. Headquarters, Advisory Team 87. "After-Action Report, Task Force 52." Xuan Loc, May 1972. Texas Tech.

Haney, Raymond, Major. Adviser, Task Force 52. Interview by Major John Cash, Military Assistance Command, Vietnam. SJS-History, 3rd Field Hospital, Saigon, 19 April 1972. Texas Tech.

Headquarters, Division Artillery, 1st Cavalry Division. "History of F Battery, 79th Artillery, 1 February 1972–31 July 1972." N.d. Texas Tech.

Headquarters, 5th Division Combat Assistance Team, Advisory Team 70. "After-Action Report, Binh Long Campaign, 1972." TRAC, 20 July 1972. CMH.

Headquarters, 1st Airborne Brigade Combat Assistance Team. "Combat After-Action Report, 1st Airborne Brigade." Saigon, 22 July 1972. CARL.

Headquarters, Third Regional Assistance Command. "Debriefing Reports of Advisers Returning from An Loc." Long Binh, 1972. CMH.

Headquarters, Third Regional Assistance Command. "Tactical Operations Center Duty Logs, April–June, 1972." Long Binh, 1972. In Robert Lester, ed., *Records of the Military Assistance Command, Vietnam, Part 1: The War in Vietnam, 1954–1973.* Bethesda, Md.: University Publications of America, 1988. MACV Historical Office Documentary Collection, microfilm reel 44.

Headquarters, Third Regional Assistance Command. "The Military Region Overview for the Period Ending 30 April 1972." Long Binh, 12 May 1972. CMH.

Headquarters, 21st Infantry Division (ARVN). "After-Action Report, Binh Long Campaign, 1972." Can Tho, 1972. CMH.

Headquarters, 21st Division Combat Assistance Team, Advisory Team 51. "Senior Officer Debriefing Report, COL Jack Conn." Can Tho, 28 February 1973. MHI.

Headquarters, U.S. Military Assistance Command, Vietnam. Army Advisory Group Study. "Subject: Sustaining U.S. Advisory Support—ARVN Division." Saigon, 16 November 1972. CARL.

Headquarters, U.S. Military Assistance Command, Vietnam. Pacification Studies Group, Office of the Director, CORDS. "Debriefing: An Loc Siege Experiences." Saigon, 27 June 1972. CARL.

Headquarters, U.S. Military Assistance Command, Vietnam. Report, "Interview with Major Larry McKay, CO 79th ARA, 3rd Bde 1st Cav Div at Bien Hoa." Saigon, 26 May 1972. CMH.

Hollingsworth, Major General James F. "Communist Invasion in Military Region III." Unpublished narrative, 1972. In Robert Lester, ed., *Records of the Military Assistance Command, Vietnam, Part 1: The War in Vietnam, 1954–1973.* Bethesda, Md.: University Publications of America, 1988. MACV Historical Office Documentary Collection, microfilm reel 44.

———. Back-channel messages to General Creighton C. Abrams. "Daily Commander's Evaluation," April–July 1972. In Robert Lester, ed., *Records of the Military Assistance Command, Vietnam, Part 1: The War in Vietnam, 1954–1973.* Bethesda, Md.: University Publications of America, 1988. MACV Historical Office Documentary Collection, microfilm reel 44.

Logan, Lieutenant Colonel Laddie B. "Senior Officer Debriefing Report." Long Binh, 7
    February 1973. MHI.

McClellan, Major General Stan L. "Vietnamization—A Point of View." Undated paper.
    MHI.

McGiffert, Brigadier General John R., Deputy Commanding General, Third Regional
    Assistance Command. Interview by Major Walter S. Dillard, Military Assistance
    Command, Vietnam. SJS-History, Saigon, 10 October 1972. MHI.

McManus, Lt. Col. Richard J. Report to Brig. Gen. McGiffert, 1 June 1972. Subj: Activi-
    ties Report. 3rd Ranger Group, 8 April–20 May 1972. CARL.

Memorandum, DCAT 70 for Brigadier General James F. Hamlet. Subject: Battle of An
    Loc—5 April 1972 to 10 May 1972. Dated 13 May 1972. Texas Tech.

Message, Hollingsworth to Gen. Vogt, CDR 7th AF, and Capt. Monger, CO USS *Han-
    cock*, 22 April 1972. CMH.

Mortensen, K. G. "The Battle of An Loc." Unpublished monograph. East St. Kilda, Aus-
    tralia, 25 April 1973. Copy in author's possession.

Smith, Captain Mark A. "Battle of Loc Ninh, RVN, 5–7 April 1972." Unpublished narra-
    tive. Fort Bragg, North Carolina, 21 October 1976. Copy in author's possession.

State of Vietnam, Ministry of National Defense. Memorandum: Principles Authorizing
    TRIM Advisers with Units and Formations of the Vietnamese National Armed
    Forces. Saigon, 10 April 1955. CARL.

Timberlake, Captain Ron, F Troop, 9th Cavalry, and Captain Michael Sloniker, A Com-
    pany, 229th Aviation, 3rd Brigade, 1st Cavalry Division. Unpublished narrative,
    1999. Texas Tech.

Tran Van Nhut, General. "The Unfinished War." Unpublished manuscript. Santa Ana,
    California, n.d. Copy in author's possession.

Ulmer, Colonel W. F. Senior Officer Debriefing Report. Third Regional Assistance Com-
    mand. Long Binh, 10 January 1973. MHI.

U.S. Army Command and General Staff College. "1972 Vietnam Counter Offensive." *RB
    100–2*. Vol. 1: *Selected Readings in Tactics*. Fort Leavenworth, Kans., n.d. CARL.

U.S. Military Assistance Command, Vietnam. Daily Operational Summary Reports to
    Joint Chiefs of Staff, March, April, May 1972. Saigon, 1972. CARL.

U.S. Military Assistance Command, Vietnam. Military History Branch. *Command His-
    tory, 1972–1973*. Saigon, 1973. CARL.

U.S. Military Assistance Command, Vietnam. Periodic Intelligence Reports (PERIN-
    TREP)—February–May 1972. Saigon, 1972. CMH.

U.S. Military Assistance Command, Vietnam. "Senior Officer Debriefing Report, COL
    Jack Conn." Saigon, February 1973. MHI.

U.S. Military Assistance Command, Vietnam. Special Intelligence Report (Declassified),
    "The Nguyen Hue Offensive—Historical Study of Lessons Learned." Saigon, Janu-
    ary 1973. CARL.

Zumwalt, Captain Marvin C., Adviser, 52d Infantry. Interview by Major John Cash,
    Military Assistance Command, Vietnam. SJS-History, 3rd Field Hospital, Saigon,
    18–19 April 1972. MHI.

OFFICIAL U.S. PUBLICATIONS

Ballard, Jack S. *Development and Employment of Fixed-Wing Gunships, 1962–1972*. The
    United States Air Force in Southeast Asia. Washington, D.C.: Office of Air Force
    History, 1982.

Berger, C., J. S. Ballard, and R. L. Bowers. *The United States Air Force in Southeast Asia: 1961–1973*. Washington, D.C.: Office of Air Force History, 1977.

Bowers, Ray L. *Tactical Airlift. The United States Air Force in Southeast Asia*. Washington, D.C.: Office of Air Force History, 1983.

Clarke, Jeffrey C. *Advice and Support: The Final Years—The U.S. Army in Vietnam*. Washington, D.C.: U.S. Army Center of Military History, 1987.

Collins, James Lawton, Jr. *The Development and Training of the South Vietnamese Army, 1950–1972*. Washington, D.C.: U.S. Government Printing Office, 1975.

Head, William P. *The Fairchild Papers: War above the Clouds—B-52 Operations during the Second Indochina War and the Effects of the Air War on Theory and Doctrine*. Maxwell Air Force Base, Ala.: Air University Press, 2002.

Lavalle, Major A. J. C., ed. *Airpower and the 1972 Spring Offensive*. United States Air Force Southeast Asia Monograph Series. Washington, D.C.: U.S. Government Printing Office, 1976.

Momyer, William W. *The Vietnamese Air Force, 1951–1975: An Analysis of Its Role in Combat*. United States Air Force Southeast Asia Monograph Series. Washington, D.C.: U.S. Government Printing Office, 1975.

Mrozek, Donald J. *Air Power and the Ground War in Vietnam: Ideas and Actions*. Maxwell Air Force Base, Ala.: Air University Press, 1988.

PAVN SOURCES

Bo Tu Lenh Thiet Giap [Armor Command]. *Mot So Tran Danh Cua Bo Doi Thiet Gap, Tap IV* (A number of battles fought by our armor troops, vol. IV). Hanoi: General Staff Printing Plant, 1983.

Le Duan. *Letters to the South*. Hanoi: Su That Publishing House, 1985.

Lich Su Quan Doi Nhan Dan Viet Nam (History of the People's Army of Vietnam). Hanoi: People's Army Publishing House, 1990.

Military History Institute of Vietnam. *The Nguyen Hue Offensive Campaign in Eastern Cochin China*. Translated by Merle L. Pribbenow. Unpublished translation, n.d. Originally published as *Chien Dich Tien Cong Nguyen Hue Mien Dong Bo—Nam 1972—Luu Hanh Noi Bo*. Hanoi: Military History Institute of the Ministry of Defense, 1988.

———. *History of the People's Army of Vietnam*. Vol. 2. Translated by Merle L. Pribbenow. Unpublished translation, n.d. Originally published as *Lich Su Quan Doi Nhan Dan Viet Nam*. Hanoi: People's Army Publishing House, 1994.

———. *Report to General Vo Nguyen Giap: A Consolidated Report on the Fight against the United States for the Salvation of Vietnam by Our People*. Translated by Duong Bui. Defense Language Institute Foreign Language Center, Presidio of Monterey, California, 1996. Originally published in Hanoi, 1987.

———. *Victory in Vietnam: The Official History of the People's Army of Vietnam, 1954–1975*. Translated by Merle L. Pribbenow. Lawrence: University Press of Kansas, 2002.

Nguyen Huu An, Colonel General, and Nguyen Tu Duong. *Chien Truong Moi: Hoi Uc* (New battlefield: A memoir). Hanoi: People's Army Publishing House, 2002.

9th Division. Translated by Foreign Broadcast Information Service (October 1995). Originally published as *Su Doan 9* (Hanoi: People's Army Publishing House, 1990).

"On the Results of Offensive Actions in South Vietnam and Challenge of Future Armed Struggle." Report by the Deputy Chief of the PAVN General, General-Lieutenant

Tran Van Quang to a session of the Soviet Politburo, 26 June 1972. Translated by U.S. Central Intelligence Agency, 2 July 1993. Texas Tech.

Tran Van Tra. *Vietnam: History of the Bulwark B2 Theater.* Vol. 5: *Concluding the 30-Year War.* Southeast Asia Report, No. 1247. Arlington, Va.: Joint Publications Research Service, 1983.

Truong Nhu Tang. *Vietcong Memoir: An Inside Account of the Vietnam War and Its Aftermath.* New York: Harcourt Brace Jovanovich, 1983.

Van Tien Dung. *Our Great Spring Victory: An Account of the Liberation of South Vietnam.* New York: Monthly Review Press, 1977.

"Vietnam: The Anti-U.S. Resistance War for National Salvation 1954–1975: Military Events." FBIS Translation JPRS 80968, 3 June 1982. CARL.

Vo Nguyen Giap. *How We Won the War.* Philadelphia: Recon Press, 1976.

STUDIES, REPORTS, MONOGRAPHS, AND VIDEOTAPES

Attack Helicopters—The Cobra. 58 min. Discovery Wings Channel, 1999. Videocassette.

BDM Corporation. *A Study of Strategic Lessons Learned in Vietnam: Omnibus Executive Summary.* McLean, Va.: BDM Corporation, April 1980.

———. *A Study of Strategic Lessons Learned in Vietnam.* Vol. 1: *The Enemy.* McLean, Va.: BDM Corporation, 1979.

———. *A Study of Strategic Lessons Learned in Vietnam.* Vol. 3: *Results of the War.* McLean, Va.: BDM Corporation, 1980.

———. *A Study of Strategic Lessons Learned in Vietnam.* Vol. 6: *Conduct of the War.* McLean, Va.: BDM Corporation, May 1980.

Bendix Aerospace Systems Division, Department of Applied Science and Technology. *Analysis of Vietnamization: Summary and Evaluation.* Ann Arbor, Mich.: Bendix Aerospace Systems Division, November 1973.

Cao Van Vien, General. *Leadership.* Indochina Monographs. Washington, D.C.: U.S. Army Center of Military History, 1981.

———. *The Final Collapse.* Indochina Monographs. Washington, D.C.: U.S. Army Center of Military History, 1985.

Cao Van Vien, General, and Lieutenant General Dong Van Khuyen. *Reflections on the Vietnam War.* Indochina Monographs. Washington, D.C.: U.S. Army Center of Military History, 1980.

Cao Van Vien, General, Lieutenant General Ngo Quang Truong, Lieutenant General Dong Van Khuyen, Major General Nguyen Duy Hinh, Brigadier General Tran Dinh Tho, Colonel Hoang Ngoc Lung, and Lieutenant Colonel Chu Xuan Vien. *The U.S. Adviser.* Indochina Monographs. Washington, D.C.: U.S. Army Center of Military History, 1980.

Collins, Major J. C. "The Battle of Loc Ninh, 5–7 April 1972." Unpublished student paper. U.S. Army War College, Carlisle Barracks, Pa., undated.

Dong Van Khuyen, Lieutenant General. *The RVNAF.* Indochina Monographs. Washington, D.C.: U.S. Army Center of Military History, 1979.

Headquarters, Pacific Command, Directorate of Operations Analysis. *Contemporary Historical Examination of Current Operations (CHECO) Report: Airlift to Besieged Areas, 7 April–31 August 1972.* Honolulu, 1973.

———. *Contemporary Historical Examination of Current Operations (CHECO) Report: The Battle for An Loc, 5 April–26 June 1972.* Honolulu, 1973.

———. *Contemporary Historical Examination of Current Operations (CHECO) Report—Kontum: Battle for the Central Highlands: 30 March–10 June 1972.* Honolulu, October 1972.

———. *Contemporary Historical Examination of Current Operations (CHECO) Report—The 1972 Invasion of Military Region I: Fall of Quang Tri and Defense of Hue.* Honolulu, March 1973.

———. *Contemporary Historical Examination of Current Operations (CHECO) Report—U.S. Air Deployments in Response to the NVA 1972 Offensive.* Honolulu, March 1973.

The Heroic Battle of An-Loc. Saigon: Government of Vietnam, n.d.

Howard, Major John D. "An Infantryman Remembers An Loc and the Air Force." U.S. Army Command and General Staff College, Fort Leavenworth, Kans., March 1974. Unpublished student paper. CARL.

———. "The War We Came to Fight: A Study of the Battle of An Loc, April–June 1972." U.S. Army Command and General Staff College, Fort Leavenworth, Kans., June 1974. Unpublished student paper. CARL.

Kellen, Konrad. *Conversations with Enemy Soldiers in Late 1968/Early 1969: A Study of Motivation and Morale.* Santa Monica, Calif.: RAND Corporation, 1970.

Metcalf, D. J. "Why Did the Defense of Quang Tri Province Fail?" U.S. Army War College, Carlisle Barracks, Pa., October 1972.

Ngo Quang Truong, Lieutenant General. *The Easter Offensive of 1972.* Indochina Monographs. Washington, D.C.: U.S. Army Center of Military History, 1980.

———. *RVNAF and U.S. Operational Cooperation and Coordination.* Indochina Monographs. Washington, D.C.: U.S. Army Center of Military History, 1980.

Nguyen Duy Hinh, Major General. *Vietnamization and the Cease-Fire.* Indochina Monographs. Washington, D.C.: U.S. Army Center of Military History, 1980.

Parker, G. J. *An Essay on Vietnamization.* Santa Monica, Calif.: RAND Corporation, March 1971.

Pham Nhat Nam. "An Loc: The Unquiet East." Translated by John C. Shafer. Unpublished monograph. Center for Southeast Asian Studies, Northern Illinois University, DeKalb, Ill., undated.

U.S. Congress. Senate. Committee on Armed Services. *Staff Report, Vietnam 1972.* 92nd Cong., 2nd sess. Washington, D.C.: U.S. Government Printing Office, 1972.

Valiant Binh Long: The 1972 Failure of Communist North Vietnam. In English and Vietnamese. Saigon: Nguyen Ba Tong Printing Company, n.d.

Willbanks, James H. *Thiet Giap! The Battle of An Loc, April 1972.* Fort Leavenworth, Kans.: U.S. Army Command and General Staff College, Combat Studies Institute, 1993.

SECONDARY SOURCES

Andradé, Dale. *America's Last Vietnam Battle: Halting Hanoi's 1972 Easter Offensive.* Lawrence: University Press of Kansas, 2001.

———. *Trial by Fire: The 1972 Easter Offensive, America's Last Vietnam Battle.* New York: Hippocrene Books, 1995.

Berman, Larry. *No Peace, No Honor: Nixon, Kissinger, and Betrayal.* New York: Free Press, 2001.

Bui Diem, with David Chanoff. *In the Jaws of History.* Boston: Houghton Mifflin, 1987.

Carhart, Tom. *Battles and Campaigns in Vietnam.* New York: Crown, 1984.

Chen Jian. *Mao's China and the Cold War.* Chapel Hill: University of North Carolina Press, 2001.

Colby, William. *Lost Victory.* Chicago: Contemporary Books, 1989.

Currey, Cecil B. *Victory at Any Cost.* Washington, D.C.: Brassey's, 1997.

Davidson, Phillip B. *Vietnam at War: The History 1946–1975.* Novato, Calif.: Presidio Press, 1988.

Doleman, Edgar C. *The Vietnam Experience: Tools of War.* Boston: Boston Publishing Company, 1984.

Dunstan, Simon. *Armor of the Vietnam Wars.* London: Osprey Press, 1985.

———. *Vietnam Tracks: Armor in Battle, 1945–75.* Novato, Calif.: Presidio Press, 1982.

Elliott, David W. P. *NLF-DRV Strategy and the 1972 Spring Offensive.* Ithaca, N.Y.: Cornell University, International Relations of East Asia, IREA Project, January 1974.

Errington, Elizabeth Jane, and B. J. C. McKercher, eds. *The Vietnam War as History.* New York: Praeger, 1990.

Esper, George. *The Eyewitness History of the Vietnam War, 1961–1975.* New York: Ballantine Books, 1983.

Fanning, Louis A. *Betrayal in Vietnam.* New Rochelle, N.Y.: Arlington House, 1976.

Fulghum, David, and Terrence Maitland. *South Vietnam on Trial, Mid-1970 to 1972.* Boston: Boston Publishing Company, 1984.

Gaiduk, Ilya V. *The Soviet Union and the Vietnam War.* Chicago: I. R. Dee, 1996.

Gilbert, Marc Jason, ed. *Why the North Won the Vietnam War.* New York: Palgrave, 2002.

Harrison, Marshall. *A Lonely Kind of War: Forward Air Controllers in Vietnam.* Novato, Calif.: Presidio Press, 1989.

Herring, George C. *America's Longest War: The United States and Vietnam, 1950–1975.* New York: Knopf, 1979.

Herrington, Stuart A. *Peace with Honor.* Novato, Calif.: Presidio Press, 1983.

———. *Silence Was a Weapon: The Vietnam War in the Villages.* Novato, Calif.: Presidio Press, 1982.

Hess, Gary R. *Vietnam and the United States: Origins and Legacy of the War.* Boston: Twayne, 1990.

Hieu Dinh Vu. *The ARVN Rangers.* Dallas: self-published, 1996.

Hunt, Richard A. *Pacification: The American Struggle for Vietnam's Hearts and Minds.* Boulder, Colo.: Westview Press, 1995.

Isaacs, Arnold R. *Without Honor: Defeat in Vietnam and Cambodia.* Baltimore, Md.: Johns Hopkins University Press, 1983.

Joes, Anthony James. *The War for South Viet Nam, 1954–1975.* New York: Praeger, 1989.

Karnow, Stanley. *Vietnam: A History.* New York: Viking Press, 1983.

Katsiaficas, George, ed. *Vietnam Documents: American and Vietnamese Views of the War.* Armonk, N.Y.: M. E. Sharpe, 1992.

Kinnard, Douglas. *The War Managers.* Wayne, N.J.: Avery, 1985.

Kissinger, Henry. *Ending the Vietnam War.* New York: Simon and Schuster, 2003.

———. *White House Years.* Boston: Little, Brown and Company, 1979.

Knappman, Edward W., ed. *South Vietnam: U.S.-Communist Confrontation in Southeast Asia, 1972–1973.* Vol. 7. New York: Facts on File, 1973.

Lam Quang Thi. *The Twenty-Five Year Century.* Denton: University of North Texas Press, 2001.

Lanning, Michael Lee, and Dan Cragg. *Inside the VC and the NVA: The Real Story of North Vietnam's Armed Forces.* New York: Fawcett Columbine, 1992.

Lewy, Guenther. *America in Vietnam.* New York: Oxford University Press, 1978.

MacDonald, Peter. *Giap: The Victor in Vietnam.* New York: W. W. Norton, 1993.

MacLear, Michael. *The Ten Thousand Day War, Vietnam: 1945–1975.* New York: St. Martin's Press, 1981.

Martin, Michael. *Angels in Red Hats: Paratroopers of the Second Indochina War.* Louisville, Ky.: Harmony House, 1995.

Martin, Michael, and McDonald Valentine Jr. *The Black Tigers: Elite Vietnamese Rangers and Their American Counterparts.* Louisville, Ky.: Harmony House, 1993.

Middleton, Drew. *Air War: Vietnam.* New York: Armon Press, 1978.

Millett, Allen Reed. *A Short History of the Vietnam War.* Bloomington: Indiana University Press, 1979.

Morrison, Wilbur H. *The Elephant and the Tiger.* New York: Hippocrene Books, 1990.

Morrocco, John. *Rain of Fire: Air War, 1969–1973.* Boston: Boston Publishing Company, 1985.

Mortensen, K. G. *The Battle of An Loc, 1972.* Parkville, Victoria, Australia: Gerald Griffin Press, 1996.

———. *Vietnam: Target for 1972 Blitzkrieg.* East St. Kilda, Australia: Gerald Griffin Press, 1972.

Natkiel, Richard. *Atlas of Battles: Strategy and Tactics Civil War to Present.* New York: Military Press, 1984.

Nguyen Cao Ky. *Buddha's Child: My Fight to Save Vietnam.* New York: St. Martin's Press, 2002.

———. *Twenty Years and Twenty Days.* New York: Stein and Day, 1976.

Nixon, Richard M. *The Real War.* New York: Warner Books, 1980.

———. *RN: The Memoirs of Richard Nixon.* New York: Warner Books, 1978.

Palmer, Dave Richard. *Summons of the Trumpet: U.S.-Vietnam in Perspective.* San Rafael, Calif.: Presidio Press, 1978.

Pike, Douglas. *PAVN: People's Army of Vietnam.* Novato, Calif.: Presidio Press, 1986.

Pimlott, John, ed. *Vietnam: The History and the Tactics.* New York: Crescent Books, 1982.

Qiang Zhai. *China and the Vietnam Wars, 1950–1975.* Chapel Hill: University of North Carolina Press, 2000.

Ryan, Cornelius. *The Last Battle.* New York: Simon and Schuster, 1966.

Schulzinger, Robert D. *A Time for War: The United States and Vietnam, 1941–1975.* New York: Oxford University Press, 1997.

Shaplen, Robert. *The Road from War: Vietnam 1965–1970.* New York: Harper and Row, 1970.

Sorley, Lewis. *A Better War: The Unexamined Victories and Final Tragedy of America's Last Years in Vietnam.* New York: Harcourt Brace, 1999.

———. *Thunderbolt, From the Battle of the Bulge to Vietnam and Beyond: General Creighton Abrams and the Army of His Times.* New York: Simon and Schuster, 1992.

Stanton, Shelby L. *Vietnam Order of Battle.* New York: Galahad Books, 1986.

Tin Nguyen. *Major General Nguyen Van Hieu, ARVN.* San Jose, Calif.: Writers Club Press, 2000.

Tucker, Spencer C. *Vietnam.* Lexington: University Press of Kentucky, 1999.

Turley, G. H. *The Easter Offensive.* Novato, Calif.: Presidio Press, 1985.

Turley, William S. *The Second Indochina War.* Boulder, Colo.: Westview Press, 1986.

Walton, C. Dale. *The Myth of Inevitable U.S. Defeat in Vietnam.* London: Frank Cass, 2002.

Warner, Denis A. *Certain Victory: How Hanoi Won the War.* Kansas City, Kans.: Sheed Andrews and McMeel, 1977.

Woodruff, Mark W. *Unheralded Victory: The Defeat of the Viet Cong and the North Vietnamese Army, 1961–1973.* Arlington, Va.: Vandemere Press, 1999.

PERIODICALS

"Adviser: Reds at An Loc Didn't Get it Together." *Pacific Stars and Stripes,* 23 May 1972.

"An Adviser's 2-Month Nightmare Ends." *Pacific Stars and Stripes,* 4 June 1972.

"After Attack on An Loc." *Los Angeles Times,* 17 April 1972.

"The Air War Grows." *Newsweek,* 24 April 1972, p. 32.

Alsop, Joseph. "Fighting of the ARVN at An Loc." *Los Angeles Times,* 9 May 1972.

———. "Lack of Reserves in South Vietnam." *Pacific Stars and Stripes,* 10 May 1972.

———. "The South's Heroic Defense of An Loc." *Pacific Stars and Stripes,* 30 May 1972.

Andradé, Dale. "Quang Tri Disaster." *Vietnam,* April 1994, pp. 30–36, 59–60.

———. "Three Days on the Run." *Vietnam,* August 1990, pp. 38–45.

"An Loc: A Battlefield in Hell." *Pacific Stars and Stripes,* 1 May 1972.

"An Loc Holds on Despite Relentless Attacks." *Los Angeles Times,* 21 April 1972.

"An Loc Seen from Above: War with Unreal Quality." *New York Times,* 10 May 1972.

"An Loc: Vietnamization in Action." *Pacific Stars and Stripes,* 15 June 1972.

"An Loc Will Test the Mettle of Vietnamization." *Washington News,* 15 April 1972.

"Army Cobras Blast Tanks Near An Loc." *Aviation Week and Space Technology,* 22 May 1972, pp. 14–15.

Arnett, Peter, and Horst Fass. "U.S. Officer, Pet Die Together on Front Line." *Washington Post,* 21 June 1972.

Baker, W. R. "Battle of the Bulge vs. Eastertide Offensive: Lessons Unlearned." *Vietnam,* April 1999, pp. 34–42.

———. "The Easter Offensive of 1972: A Failure to Use Intelligence." *Military Intelligence,* January–March 1998, pp. 40–42, 60.

"A Battlefield in Hell." *Pacific Stars and Stripes,* 1 May 1972.

"Battle for An Loc Ends in Crucial Red Setback." *Pacific Stars and Stripes,* 18 June 1972.

"Battle 60 Miles from Saigon." *Pacific Stars and Stripes,* 4 April 1972.

Beecher, William. "Vietnamization—A Few Loose Ends." *Army,* November 1970, pp. 13–17.

"Biggest B-52 Raids of War Pound Reds Besieging An Loc." *Los Angeles Times,* 12 May 1972.

Black, Charles. "An Loc Is Key to Saigon." *Columbus Enquirer* (Georgia), 17 May 1972.

———. "Hanoi's Troops—Good Soldiers." *Columbus Enquirer* (Georgia), 19 May 1972.

———. "Mistakes Help An Loc Allied Force." *Columbus Enquirer* (Georgia), 20 May 1972.

"'Blue Max' and An Loc." *Armed Forces Journal,* June 1972, p. 17.

"Both Sides Claim An Loc." *Pacific Stars and Stripes,* 18 April 1972.

Boyne, Walter J. "The Easter Halt." *Air Force,* September 1998, pp. 60–65.

"'Can You Hold Out for Just Eight More Minutes?'" *Life,* 21 April 1972.

Clarke, Philip C. "The Battle That Saved Saigon." *Reader's Digest,* March 1973, pp. 151–56.

———. "Defying the Odds at An Loc." *American Legion Magazine,* April 2000, p. 39.

"Colonel Willey's Last Battle." *San Francisco Chronicle*, 21 June 1972.

"Copters Rescue An Loc Wounded." *Los Angeles Times*, 11 June 1972.

Daley, Jerome R. "The AH1G Versus Enemy Tanks at An Loc." *Armor*, July–August 1972, pp. 42–43.

Daniel, Leon. "An Loc Rapidly Becoming a Pile of Rubble." *Pacific Stars and Stripes*, 23 April 1972.

———. "Not Much Left to Defend in War-Shattered An Loc." *Pacific Stars and Stripes*, 1 May 1972.

Dillard, Walter Scott, and John Francis Shortal. "Easter Invasion Repulsed." *Vietnam*, winter 1988, pp. 51–56.

Do Duc Thinh. "Hai Thang Tu Thu An Loc" (Two months defending An Loc). *Dac San GD81/BCND* (81st Airborne Ranger Family). Issue 2, 1 July 1998.

"'The Dying Is Over'—but Not Quite." *Pacific Stars and Stripes*, 16 June 1972.

"Escalation in the Air, Ordeal on the Ground." *Time*, 24 April 1972, pp. 26–28.

"1st Cav Unit Receives Presidential Citation." *Army Times*, 5 June 1974, p. 29.

Grayson, Eugene H., Jr. "Great Spring Victory." *Vietnam*, June 1992, pp. 18–24.

Hackworth, David H. "Our Advisers Must Pass the Ball." *Army*, May 1971, pp. 61–62.

Halloran, Bernard F. "Soviet Armor Comes to Vietnam." *Army*, August 1972, pp. 18–23.

"Hanoi's High-Risk Drive for Victory." *Time*, 15 May 1972, pp. 8–15.

"Hanoi's Strategy: Hit Them Everywhere." *Newsweek*, 8 May 1972, pp. 53–54.

Hayward, Henry S. "Siege of An Loc Intensifies as Hue Defenders Dig In." *Christian Science Monitor*, 13 May 1972.

Hebert, Gerard. "Both Sides Claim An Loc." *Pacific Stars and Stripes*, 18 April 1972.

"Honored at Last." (Greensboro, N.C.) *News and Record*, 25 July 1999.

Howard, Major John D. "An Loc: A Study in U.S. Power." *Army*, September 1975, pp. 18–24.

———. "They Were Good Ol' Boys!" *Air University Review*, January–February 1975, pp. 26–39.

"Human Wave Attacks Batter An Loc." *Pacific Stars and Stripes*, 22 April 1972.

"In Furious Battle." *Newsweek*, 24 April 1972, pp. 31–33.

"Lai Khe: The Cav at Work." *Armed Forces Journal*, June 1972, p. 18.

"Lessons Learned—the Hard Way—on Rt. 13." *Pacific Stars and Stripes*, 29 June 1972.

"Major Ran for His Life 4 Days—and Won." *Pacific Stars and Stripes*, 29 April 1972.

McArthur, George. "It Became Sinful." *Vietnam*, April 1995, pp. 23–28, 66.

McCarthy, Dave. "Community to Mark Fallen Vet's Sacrifice." *Providence Journal* (Rhode Island), 7 April 2004.

McGowan, Sam. "Easter Airlift." *Vietnam*, April 1994, pp. 46–50.

"Media Fail to Convey Good News from An Loc." *Baltimore Sun*, 16 June 1972.

"The Miscalculation Is Mutual." *Newsweek*, 1 May 1972, pp. 49–52.

Moore, James K. "Giap's Giant Mistake." *Vietnam*, February 1992, pp. 26–32.

"New Arms, More Bombs." *Time*, 5 June 1972, pp. 28–30.

Nguyen Quoc Khue. "LD3/BDQ Voi Tran Chien An Loc/Binh Long" (3rd Ranger Group and the battle of An Loc/Binh Long). *Tap San Biet Dong Quan* [Ranger Magazine], issue 7, 2003, pp. 77–121. (Translated by Merle L. Pribbenow.)

"Nixon's Vietnam Gamble." *Newsweek*, 22 May 1972, pp. 18–20.

"No One Could Survive, But They Did." *Pacific Stars and Stripes*, 2 May 1972.

"N. Viet Tactics." *Washington Post*, 8 May 1972.

"One Saigon Advance Unit Breaks through to An Loc." *New York Times*, 10 June 1972.

"On Highway 13: The Long Road to An Loc." *Time*, 24 April 1972, p. 27.

Osnos, P. "South Vietnamese Refugees Tired, Resigned, Homesick." *Washington Post,* 7 May 1972.

Parker, Maynard. "Vietnam: The War That Won't End." *Foreign Affairs,* January 1975, pp. 252–75.

"The President Battles on Three Fronts." *Time,* 1 May 1972, pp. 11–18.

"Rating the ARVN: Lessons from An Loc." *Christian Science Monitor,* 20 May 1972.

Rauch, Rudolph. "A Record of Sheer Endurance." *Time,* 26 June 1972, pp. 25–26.

"Reds Cut Viet Road Links." *Pacific Stars and Stripes,* 10 April 1972.

"Reds Execute Saigon Soldiers in Loc Ninh." *Los Angeles Times,* 14 April 1972.

"Reds Fire on Refugees." *Pacific Stars and Stripes,* 15 June 1972.

"Reds Seize Part of An Loc." *Pacific Stars and Stripes,* 15 April 1972.

"The Relief of An Loc." *Newsweek,* 26 June 1972, pp. 34.

"Report Few Left in An Loc." *Pacific Stars and Stripes,* 2 June 1972.

"Road to Victory Lined with Bodies: An Loc—The Battle That Couldn't Be Lost." *Los Angeles Times,* 19 June 1972.

Saar, John. "A Nervous Air Mission to An Loc and Back." *Life,* 12 May 1972, pp. 36–37.

———. "Report from the Inferno." *Life,* 28 April 1972, pp. 30–36.

Schaefer, Allen. "Report Few NVA Left in An Loc." *Pacific Stars and Stripes,* 2 June 1972.

Schanberg, S. H. "Saigon's Pilots Shun Dangers of An Loc." *New York Times,* 24 June 1972.

———. "U.S. Pilot Tells of 6 Days at An Loc in a Bunker beneath the Storm." *New York Times,* 29 May 1972.

Schemmer, Benjamin F. "Bien Hoa Air Base: Short on Toilet Paper, but Long on Teamwork." *Armed Forces Journal,* June 1972, pp. 15–17.

Serong, F. P. "The 1972 Easter Offensive." *Southeast Asia Perspectives,* summer 1974.

"Settling in for the Third Indochina War." *Time,* 8 May 1972, pp. 28–30.

"Siege at An Loc Intensifies." *Christian Science Monitor,* 13 May 1972.

Sorley, Lewis. "Courage and Blood: South Vietnam's Repulse of the 1972 Easter Invasion." *Parameters,* summer 1999, pp. 38–56.

———. "Reassessing the ARVN." *Vietnam,* April 2003, pp. 43–48, 65.

"South Viet Nam: Pulling Itself Together." *Time,* 22 May 1972, pp. 15–17.

Stacey, K. N. "North Vietnamese Armor Operations: The Lessons of 1972 and 1975." *Armor,* July–August 1981, pp. 48–53.

"The Strength and Weakness of the ARVN." *Pacific Stars and Stripes,* 18 June 1972.

"Stubborn Reds Make It Tough on Highway 13." *Pacific Stars and Stripes,* 17 June 1972.

"S. Viet Armor Ineffective in Fight for Road." *Los Angeles Times,* 16 April 1972.

"A Tale of Two Broken Cities." *Time,* 15 January 1973, pp. 19–20.

"Tells How Reds Died: Chained Inside of Tanks." *Pacific Stars and Stripes,* 18 April 1972.

"Their Sin—to Leave An Loc." *Pacific Stars and Stripes,* 15 June 1972.

Thimmesch, Nick. "A Grisly Story." *Pacific Stars and Stripes,* 13 May 1972.

"3 Americans Held, Photographer Says." *New York Times,* 15 July 1972.

Tokar, Major John A. "Supply by Sky: An Loc Airlift." *Vietnam,* December 2000, pp. 35–40, 65.

"The Toll in Battered An Loc—Unknown, But in Hundreds." *Pacific Stars and Stripes,* 17 June 1972.

"Touchy Times for American Advisers." *Newsweek,* 29 May 1972, p. 41.

"Tough Viet Troops Hunt a Fight—Find It." *Pacific Stars and Stripes,* 11 April 1972.

Ulmer, Colonel Walter F., Jr. "Anti-Aircraft Employment on a Battlefield in South Viet-
    nam." *Armor,* May–June 1974, p. 24.
———. "Notes on Enemy Armor at An Loc." *Armor,* January–February 1973, pp. 14–20.
Ulsamer, Edgar. "Airpower Halts an Invasion." *Air Force Magazine,* September 1972, p. 61.
"U.S. General Dies in An Loc Shelling." *New York Times,* 10 July 1972.
"A Very Long Road, Where Death Is the Only Easy Rider." *Pacific Stars and Stripes,* 14
    April 1972.
"Vietnam: The Specter of Defeat." *Newsweek,* 15 May 1972, pp. 20–22.
"Vietnamization: A Policy under the Gun." *Time,* 17 April 1972, pp. 33–40.
"Vietnamization Makes Steady Gains." *Army,* November 1970, pp. 44–45.
"Vietnamization: Will It Work?" *Newsweek,* 9 February 1970, p. 32.
"Viets on Way to Victory at An Loc—Top Adviser." *Pacific Stars and Stripes,* 23 April
    1972.
Ward, Ian. "North Vietnam's Blitzkrieg—Why Giap Did It: Report from Saigon." *Conflict
    Studies,* October 1972, pp. 1–11.
"War's Cruel Fate Puts Tiny Town on the Map." *Pacific Stars and Stripes,* 24 April 1972.
"The War That Won't Go Away." *Newsweek,* 17 April 1972, pp. 16–21.
Weller, Jac. "RVNAF Training: The Vital Element in Vietnamization." *Military Review,*
    October 1972, pp. 36–49.
Whitney, C. R. "Focus on An Loc Shifts to Relief Column." *New York Times,* 27 May
    1972.

INDEX

JAMES H. WILLBANKS, lieutenant colonel, U.S. Army (Ret.), was an adviser during the battle of An Loc in 1972. He retired in 1992 after 23 years' service and has since been on the faculty of the U.S. Army Command and General Staff College, Fort Leavenworth, Kansas. He completed his B.A. at Texas A&M University and received his M.A. and Ph.D. degrees from the University of Kansas. He is the author of *Abandoning Vietnam*, a study of Vietnamization (2004), and a forthcoming book on the Tet Offensive.